Knitting Outside the Box

Bristol Ivy

POM POM PRESS

LONDON

Knitting Outside the Box
Published in 2017 by Pom Pom Press
Text (c) 2017 Bristol Ivy
Pattern Photography (c) 2017 Amy Gwatkin
Stitch Dictionary Photography (c) 2017 Juju Vail

ISBN: 978-0-9934866-6-1
A catalogue record for this book
is available from the British Library.

Editors   Lydia Gluck & Meghan Fernandes
Associate Editor   Amy Collins
Design & Layout   James Lunn for People of Print
Media Manager   Sophie Scott
US Account Manager   Gayle Taliaferro Gilner
Technical Editors   Jemima Bicknell, Jen Arnall-Culliford,
                                 Kate Atherley, Minh Nguyen & Rachel Atkinson
                                 Bristol Ivy
Illustrations
Schematic Illustrations   Lydia Gluck
Copy Editor   Annie Prime

Models   Natasha Culzac & Jacqueline Ilumoka
Photographer's Assistants   Esther Theaker & Chanel Baker
Hair & Makeup   Jenny Green
Project Assistants   Iesha Parker & Alice Sleight
Jewellery provided by   Jasmin Rowlandson
Sample Knitters   Averi Moore, Addison Aliprandi,
                                 Darlene Ivy, Minh Nguyen, Jessica Krop,
                                 Bonnie Politano & Kate Cruse

For pattern corrections, please visit:
pompommag.com/errata

Printed in the UK by Pureprint Group Limited
End Paper Colorplan Marrs Green 135gsm from G . F Smith
Typefaces supplied by Colophon Foundry

POM POM PRESS
B203 Lighthouse Space
89A Shacklewell Lane
London E8 2EB
United Kingdom

pompommag.com

Lydia Gluck & Meghan Fernandes
London, July 2017

In June of 2015, we met with Bristol Ivy in a Columbus, Ohio diner to chat about the possibility of publishing her book. We hadn't yet published any books, and Bristol would become the second author ever to sign on with us. She took a leap of faith working with Pom Pom Press, and it has been an honour to help share her creativity and innovation with the knitting community.

The concept behind this book was one we were familiar with: we had seen Bristol give a talk with the same name at Unravel festival. As soon as we saw her proposal we knew we wanted to help create the concrete, bound version of Bristol's idea. As knitters we knew that a book exploring her design process, and her affinity with knitted fabric and the ways it can be manipulated, would be something new. We couldn't wait to add it to our own knitting libraries.

Knitting Outside the Box is by far the biggest publication we've ever undertaken, and we couldn't be prouder of it. It is a veritable treasure trove of inspiration, practical knowledge, gorgeous photographs, and an insight into the brilliant mind of one of the knitting world's most exceptionally talented designers.

If there is one thing we have learned from working with Bristol Ivy over the past three years (if you count her early work for *Pom Pom Quarterly*) it is that she is generous of mind, spirit, and knowledge. We are certain you will feel this generosity in the following pages.

Bristol Ivy
Portland, Maine, July 2017

I'm a daydreamer. Long car rides as a child were spent alternately with my nose deep in a book or with my gaze on some distant horizon, creating impossible worlds and preposterous tales that always vanished with a sigh as we pulled into the driveway home. As a teenager, I lived and breathed the art of making, spending my days writing, taking photos, making collages, binding books, dancing, building sets... and still finding time for daydreams. However, in addition to dreaming of faraway lands and scenarios in which I was the witty, effortlessly cool, world-famous heroine, I dreamt of the things I could make. I dreamt of the work of my hands.

When I picked up knitting again as a freshman in college (after a brief variegated-neon-acrylic stint as a kid), it felt like coming home. My first year of college wasn't easy; I was away from my family, halfway across the country, trying to embody and manifest that effortless heroine of my daydreams with less-than-stellar results. But the concrete, tactile growth of the fabric, stitch by stitch, row by row, was the antidote to this uncertain, stomach-clenching identity crisis. These stitches, these clumsy twists of yarn around needles, captivated me, energised me, and sent me dreaming down a whole new path. This was a world that made sense to me, that made sense to my hands. I found anchors for who I was in the action of my fingers, unwittingly echoing a Louise Bourgeois quote I would discover years later: "I am not what I am, I am what I do with my hands". My daydreams changed. I stopped asking 'what now?' and started asking 'what if?'.

Fourteen years later, I'm still asking 'what if?'. My hands move steadily now in the rhythm of the stitches, my movements smaller and more refined than when I was 18. I don't have to look at my knitting. I've gone whole evenings with the steady tick of needle on needle as the background metronome to whatever British murder mystery I've found on Netflix, never looking down. But this familiarity doesn't mean contentment—it doesn't mean the daydreaming is done. Instead, it means that I dream all the time. I dream about the possibilities, the opportunities, the moments when I have to drop everything and give an idea a try. And it means that I want to be able to share the same sense of freedom and joy that experimentation with knitting has given me. I want to share it with you.

This book is my attempt to capture some of what knitting means to me, and some of the possibilities inherent in knitted fabric. From my years of daydreaming, swatching, ripping, and designing, what I've written here is what I've come to understand—both in my brain and in my fingers. This book is equal parts creative exercise, technical textbook, and a peek inside my design process. My hope is that it inspires you to see knitting not just as a hobby, but as an extension of you: of your hands, of your brain, of your ideas. I hope it inspires you to step outside your comfort zone (or, dare I say, out of the box) and push boundaries to get what you truly want out of your knitting. And I hope it inspires you to dream.

"I go to seek a Great Perhaps"

Francois Rabelais

It's no coincidence that comfort and safety are associated with warm, woolly things. There is joy, reassurance, and relaxation in cocooning ourselves in the familiar and the known—sometimes in the literal sense. We've all had days where the only thing that makes us feel better is that one shawl or sweater, even if it's worn beyond recognition and too threadbare to leave the house. But it makes us feel like ourselves, and there is no greater pleasure.

The same is true of knitting. I find such comfort in knitting a shape that's familiar and that my hands can trace of their own volition as I while away the hours. But there is also joy in taking charge of your knitting, asking 'what if?', and maybe, just maybe, taking it somewhere it hasn't been before.

In the modern knitting world, we are spoiled for choice. We are surrounded by a daily kaleidoscope of beautiful new patterns. There are hundreds upon thousands of variations on the same basic ideas, each developing differently as it comes through the hands and mind of a different maker. But even these many options that we are given to explore limit us to following other people's visions, other people's ideas. I want to make room for *your* ideas.

This book evolved from a class I've been teaching for four years, coincidentally titled "Knitting Outside the Box". One of the most important things in that class that I strive to impress on my students is: **just because something has always been done a certain way, it doesn't mean it must be done that way. Knitting has traditions, but knitting doesn't have rules.**

Many of us come to knitting with the assumption that, based on everything we've seen, knitting has to be done a certain way. But when you seek the reasoning behind this, the logic dissolves. For example, our knowledge of the world of knitting says, "sweaters must be knit in the round from the top down or pieced from the bottom up". Yes, this is what we most commonly see. But why should that limit us? Why can't we start a sweater from the side, or from a corner, or even from the centre out? Why do we have to knit cables or lace symmetrically? Why must our socks match? At the end of the day, there are no hard and fast answers to these questions, or any others of knitting tradition. We are free to take knitting, this art form we love and take such comfort in, and make it our own. There is great power in taking something from which we derive such joy and security, and making it something that pushes our boundaries and challenges us to take a few steps outside our comfort zone.

Once we take those steps, a whole new world opens up to us, but this time, we are in control. The techniques we love or the activities we enjoy become the focal points and anchors for our exploration. This is one of the things that I love about knitting: we are all uniquely shaped by our knitting histories, our preferences, the actions of our hands. There are often techniques we enjoy more than others, and so our brains want to steer us in that direction. But when working from other people's patterns, we don't always get that choice.

For example, I personally find ssk decreases far easier than k2tog decreases (for no reason I can rightly understand). So, if given the choice of which uni-directional decrease to use, I'm going left! Likewise, certain stitch patterns just make sense to me: brioche, chevrons, antler cables, garter ridge, drop stitches—these all click with the way my brain works. But I may not have the opportunity to find an existing design that satisfies all of those existing preferences. I could keep knitting other people's work, shaped by other people's preferences, grumping about having to do k2togs all the time, or I could take what I love and use it to create something of my very own. I want to give you that same opportunity and licence to start using your preferences to mould, shape, and explore your own ideas. There are things you understand and love from your knitting history that are specific to you, and these will shape how you view the inspiration around you. They will be the lenses through which you view the world, and they will give form to your ideas. I hope this book will help you along this path.

Knitting Outside the Box is broken up into three parts. The first is a series of exercises designed to help you look at your knitting in different ways: in different combinations, from different directions, and with different constructions. They will ask you to look at knitting from divergent perspectives, perhaps ones you haven't yet attempted, and to imagine how you can bring your own experience into play.

There are also three patterns in this section, all designed as a result of my own experiences using these same exercises. This is not an unusual circumstance; these are exercises I still use frequently in my designing life. Whether it's playing around when I'm on long phone calls (sorry, everyone I talk to), when I'm stuck with the designer's version of writer's block, or when I want to shake things up and break out of my comfort zone, they are invaluable for providing me with fresh ideas or new angles on knitting. I encourage you to give them a try!

Once you have the ideas, however, it can be tricky to figure out how to make them work. That's where the next section of the book comes in. Here, I discuss three different methods (and the maths and physics behind them) for how you can physically manifest the ideas you've created. With increases and decreases, short rows, and stitch patterns that manipulate your gauge, you have three solid tools to use individually or to mix and match to achieve what you want out of your knitting.

There are nine patterns in this section, three for each technique. With all of them, I wanted to show what it would look like when the technique was used in isolation, and what it would look like when combined with one of its partners. They are examples only, and I hope they illustrate just how many possibilities are inherent in these three different techniques.

The final section is when we let it all go and do exactly what we want. Here, I take you step by step through three ideas from the spark of creation, to pattern writing, to the knitting process (and sometimes

back through the sequence a few times before I got it right!). I wanted to show concrete examples of how ideas can move into reality, and also show that there is often more than one right answer—as well as more than one wrong answer! In the end, the most important thing is that you get the results you want, and do so on your own terms.

My final words about this book: as I said above, knitting has traditions, but no rules. So what about the statements I make in this book? They are as ephemeral and subjective as any other knitting 'rule'. They are based on my own personal experience, thought processes, and knitting history, and they may not jive with yours. So challenge them. Set out to prove them wrong. Put your own spin on them. Yell at me and throw the book across the room. Rules are made to be broken, and my work is not exempt from that. But even if we somehow disagree on the mechanics, I hope we will agree on the ideology: you are completely, utterly, infallibly, 100% in charge of your own knitting destiny. Knitting is a blank slate: it is an amorphous, inchoate, and imminently malleable art form, and it is yours to do with whatever you wish. So let's have some fun.

PART I

LETTING GO AND GETTING CREATIVE

MASH-UP

EXERCISE ONE

Knitters are visual people. We are textile magpies, collecting shapes, stitch patterns, and covert photos of other people's sweaters from myriad waiting rooms and queues across the world. We are drawn to the visual aspects of our art form, and often seek to incorporate what we see around us into what we make with our hands. But often it's difficult to know where to start! In this exercise, we'll start from an art form that we already know and understand: existing knitting patterns. We can take these, note what interests us about them, and put them together them in whole new combinations: mash-ups.

This concept was first introduced to me by Brenda Dayne's *Cast On* podcast (well worth a listen to all the back archives). In Episode 34 (appropriately named *Knitting Mash-Up*) from way back in 2006, she talked about how she had chosen the stitch pattern from one design and combined it with the construction from another to create something new. This final project was something that was the best of all possible worlds—not only did it satisfy the creative itch, but it did so while letting her reference things that she was already comfortable with. This concept can be broadened into a creative exercise for all knitters: what would you create if you could have the best of all worlds?

This may seem intimidating, but you've most likely done a fair bit of mashing up on your own already. Have you ever switched out a stitch pattern for one you liked better? Mash-up. Substituted one sock heel for another? Mash-up. Or chose to work the pattern in a different weight or type of yarn? Even that is a mash-up. You're using your knitting knowledge and preferences —stitch patterns, sock heels, yarn weight and drape—to make sure you create exactly the item you want. We're just going to take it one step further!

The first step in a knitting mash-up is to go on the hunt. What patterns do you love? Have you seen something in a magazine recently that struck you? Take pieces that have caught your eye and start breaking them down into components. Components can be any number of things: garment silhouette, stitch pattern, direction of knitting, placement of motif, colour combinations, and so on. Think of these as the building blocks that come together as a single garment. Like building blocks, they can be taken apart and recombined to create something entirely new.

Let's take a look at some of the images from *Pom Pom Quarterly* that have caught my eye and resonated with me over the years. Though I didn't go into the archives with any particular agenda, the same motifs and structures cropped up again and again. There were a few basic themes: geometric colourwork and stripes (Iara by Renee Callahan, Onda by Lydia Gluck, Mysa by Kate Gagnon Osborn, and Contigo by Meghan Fernandes); wide front bands (Onda, Mysa, and my own Callas); strong architectural, diagonal stitch patterns and chevrons (Iara, Right Angle by Georgia Farrell, Delineate by Olga Buraya-Kefelian, Deco City by Amy van de Laar, Sceles by Anna Maltz, Quadrillion by Meghan Fernandes, and my own Florence); and boxy shapes (Callas, Quadrillion, Sceles, Mysa, Delineate, and Right Angle). These elements were obviously piquing my interest, so I decided to pull some of each of them and sketch a few ideas.

Once you have some aspects in mind, there are two ways to approach a mash-up: imitation and inspiration. Both are completely valid, and just depend on how attached you are to the original designs. With imitation, you can pull the exact ideas off the page and combine them together to create something new that clearly references something existing. So, for instance, if I were really attached to the colourwork from Lydia's Onda and the construction of my Callas, I could easily cut and paste one onto the other without changing very much. I could keep the basic construction of Callas, but leave off the front band during the original knitting, then

Below top left
Mysa by Kate Gagnon Osborn
Pom Pom Issue 12 – Spring 2015
Photo by Ana Mercedes

Below top right
Quadrillion by Meghan Fernandes
Pom Pom Issue 6 – Autumn 2013
Photo by Juju Vail

Below bottom left
Callas by Bristol Ivy
Pom Pom Issue 15 – Winter 2015
Photo by Juju Vail

Below bottom right
Onda by Lydia Gluck
Pom Pom Issue 2 – Autumn 2012
Photo by Juju Vail

Opposite
Mash-up sketch

pick up and knit the band à la Onda afterwards. As long as my pick-up numbers worked with the Onda chart, I'd be good to go! Or, if I wanted to take both designs as inspiration, I could riff off the general ideas—colourwork, boxy shape, angled wide fronts, moving lines of ribbing—and create something entirely new. Here I am not tied to the literal idea of what the garment is; I am working with my own perception of the garment and going from there. I might use similar colourwork bands at the hem instead of ribbing, or keep the shape of Onda but create a new colourwork chart that mimics the moving lines of Callas. I might even keep the cocoon shape of Callas but start from the centre out, from a colourwork panel at the centre back. The best part about knitting mash-ups is that there's no one to tell you to stop—the only limit is your imagination. If you want to stay close to the original designs or work solely with details from the original patterns, awesome. If you want to go so wide-ranging that your finished piece is miles away from where you started, fantastic. Like I said before, there are no rules in knitting—it is there to be an expression of your interests, preferences, and inspirations, and no one can tell you that it should be otherwise.

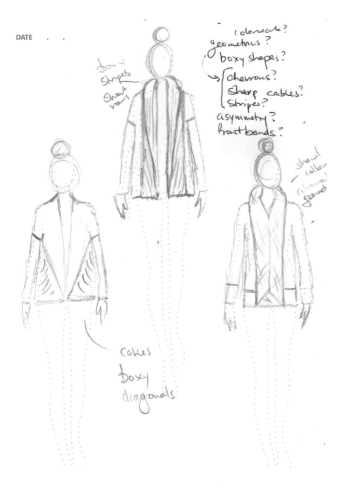

Once you've decided how you're going to approach the designs you've chosen, working from imitation, inspiration, or a combination of the two, get moving! Sketching, list-making, collaging—whatever best enables you to record your ideas in a way that you'll understand later. I tend to go for a combination of reference photos, sketches in my Fashionary notebook, and notes to myself in the margins. This time, while I was sketching, I came up with three ideas based on the elements that were piquing my interest from the patterns opposite. The first idea combined elements of inspiration from Quadrillion (the allover cables, focusing on cable patterns that trended more towards architectural and angled rather than organic and curving), parts of Sceles and Right Angle (the boxy shape), and one final part from Callas (the wide front bands). It took the diagonal concept even further by decreasing away the cables and replacing it with smooth stockinette across the fronts, to keep the whole piece from becoming too heavy.

Concept number two took the same boxy shape and the same front bands, but replaced the cables with smooth stockinette. The front bands themselves became the centrepiece, picked up and worked after all the rest of the garment was complete. They would be striped, but shaped with short rows so that the stripes created wedges at the hem and the neck, bringing in shades of Mysa and Onda.

The final concept was a pullover, with a twist. It would be a more fitted shape than the others, but the focus would still sit on the centre front. I was intrigued by the construction of Mysa—a central panel picked up and worked after the rest of the body was complete, and then joined together to create a pullover—and wondered if you couldn't do something similar with colourwork like Onda instead of stockinette. Since this one would be more substantial than either Mysa or Onda, I added a shawl collar to the neck to add weight and cosiness there, too.

Each of these designs is valid and would be fun to pursue, but the final step of a mash-up is to take a step back and assess your ideas critically. Ask yourself a few questions: would I wear it or would the recipient wear it? Would I enjoy knitting it? Is it too simple or too complicated to hold my interest? If I'm not going to love the knitting process, do I want the finished product enough to push through? If you've answered any of the above questions dubiously, see what you can change about your design to bring it more within your comfort zone. This may involve taking out some of the very elements that link it to your original inspirations, but as long as it's something that you want to knit and/or wear, then it's worth making those modifications. For me, I knew that the cabled design was something that would fit in with the other pieces in this book, and something that I would love in my wardrobe. I may come back to the other two pieces, but I might make certain tweaks to make them more knittable and wearable. Could I make the colourwork pullover into a cardigan and eliminate the potentially confusing construction? Could I make the short row cardigan into a pullover to make it more interesting? I'll keep these sketches in my notebook and revisit them in the future, when perhaps some new knitting inspiration will be the key to their perfection!

This is another fabulous aspect of knitting mash-ups: you never have to consider them complete if you don't want to. Often I will have an idea and sketch it, but only a few years later finally have the right references to figure out how to make it work elegantly. As a mini exercise, look back at some of your previous knitting projects and see what you might change if you knew then what you know now. What attributes might you add or take away? Is there another stitch pattern you prefer now? Keep exploring, playing, and breaking down all the garments you see into their components, and think about what I've written here is what I've come to understand changes would make them your own.

You can even take your knitting mash-ups out of the concrete realm of physical attributes and ask yourself about how the item makes you feel. Do the colours give you a particular emotion? Does the shape signify something to you? When you wear it do you want to feel the way that the model looks in the photos? We often unconsciously gravitate towards the emotions behind a garment, which are also entirely valid points of reference for later creativity. Ask yourself what you might change if you wanted the garment to feel a certain way at the end of the process. What would you change if you wanted it to be cosy? Or if you wanted it to be polished and sleek? These are all great ways to push your creativity and make sure you end up with your perfect garment.

As you can see, knitting mash-ups are a great way to jump start the creative process while playing to the visual imagery that is most knitters' strength. Give it a try and see what components resonate with you, then see just how far you can take them.

PINA
—
CARDIGAN

Pina Bausch, German choreographer

Pina

Sizes:

1 (2, 3, 4, 5, 6, 7, 8)

Finished bust circumference:

140 (140, 140, 150.5, 150.5, 150.5, 167, 167) cm / 55¼ (55¼, 55¼, 59¼, 59¼, 59¾, 65¾, 65¾)" – to be worn with 19.5-64 cm / 7¾-25¼" positive ease.

Important sizing note:

Pina is intended to be worn with lots of positive ease around the bust but it has fitted sleeves. Therefore please select your size based on the following finished upper arm circumference:

30 (32.5, 34.5, 37.5, 40.5, 45, 48, 51) cm / 12 (12¾, 13½, 14¾, 16, 17¾, 18¾, 20)"

Model has 86 cm / 34" bust, stands 183 cm / 6'0" tall, and is wearing size 2.

Yarn: Yarn on the House

Big Sister (DK weight; 80% superwash Merino wool, 10% cashmere, 10% nylon polyamide; 211 m / 231 yds per 100 g skein)

Shade: Mint; 8 (8, 8, 9, 9, 9, 10, 10) skeins

Gauge:

19.5 sts & 27 rows = 10 cm / 4" over stocking stitch on 4.5 mm needles after blocking.

27 sts & 27 rows = 10 cm / 4" over stitches 20-33 of Chart E on 4.5 mm knitting needles after blocking.

Needles:

4 mm / US 6 **AND** 4.5 mm / US 7 knitting needles

4 mm / US 6 **AND** 4.5 mm / US 7 needles suitable for working small circumferences in the round

Always use a needle size that will result in the correct gauge after blocking.

Notions:

3 stitch markers, locking stitch markers for Japanese Short Rows (JSR), cable needle, stitch holders or scrap yarn, tapestry needle, t-pins and blocking wires

Notes:

Pina is constructed in pieces from the bottom up. Shaping occurs to transition the body from cables to stocking stitch, and shaping is worked at the neck edge. Shoulders are shaped with short rows, and sleeves are picked up and knit down after seaming.

CHARTS – WRITTEN INSTRUCTIONS

Chart A (Front Band Cable)

Worked over 18 sts and 24 rows.
ROW 1 (RS): 3/3 LC, k6, 3/3 RC.
ROW 2 (WS and all following WS rows): Purl.
ROW 3: Knit.
ROW 5: K3, 3/3 RC, 3/3 LC, k3.
ROW 7: Knit.
ROW 8 (WS): Purl.
ROWS 9-24: Rep rows 1-8 twice more.

Chart B (Left Front Cable Panel)

SIZES 1, 2 & 3 ONLY:
Worked over 64 sts and 24 rows.
ROW 1 (RS): 3/3 LC, k6, 3/3 RC, p1, k2, [k2, 2/2 RC] 4 times, p1, 3/3 LC, k6, 3/3 RC.
ROW 2 (WS and all following WS rows): P18, k1, p26, k1, p18.
ROW 3: K18, p1, k2, [2/2 RC, k2] 4 times, p1, k18.
ROW 5: K3, 3/3 RC, 3/3 LC, k3, p1, [2/2 RC, k2] 4 times, k2, p1, k3, 3/3 RC, 3/3 LC, k3.
ROW 7: K18, p1, k2, [k2, 2/2 RC] 4 times, p1, k18.
ROW 9: 3/3 LC, k6, 3/3 RC, p1, k2, [2/2 RC, k2] 4 times, p1, 3/3 LC, k6, 3/3 RC.
ROW 11: K18, p1, [2/2 RC, k2] 4 times, k2, p1, k18.
ROW 13: K3, 3/3 RC, 3/3 LC, k3, p1, k2, [k2, 2/2 RC] 4 times, p1, k3, 3/3 RC, 3/3 LC, k3.
ROW 15: K18, p1, k2, [2/2 RC, k2] 4 times, p1, k18.
ROW 17: 3/3 LC, k6, 3/3 RC, p1, [2/2 RC, k2] 4 times, k2, p1, 3/3 LC, k6, 3/3 RC.

ROW 19: K18, p1, k2, [k2, 2/2 RC] 4 times, p1, k18.
ROW 21: K3, 3/3 RC, 3/3 LC, k3, p1, k2, [2/2 RC, k2] 4 times, p1, k3, 3/3 RC, 3/3 LC, k3.
ROW 23: K18, p1, [2/2 RC, k2] 4 times, k2, p1, k18.
ROW 24 (WS): P18, k1, p26, k1, p18.

SIZES 4, 5 & 6 ONLY:
Worked over 73 sts and 24 rows.
ROW 1 (RS): 2/2 LC, k4, p1, 3/3 LC, k6, 3/3 RC, p1, k2, [k2, 2/2 RC] 4 times, p1, 3/3 LC, k6, 3/3 RC.
ROW 2 (WS and all following WS rows): P18, k1, p26, k1, p18, k1, p8.
ROW 3: K2, 2/2 LC, k2, p1, k18, p1, k2, [2/2 RC, k2] 4 times, p1, k18.
ROW 5: K4, 2/2 LC, p1, k3, 3/3 RC, 3/3 LC, k3, p1, [2/2 RC, k2] 4 times, k2, p1, k3, 3/3 RC, 3/3 LC, k3.
ROW 7: 2/2 LC, k4, p1, k18, p1, k2, [k2, 2/2 RC] 4 times, p1, k18.
ROW 9: K2, 2/2 LC, k2, p1, 3/3 LC, k6, 3/3 RC, p1, k2, [2/2 RC, k2] 4 times, p1, 3/3 LC, k6, 3/3 RC.
ROW 11: K4, 2/2 LC, p1, k18, p1, [2/2 RC, k2] 4 times, k2, p1, k18.
ROW 13: 2/2 LC, k4, p1, k3, 3/3 RC, 3/3 LC, k3, p1, k2, [k2, 2/2 RC] 4 times, p1, k3, 3/3 RC, 3/3 LC, k3.
ROW 15: K2, 2/2 LC, k2, p1, k18, p1, k2, [2/2 RC, k2] 4 times, p1, k18.
ROW 17: K4, 2/2 LC, p1, 3/3 LC, k6, 3/3 RC, p1, [2/2 RC, k2] 4 times, k2, p1, 3/3 LC, k6, 3/3 RC.
ROW 19: 2/2 LC, k4, p1, k18, p1, k2, [k2, 2/2 RC] 4 times, p1, k18.
ROW 21: K2, 2/2 LC, k2, p1, k3, 3/3 RC, 3/3 LC, k3, p1, k2, [2/2 RC, k2] 4 times, p1, k3, 3/3 RC, 3/3 LC, k3.
ROW 23: K4, 2/2 LC, p1, k18, p1, [2/2 RC, k2] 4 times, k2, p1, k18.
ROW 24 (WS): P18, k1, p26, k1, p18, k1, p8.

SIZES 7 & 8 ONLY:
Worked over 82 sts and 24 rows.
ROW 1 (RS): K4, 2/2 RC, p1, 2/2 LC, k4, p1, 3/3 LC, k6, 3/3 RC, p1, k2, [k2, 2/2 RC] 4 times, p1, 3/3 LC, k6, 3/3 RC.
ROW 2 (WS and all following WS rows): P18, k1, p26, k1, p18, [k1, p8] twice.

ROW 3: K2, 2/2 RC, k2, p1, k2, 2/2 LC, k2, p1, k18, p1, k2, [2/2 RC, k2] 4 times, p1, k18.

ROW 5: 2/2 RC, k4, p1, k4, 2/2 LC, p1, k3, 3/3 RC, 3/3 LC, k3, p1, [2/2 RC, k2] 4 times, k2, p1, k3, 3/3 RC, 3/3 LC, k3.

ROW 7: K4, 2/2 RC, p1, 2/2 LC, k4, p1, k18, p1, k2, [k2, 2/2 RC] 4 times, p1, k18.

ROW 9: K2, 2/2 RC, k2, p1, k2, 2/2 LC, k2, p1, 3/3 LC, k6, 3/3 RC, p1, k2, [2/2 RC, k2] 4 times, p1, 3/3 LC, k6, 3/3 RC.

ROW 11: 2/2 RC, k4, p1, k4, 2/2 LC, p1, k18, p1, [2/2 RC, k2] 4 times, k2, p1, k18.

ROW 13: K4, 2/2 RC, p1, 2/2 LC, k4, p1, k3, 3/3 RC, 3/3 LC, k3, p1, k2, [k2, 2/2 RC] 4 times, p1, k3, 3/3 RC, 3/3 LC, k3.

ROW 15: K2, 2/2 RC, k2, p1, k2, 2/2 LC, k2, p1, k18, p1, k2, [2/2 RC, k2] 4 times, p1, k18.

ROW 17: 2/2 RC, k4, p1, k4, 2/2 LC, p1, 3/3 LC, k6, 3/3 RC, p1, [2/2 RC, k2] 4 times, k2, p1, 3/3 LC, k6, 3/3 RC.

ROW 19: K4, 2/2 RC, p1, 2/2 LC, k4, p1, k18, p1, k2, [k2, 2/2 RC] 4 times, p1, k18.

ROW 21: K2, 2/2 RC, k2, p1, k2, 2/2 LC, k2, p1, k3, 3/3 RC, 3/3 LC, k3, p1, k2, [2/2 RC, k2] 4 times, p1, k3, 3/3 RC, 3/3 LC, k3.

ROW 23: 2/2 RC, k4, p1, k4, 2/2 LC, p1, k18, p1, [2/2 RC, k2] 4 times, k2, p1, k18.

ROW 24 (WS): P18, k1, p26, k1, p18, [k1, p8] twice.

Chart C (Left Travelling Cable)

Worked over 10 sts and 24 rows.

ROW 1 (RS): P1, 2/2 LC, k4, p1.

ROW 2 (WS and all following WS rows): K1, p8, k1.

ROW 3: P1, k2, 2/2 LC, k2, p1.

ROW 5: P1, k4, 2/2 LC, p1.

ROW 6 (WS): K1, p8, k1.

ROWS 7-24: Rep rows 1-6 a further 3 times.

Chart D (Right Travelling Cable)

Worked over 10 sts and 24 rows.

ROW 1 (RS): P1, k4, 2/2 RC, p1.

ROW 2 (WS and all following WS rows): K1, p8, k1.

ROW 3: P1, k2, 2/2 RC, k2, p1.

ROW 5: P1, 2/2 RC, k4, p1.

ROW 6 (WS): K1, p8, k1.

ROWS 7-24: Rep rows 1-6 a further 3 times.

Chart E (Right Front Cable Panel)

SIZES 1, 2 & 3 ONLY:

Worked over 64 sts and 24 rows.

ROW 1 (RS): 3/3 LC, k6, 3/3 RC, p1, [2/2 LC, k2] 4 times, k2, p1, 3/3 LC, k6, 3/3 RC.

ROW 2 (WS and all following WS rows): P18, k1, p26, k1, p18.

ROW 3: K18, p1, [k2, 2/2 LC] 4 times, k2, p1, k18.

ROW 5: K3, 3/3 RC, 3/3 LC, k3, p1, k2, [k2, 2/2 LC] 4 times, p1, k3, 3/3 RC, 3/3 LC, k3.

ROW 7: K18, p1, [2/2 LC, k2] 4 times, k2, p1, k18.

ROW 9: 3/3 LC, k6, 3/3 RC, p1, [k2, 2/2 LC] 4 times, k2, p1, 3/3 LC, k6, 3/3 RC.

ROW 11: K18, p1, k2, [k2, 2/2 LC] 4 times, p1, k18.

ROW 13: K3, 3/3 RC, 3/3 LC, k3, p1, [2/2 LC, k2] 4 times, k2, p1, k3, 3/3 RC, 3/3 LC, k3.

ROW 15: K18, p1, [k2, 2/2 LC] 4 times, k2, p1, k18.

ROW 17: 3/3 LC, k6, 3/3 RC, p1, k2, [k2, 2/2 LC] 4 times, p1, 3/3 LC, k6, 3/3 RC.

ROW 19: K18, p1, [2/2 LC, k2] 4 times, k2, p1, k18.

ROW 21: K3, 3/3 RC, 3/3 LC, k3, p1, [k2, 2/2 LC] 4 times, k2, p1, k3, 3/3 RC, 3/3 LC, k3.

ROW 23: K18, p1, k2, [k2, 2/2 LC] 4 times, p1, k18.

ROW 24 (WS): P18, k1, p26, k 1, p18.

SIZES 4, 5 & 6 ONLY:

Worked over 73 sts and 24 rows.

ROW 1 (RS): 3/3 LC, k6, 3/3 RC, p1, [2/2 LC, k2] 4 times, k2, p1, 3/3 LC, k6, 3/3 RC, p1, k4, 2/2 RC.

ROW 2 (WS and all following WS rows): P8, k1, p18, k1, p26, k1, p18.

ROW 3: K18, p1, [k2, 2/2 LC] 4 times, k2, p1, k18, p1, k2, 2/2 RC, k2.

ROW 5: K3, 3/3 RC, 3/3 LC, k3, p1, k2, [k2, 2/2 LC] 4 times, p1, k3, 3/3 RC, 3/3 LC, k3, p1, 2/2 RC, k4.

ROW 7: K18, p1, [2/2 LC, k2] 4 times, k2, p1, k18, p1, k4, 2/2 RC.

ROW 9: 3/3 LC, k6, 3/3 RC, p1, [k2, 2/2 LC] 4 times, k2, p1, 3/3 LC, k6, 3/3 RC, p1, k2, 2/2 RC, k2.

ROW 11: K18, p1, k2, [k2, 2/2 LC] 4 times, p1, k18, p1, 2/2 RC, k4.

ROW 13: K3, 3/3 RC, 3/3 LC, k3, p1, [2/2 LC, k2] 4 times, k2, p1, k3, 3/3 RC, 3/3 LC, k3, p1, k4, 2/2 RC.

ROW 15: K18, p1, [k2, 2/2 LC] 4 times, k2, p1, k18, p1, k2, 2/2 RC, k2.

SIZES 7 & 8 ONLY:

Worked over 82 sts and 24 rows.

ROW 1 (RS): 3/3 LC, k6, 3/3 RC, p1, [2/2 LC, k2] 4 times, k2, p1, 3/3 LC, k6, 3/3 RC, p1, k4, 2/2 RC, p1, 2/2 LC, k4.

ROW 2 (WS and all following WS rows): [P8, k1] twice, p18, k1, p26, k1, p18.

ROW 3: K18, p1, [k2, 2/2 LC] 4 times, k2, p1, k18, p1, k2, 2/2 RC, k2, p1, k2, 2/2 LC, k2.

ROW 5: K3, 3/3 RC, 3/3 LC, k3, p1, k2, [k2, 2/2 LC] 4 times, p1, k3, 3/3 RC, 3/3 LC, k3, p1, 2/2 RC, k4, p1, k4, 2/2 LC.

ROW 7: K18, p1, [2/2 LC, k2] 4 times, k2, p1, k18, p1, k4, 2/2 RC, p1, 2/2 LC, k4.

ROW 9: 3/3 LC, k6, 3/3 RC, p1, [k2, 2/2 LC] 4 times, k2, p1, 3/3 LC, k6, 3/3 RC, p1, k2, 2/2 RC, k2, p1, k2, 2/2 LC, k2.

ROW 11: K18, p1, k2, [k2, 2/2 LC] 4 times, p1, k18, p1, 2/2 RC, k4, p1, k4, 2/2 LC.

ROW 13: K3, 3/3 RC, 3/3 LC, k3, p1, [2/2 LC, k2] 4 times, k2, p1, k3, 3/3 RC, 3/3 LC, k3, p1, k4, 2/2 RC, p1, 2/2 LC, k4.

ROW 15: K18, p1, [k2, 2/2 LC] 4 times, k2, p1, k18, p1, k2, 2/2 RC, k2, p1, k2, 2/2 LC, k2.

ROW 17: 3/3 LC, k6, 3/3 RC, p1, k2, [k2, 2/2 LC] 4 times, p1, 3/3 LC, k6, 3/3 RC, p1, 2/2 RC, k4, p1, k4, 2/2 LC.

ROW 19: K18, p1, [2/2 LC, k2] 4 times, k2, p1, k18, p1, k4, 2/2 RC, p1, 2/2 LC, k4.

ROW 21: K3, 3/3 RC, 3/3 LC, k3, p1, [k2, 2/2 LC] 4 times, k2, p1, k3, 3/3 RC, 3/3 LC, k3, p1, k2, 2/2 RC, k2, p1, k2, 2/2 LC, k2.

ROW 23: K18, p1, k2, [k2, 2/2 LC] 4 times, p1, k18, p1, 2/2 RC, k4, p1, k4, 2/2 LC.

ROW 24 (WS): [P8, k1] twice, p18, k1, p26, k1, p18.

PATTERN BEGINS

LEFT FRONT

Using smaller needles and the long-tail method, cast on 84 (84, 84, 91, 91, 91, 98, 98) sts. Do not join.

SIZES 1, 2 & 3 ONLY:
SET-UP ROW (WS): [P2, k2] twice, p18, PM, k1, p2, k2, p2, k1, p3, k2, p4, k2, p3, k1, p2, k1, [p3, k1] 3 times, p2, k2, p3, k2, p4, k2, p3, k1, p1.

SIZES 4, 5 & 6 ONLY:
SET-UP ROW (WS): [P2, k2] twice, p18, PM, k1, p2, k2, p2, k1, p3, k2, p4, k2, p3, k1, p2, k1, [p3, k1] 3 times, p2, k2, p3, k2, p4, k2, p3, k1, p2, k2, p2, k1, p1.

SIZES 7 & 8 ONLY:
SET-UP ROW (WS): [P2, k2] twice, p18, PM, k1, p2, k2, p2, k1, p3, k2, p4, k2, p3, k1, p2, k1, [p3, k1] 3 times, p2, k2, p3, k2, p4, k2, p3, k1, p2, k2, p2, k1, p2, k2, p2, k1, p1.

ALL SIZES AGAIN:
NEXT ROW (RS): Knit the knits and purl the purls to marker, SM, k18, [p2, k2] twice.
NEXT ROW (WS): [P2, k2] twice, p18, SM, knit the knits and purl the purls to end.

Commence Chart

ROW 1 (RS): Knit the knits and purl the purls to marker, SM, reading from the Chart or Written Instructions, work row 1 of Chart A across next 18 sts, [p2, k2] twice.
ROW 2 (WS): [P2, k2] twice, work row 2 of Chart A to marker, SM, knit the knits and purl the purls to end.
ROWS 3-14: Working next row of chart A, rep rows 1-2 a further 6 times.
Change to larger needles.

SIZES 1, 2 & 3 ONLY:
NEXT ROW (RS)(Inc): K1, p1, k3, pfb, p1, k1/R, k4, k1/L, pfb, p1, k3, pfb, p1, k2, [pfb, k3, k1/L] 3 times, pfb, k2, p1, k3, pfb, p1, k1/R, k4, k1/L, pfb, p1, k3, PM, p1, k2, pfb, p1, k2, k1/L, p1, SM, work row 15 of Chart A, [p2, k2] twice. *102 sts*
NEXT ROW (WS): [P2, k2] twice, work row 16 of Chart A, SM, k1, p8, k1, SM, p18, k1, p26, k1, p18, k1, p1.

SIZES 4, 5 & 6 ONLY:
NEXT ROW (RS)(Inc): K1, p1, k2, pfb, p1, k2, k1/L, p1, k3, pfb, p1, k1/R, k4, k1/L, pfb, p1, k3, pfb, p1, k2, [pfb, k3, k1/L] 3 times, pfb, k2, p1, k3, pfb, p1, k1/R, k4, k1/L, pfb, p1, k3, PM, p1, k2, pfb, p1, k2, k1/L, p1, SM, work row 15 of Chart A, [p2, k2] twice. *111 sts*
NEXT ROW (WS): [P2, k2] twice, work row 16 of Chart A, SM, k1, p8, k1, SM, p18, k1, p26, k1, p18, k1, p8, k1, p1.

SIZES 7 & 8 ONLY:
NEXT ROW (RS)(Inc): K1, p1, k1/R, k2, pfb, p1, k2, p1, k2, pfb, p1, k2, k1/L, p1, k3, pfb, p1, k1/R, k4, k1/L, pfb, p1, k3, pfb, p1, k2, [pfb, k3, k1/L] 3 times, pfb, k2, p1, k3, pfb, p1, k1/R, k4, k1/L, pfb, p1, k3, PM, p1, k2, pfb, p1, k2, k1/L, p1, SM, work row 15 of Chart A, [p2, k2] twice. *120 sts*
NEXT ROW (WS): [P2, k2] twice, work row 16 of Chart A, SM, k1, p8, k1, SM, p18, k1, p26, k1, p18, k1, p8, k1, p8, k1, p1.

ALL SIZES AGAIN:
NEXT ROW (RS)(Inc): K1, p1, starting where indicated for your size, work row 1 of Chart B to marker, SM, work row 1 of Chart C to marker, SM, M1L, PM, work row 1 of Chart A, [p2, k2] twice. *103 (103, 103, 112, 112, 112, 121, 121) sts*
NEXT ROW (WS): [P2, k2], work row 2 of Chart A to marker, SM, p1, SM, work row 2 of Chart C to marker, SM, work row 2 of Chart B to last 2 sts, k1, p1.

NOTE: *During the following section, Chart A continues up the front edge, while Chart C is shifted across the fabric, and in doing so, the stitches of Chart B are consumed. Read the following steps but **do not** knit. Then follow instructions listed for your size. The decrease or shift rows in the next section are first explained, and then listed in the combination worked for each size. Note your size and follow the instructions for repeating the rows as needed for your size. If, during the decreases or shifts, there are not enough stitches to complete a cable cross in Chart B, work those stitches in St st.*

RS SHIFT ROW: Patt to 2 sts before first marker, k2tog, SM, work Chart C to marker, SM, M1L, k to marker, SM, work Chart A, [p2, k2] twice.

WS SHIFT ROW: [P2, k2] twice, work Chart A to marker, SM, p to marker, M1P, SM, work Chart C to marker, SM, p2tog, patt to end.

RS DECREASE AND SHIFT ROW: Patt to 3 sts before first marker, k3tog, SM, work Chart C to marker, SM, M1L, k to marker, SM, work Chart A, [p2, k2] twice. *1 st dec*

Continue Work from Here

SIZES 1, 2 & 3 ONLY:
Continuing in patt as set, [work RS Decrease and Shift Row every RS row] twice, [work RS Shift Row every RS row twice, then work RS Decrease and Shift Row once] 14 times, then [work RS Decrease and Shift Row every 4th row] twice. *85 sts*

SIZES 4, 5 & 6 ONLY:
Continuing in patt as set, [work RS Decrease and Shift Row, then WS Shift Row] 4 times, [work RS Decrease and Shift Row every RS row] 4 times, then [work RS Shift Row every RS row twice, then work RS Decrease and Shift Row once] 13 times, then work RS Shift Row once more. *91 sts*

SIZES 7 & 8 ONLY:
Continuing in patt as set, [work RS Decrease and Shift Row every RS row] 6 times, [work RS Decrease and Shift Row, then WS Shift Row, then RS Shift Row, then WS Shift Row] 6 times, then [work RS Shift Row every RS row twice, then work RS Decrease and Shift Row once] 10 times. *99 sts*

ALL SIZES AGAIN:
NEXT ROW (WS): Patt to end, removing final marker in the row.

With RS facing, PLM at right edge of piece to mark beg of armhole.

Please read remaining section carefully, as Armhole Shift Rows and Neck Decreases will occur **AT THE SAME TIME**. During the Armhole Shift Rows, all Chart C sts will be consumed.

ARMHOLE SHIFT ROW (RS): K1, ssp, work rem sts from Chart C to marker as set, SM, M1L, work St st to marker, SM, work Chart A as est, [p2, k2] twice.

Rep Armhole Shift Row every RS row a further 9 times. Remove first marker on final row. The only marker remaining is between Chart A and the St st section.

NEXT ROW (WS): Patt to end.
NEXT ROW (RS): K1, p1, patt to marker, SM, work Chart A as est, [p2, k2] twice.

Neck Decreases

And **AT THE SAME TIME**, beg at first Armhole Shift Row, work neck dec as foll:
NEXT ROW (RS)(Neck Dec): Patt to 2 sts before marker, k2tog, SM, patt to end.
1 st dec

Rep Neck Dec Row every 2 (2, 2, 2, 2, 4, 4, 4) rows a further 4 (2, 1, 2, 1, 11, 9, 7) times, then every 4 (4, 4, 4, 4, 6, 6, 6) rows 6 (8, 9, 10, 11, 1, 3, 5) times. *74 (74, 74, 78, 78, 78, 86, 86) sts*

Work straight in patt as set until piece measures 15 (16.5, 17, 19, 20.5, 23, 24, 25.5) cm / 6 (6½, 6¾, 7½, 8, 9, 9½, 10)" from locking stitch marker, ending with a RS row.

Commence Shoulder Short Rows

SIZES 1, 2, 3, 4, 5 & 6 ONLY:
SHORT ROW 1 (WS): Patt to 2 sts before end, turn and PLM for JSR.
SHORT ROW 2 (RS): Patt to end.
SHORT ROW 3: Patt to 2 sts before previous turn, turn and PLM for JSR.
SHORT ROW 4: Patt to end.

Rep short rows 3-4 a further 12 (12, 12, 6, 6, 6, –, –) times.

SIZES 7 & 8 ONLY:
SHORT ROW 1 (WS): Patt to 3 sts before end, turn and PLM for JSR.
SHORT ROW 2 (RS): Patt to end.

ALL SIZES AGAIN:
NEXT SHORT ROW (WS): Patt to 3 sts before previous turn, turn and PLM for JSR.
NEXT SHORT ROW (RS): Patt to end.

Rep last 2 short rows a further 5 (5, 5, 11, 11, 11, 18, 18) times.

NEXT SHORT ROW (WS): Patt to end resolving all short rows through the back loop.
NEXT ROW (RS): Patt to end.

Place 48 (48, 48, 52, 52, 52, 60, 60) sts to the right of marker on stitch holder or scrap yarn. *26 sts on needle*

Work straight over rem sts for 3 cm / 1¼". Place all sts on stitch holder or scrap yarn. Break working yarn and set aside.

RIGHT FRONT

Using smaller needles and the long-tail method, cast on 84 (84, 84, 91, 91, 91, 98, 98) sts. Do not join.

SIZES 1, 2 & 3 ONLY:
NEXT ROW (WS): P1, k1, p3, k2, p4, k2, p3, k2, p2, [k1, p3] 3 times, k1, p2, k1, p3, k2, p4, k2, p3, k1, p2, k2, p2, k1, PM, p18, [k2, p2] twice.

SIZES 4, 5 & 6 ONLY:
NEXT ROW (WS): P1, k1, p2, k2, p2, k1, p3, k2, p4, k2, p3, k2, p2, [k1, p3] 3 times, k1, p2, k1, p3, k2, p4, k2, p3, k1, p2, k2, p2, k1, PM, p18, [k2, p2] twice.

SIZES 7 & 8 ONLY:
NEXT ROW (WS): P1, k1, p2, k2, p2, k1, p2, k2, p2, k1, p3, k2, p4, k2, p3, k2, p2, [k1, p3] 3 times, k1, p2, k1, p3, k2, p4, k2, p3, k1, p2, k2, p2, k1, PM, p18, [k2, p2] twice.

ALL SIZES AGAIN:
NEXT ROW (RS): [K2, p2] twice, k18, SM, knit the knits and purl the purls to end.
NEXT ROW (WS): Knit the knits and purl the purls to marker, SM, p18, [k2, p2].

Commence Charts

NEXT ROW: [K2, p2] twice, reading from Chart or Written Instructions, work row 1 of Chart A to marker, SM, knit the knits and purl the purls to end.
NEXT ROW: Knit the knits and purl the purls to marker, SM, work row 2 of Chart A, [k2, p2] twice.

Working next row of chart, work last 2 rows a further 6 times, working to end of row 14 of Chart A. Change to larger needles.

SIZES 1, 2 & 3 ONLY:
NEXT ROW (RS)(Inc): [K2, p2] twice, work row 15 of Chart A, SM, p1, k1/R, k2, pfb, p1, k2, p1, PM, k3, pfb, p1, k1/R, k4, k1/L, pfb, p1, k3, p1, k2, [pfb, k1/R, k3] 3 times, pfb, k2, pfb, p1, k3, pfb, p1, k1/R, k4, k1/L, pfb, p1, k3, p1, k1. *102 sts*
NEXT ROW (WS): P1, k1, p18, k1, p26, k1, p18, SM, k1, p8, k1, SM, work row 16 of Chart A, [k2, p2] twice.

SIZES 4, 5 & 6 ONLY:
NEXT ROW (RS)(Inc): [K2, p2] twice, work row 15 of Chart A, SM, p1, k1/R, k2, pfb, p1, k2, p1, PM, k3, pfb, p1, k1/R, k4, k1/L, pfb, p1, k3, p1, k2, [pfb, k1/R, k3] 3 times, pfb, k2, pfb, p1, k3, pfb, p1, k1/R, k4, k1/L, pfb, p1, k3, p1, k1/R, k2, pfb, p1, k2, p1, k1. *111 sts*
NEXT ROW (WS): P1, k1, p8, k1, p18, k1, p26, k1, p18, SM, k1, p8, k1, SM, work row 16 of Chart A, [k2, p2] twice.

SIZES 7 & 8 ONLY:
NEXT ROW (RS)(Inc): [K2, p2] twice, work row 15 of Chart A, SM, p1, k1/R, k2, pfb, p1, k2, p1, PM, k3, pfb, p1, k1/R, k4, k1/L, pfb, p1, k3, p1, k2, [pfb, k1/R, k3] 3 times, pfb, k2, pfb, p1, k3, pfb, p1, k1/R, k4, k1/L, pfb, p1, k3, p1, k1/R, k2, pfb, p1, k2, p1, k2, pfb, p1, k2, k1/R, p1, k1. *120 sts*
NEXT ROW (WS): P1, k1, p8, k1, p8, k1, p18, k1, p26, k1, p18, SM, k1, p8, k1, SM, work row 16 of Chart A, [k2, p2] twice.

ALL SIZES AGAIN:
NEXT ROW (RS): [K2, p2] twice, work row 1 of Chart A, SM, M1R, PM, work row 1 of Chart D to marker, SM, ending where indicated for your size, work row 1 of Chart E to last 2 sts, p1, k1. *103 (103, 103, 112, 112, 112, 121, 121) sts*
NEXT ROW (WS): P1, k1, work row 2 of Chart E to marker, SM, work row 2 of Chart D to marker, p1, SM, work row 2 of Chart A to last 4 sts, p2, k2.

NOTE: *During the following section, Chart A continues up the front edge, while Chart D is shifted across the fabric, and in doing so, the stitches of Chart E are consumed. Read* *the following steps but **do not** knit. Then follow instructions listed for your size. The decrease or shift rows in the next section are first explained, and then listed in the combination worked for each size. Note your size and follow the instructions for repeating the rows for your size. If, during the decreases or shifts, there are not enough stitches to complete a cable cross in the Right Front Cable Panel, work those stitches in St st.*

RS SHIFT ROW: [K2, p2] twice, work Chart A to marker, SM, k to marker, M1R, SM, work Chart D to marker, SM, ssk, patt to end.

WS SHIFT ROW: Patt to 2 sts before marker, ssp, SM, work Chart D to marker, SM, M1PR, p to marker, SM, work Chart A to last 8 sts, [k2, p2] twice.

RS DECREASE AND SHIFT ROW: [K2, p2] twice, work Chart A to marker, SM, k to marker, M1R, SM, work Chart D to marker, SM, sssk, patt to end. *1 st dec*

Continue Work from Here

SIZES 1, 2 & 3 ONLY:
Continuing in patt as set, [work RS Decrease and Shift Row every RS row] twice, [work RS Shift Row every RS row twice, then work RS Decrease and Shift Row once] 14 times, then [work RS Decrease and Shift Row every 4th row] twice. *85 sts*

SIZES 4, 5 & 6 ONLY:
Continuing in patt as set, [work RS Decrease and Shift Row, then WS Shift Row] 4 times, [work RS Decrease and Shift Row every RS row] 4 times, then [work RS Shift Row every RS row twice, then work RS Decrease and Shift Row once] 13 times, then work RS Shift Row once more. *91 sts*

SIZES 7 & 8 ONLY:
Continuing in patt as set, [work RS Decrease and Shift Row every RS row] 6 times, [work RS Decrease and Shift Row, then WS Shift Row, then RS Shift Row, then WS Shift Row] 6 times, then [work RS Shift Row every RS row twice, then work RS Decrease and Shift Row once] 10 times. *99 sts*

ALL SIZES AGAIN:
NEXT ROW (WS): Patt to end.
With RS facing, PLM at left edge of piece to mark beg of armhole.

Please read remaining section carefully, as Armhole Shift Rows and Neck Decreases will occur **AT THE SAME TIME**. During the Armhole Shift Rows, all Chart D sts will be consumed.

ARMHOLE SHIFT ROW (RS): [K2, p2] twice, work Chart A, SM, k to marker, M1R, SM, work Chart D to last 3 sts, p2tog, k1.

Rep Armhole Shift Row every RS row a further 9 times and remove second marker on final row. The only marker remaining is between Chart A and the St st section.

NEXT ROW (WS): Patt to end.
NEXT ROW (RS): [K2, p2] twice, work Chart A as est, SM, patt to last 2 sts, p1, k1. Work straight in patt as est until piece measures 15 (16.5, 17, 19, 20.5, 23, 24, 25.5) cm / 6 (6½, 6¾, 7½, 8, 9, 9½, 10)" from locking st marker, ending with a WS row.

Neck Decreases

And **AT THE SAME TIME**, beg at first armhole shift row, work neck decs as foll:

NEXT ROW (RS)(Neck Dec): Patt to marker, SM, ssk, patt to end. *1 st dec*

Rep Neck Dec row every 2 (2, 2, 2, 2, 4, 4, 4) rows a further 4 (2, 1, 2, 1, 11, 9, 7) times, then every 4 (4, 4, 4, 4, 6, 6, 6) rows 6 (8, 9, 10, 11, 1, 3, 5) times. *74 (74, 74, 78, 78, 78, 86, 86) sts*

Shoulder Short Rows

SIZES 1, 2, 3, 4, 5 & 6 ONLY:
SHORT ROW 1 (RS): Patt to 2 sts before end, turn and PLM for JSR.
SHORT ROW 2 (WS): Patt to end.
SHORT ROW 3: Patt to 2 sts before previous turn, turn and PLM for JSR.
SHORT ROW 4: Patt to end.

Rep short rows 3-4 a further 12 (12, 12, 6, 6, 6, –, –) times.

SIZES 7 & 8 ONLY:
NEXT ROW (RS): Patt to 3 sts before end, turn and PLM for JSR.
NEXT ROW (WS): Patt to end.

ALL SIZES AGAIN:
NEXT SHORT ROW (RS): Patt to 3 sts before previous turn, turn and PLM for JSR.
NEXT SHORT ROW (WS): Patt to end.

Rep last 2 short rows a further 5 (5, 5, 11, 11, 11, 18, 18) times.

NEXT ROW (RS): Patt across all sts, resolving all short rows through the back loop.
NEXT ROW (WS): Patt to end.

Place 48 (48, 48, 52, 52, 52, 60, 60) sts to the left of marker on stitch holder or scrap yarn. *26 sts on needle*

Work straight over rem sts for 3 cm / 1¼". Place all sts on stitch holder or scrap yarn. Break yarn and set aside.

BACK

Using smaller needles and the long-tail method, cast on 114 (114, 114, 122, 122, 122, 138, 138) sts. Do not join.

SET-UP ROW (WS): [P2, k2] 12 (12, 12, 13, 13, 13, 15, 15) times, PM, p18, PM, [k2, p2] 12 (12, 12, 13, 13, 13, 15, 15) times to end.

Knit the knits and purl the purls for 2 rows.

Commence Charts

ROW 1 (RS): [K2, p2] to marker, SM, reading from the Chart or Written Instructions, work row 1 of Chart A, SM, [p2, k2] to end.
ROW 2 (WS): [P2, k2] to marker, SM, work row 2 of Chart A, SM, [k2, p2] to end.

Work straight in patt as set for a further 14 rows. Change to larger needles.

NEXT ROW (RS): K to marker, SM, work Chart A, SM, k to end.
NEXT ROW (WS): P to marker, SM, work Chart A, SM, p to end.

Work straight in patt as set until Back length matches Fronts to armhole marker, ending with a WS row. PLM in either edge to mark beg of armhole.

Work straight in patt as set until piece measures 15 (16.5, 17, 19, 20.5, 23, 24, 25.5) cm / 6 (6½, 6¾, 7½, 8, 9, 9½, 10)" from locking st marker, ending with a WS row.

Begin Shoulder Short Rows

SIZES 1, 2, 3, 4, 5 & 6 ONLY:
SHORT ROW 1 (RS): Patt to 2 sts before end, turn and PLM for JSR.
SHORT ROW 2 (WS): Patt to 2 sts before end, turn and PLM for JSR.
SHORT ROW 3: Work in pattern as est to 2 sts before previous turn, turn and PLM for JSR.
SHORT ROW 4: Patt to 2 sts before previous turn, turn and PLM for JSR.

Rep short rows 3-4 a further 12 (12, 12, 6, 6, 6, –, –) times.

SIZES 7 & 8 ONLY:
SHORT ROW 1 (RS): Patt to 3 sts before end, turn and PLM for JSR.
SHORT ROW 2 (WS): Patt to 3 sts before end, turn and PLM for JSR.

ALL SIZES AGAIN:
NEXT SHORT ROW (RS): Patt to 3 sts before last marker, turn and PLM for JSR.
NEXT SHORT ROW (WS): Patt to 3 sts before last marker, turn and PLM for JSR.

Rep last 2 short rows a further 5 (5, 5, 11, 11, 11, 18, 18) times.

NEXT SHORT ROW (RS): Patt across all sts in, resolving all short rows through the back loop.
NEXT ROW (WS): Patt to end, resolving all rem short rows. **Do not** break yarn.

Steam-block pieces. With RSs together and WSs facing out, and starting with right shoulder, join right shoulder front and back together using 3-needle cast off across 48 (48, 48, 52, 52, 52, 60, 60) shoulder sts, cast off centre 18 sts on back, then join left shoulder front and back together using 3-needle cast off across rem 48 (48, 48, 52, 52, 52, 60, 60) shoulder sts. Seam sides from hem to armhole markers.

SLEEVES

Using larger needles and beg at underarm, pick up and k58 (62, 66, 72, 78, 86, 92, 98) sts in armhole. Join to work in the round and PM to indicate beg of round.

NEXT ROUND: Knit.
NEXT ROUND (DEC): K1, ssk, k to 3 sts before end, k2tog, k1. *2 sts dec*

Rep Dec round every 10 (8, 6, 6, 4, 4, 2, 2) rounds a further 8 (10, 7, 11, 6, 18, 3, 9) times, then every 0 (0, 8, 8, 6, 6, 4, 4) rounds 0 (0, 5, 2, 10, 2, 20, 17) times. *40 (40, 40, 44, 44, 44, 44, 44) sts*

Work straight in St st as set until Sleeve measures 35.5 cm / 14" from pick-up.

Change to smaller needles.

RIB ROUND: [K2, p2] to end.
Rep Rib round until rib measures 5 cm / 2".
Cast off using sewn or stretchy method.

FINISHING

Place both sets of held Chart A sts onto needles and, with RSs together and WSs facing out, join together using 3-needle cast off. Seam to centre back neck.

Weave in all ends and block to measurements.

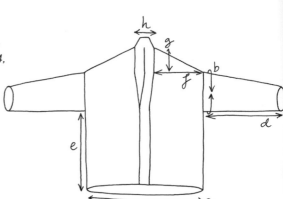

PINA SCHEMATIC KEY

a. Back width:
57 (57, 57, 61, 61, 61, 69.5, 69.5) cm / 22¼ (22¼, 22¼, 24, 24, 24, 27¼, 27¼)"
b. Upper arm circumference:
30 (32.5, 34.5, 37.5, 40.5, 45, 48, 51) cm / 12 (12¾, 13½, 14¾, 16, 17¾, 18¾, 20)"
c. Cuff circumference:
21 (21, 21, 23, 23, 23, 23, 23) cm / 8¼ (8¼, 8¼, 9, 9, 9, 9, 9)"
d. Sleeve length: 40.5 cm / 16"
e. Body length: 44 cm / 17¼"
f. Shoulder width:
25 (25, 25, 27.5, 27.5, 27.5, 31.5, 31.5) cm / 9¾ (9¾, 9¾, 10¾, 10¾, 10¾, 12½, 12½)"
g. Shoulder drop: 15 cm / 6"
h. Back neck width: 7 cm / 2¾"

Chart A (Front Band Cable)   Chart C (Left Travelling Cable) 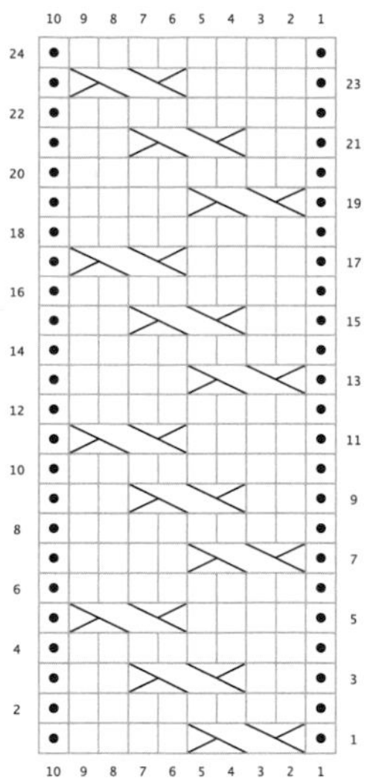   Chart D (Right Travelling Cable)

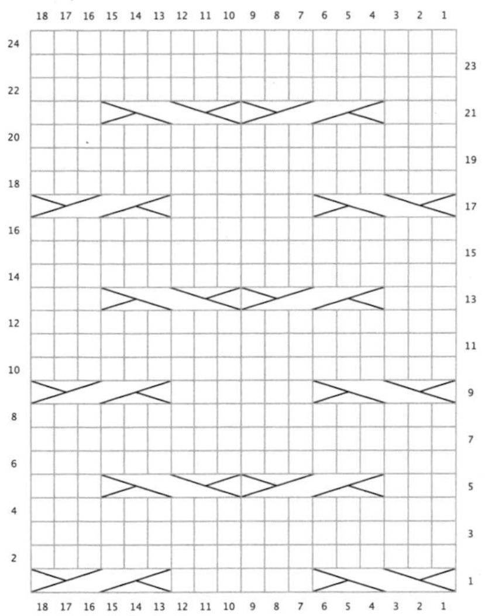

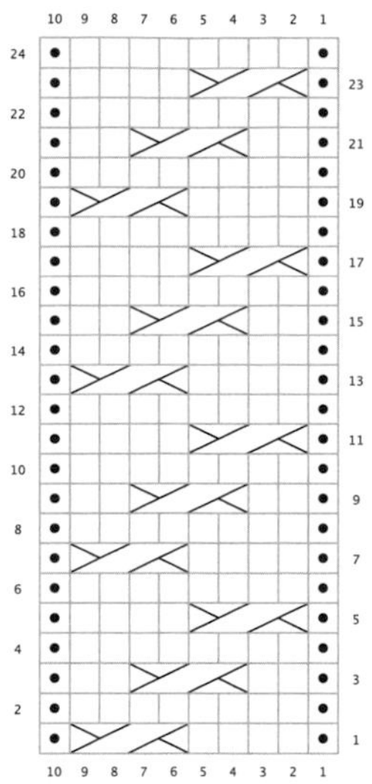

RS: knit / WS: purl

RS: purl / WS: knit

2/2 LC

2/2 RC

3/3 LC

3/3 RC

Begin sizes 1, 2 & 3

Begin sizes 1, 2 & 3

Begin sizes 7 & 8

Repeat (work 3 times in total)

End sizes 1, 2 & 3

End sizes 4, 5 & 6

End sizes 7 & 8

Chart B (Left Front Cable Panel)

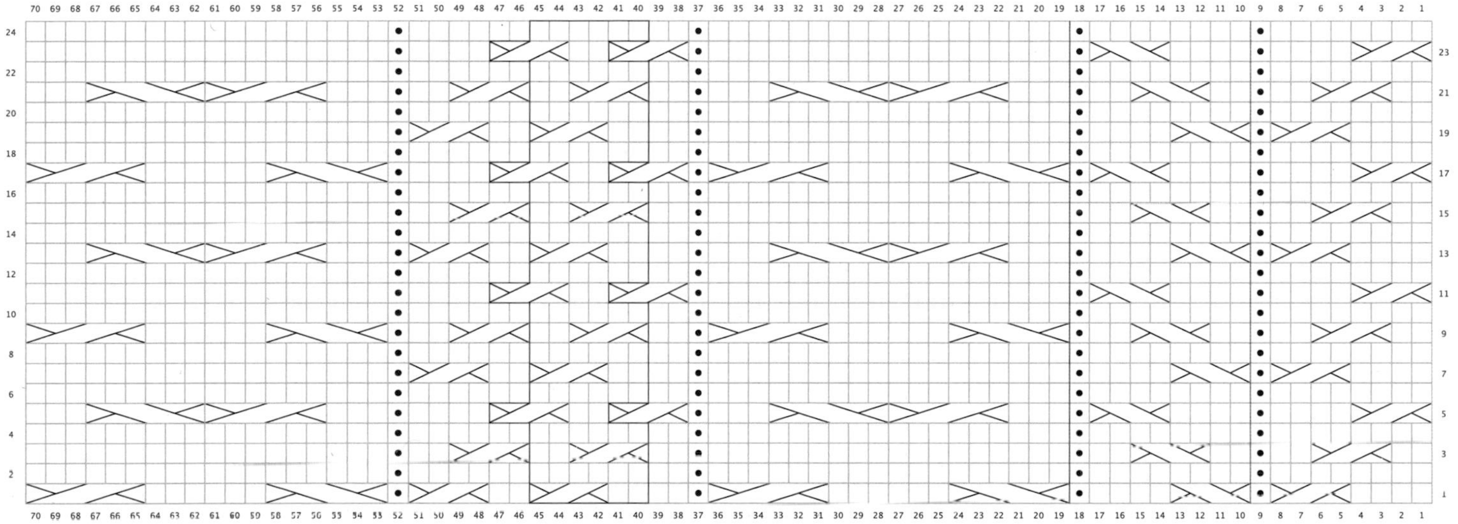

Chart E (Right Front Cable Panel)

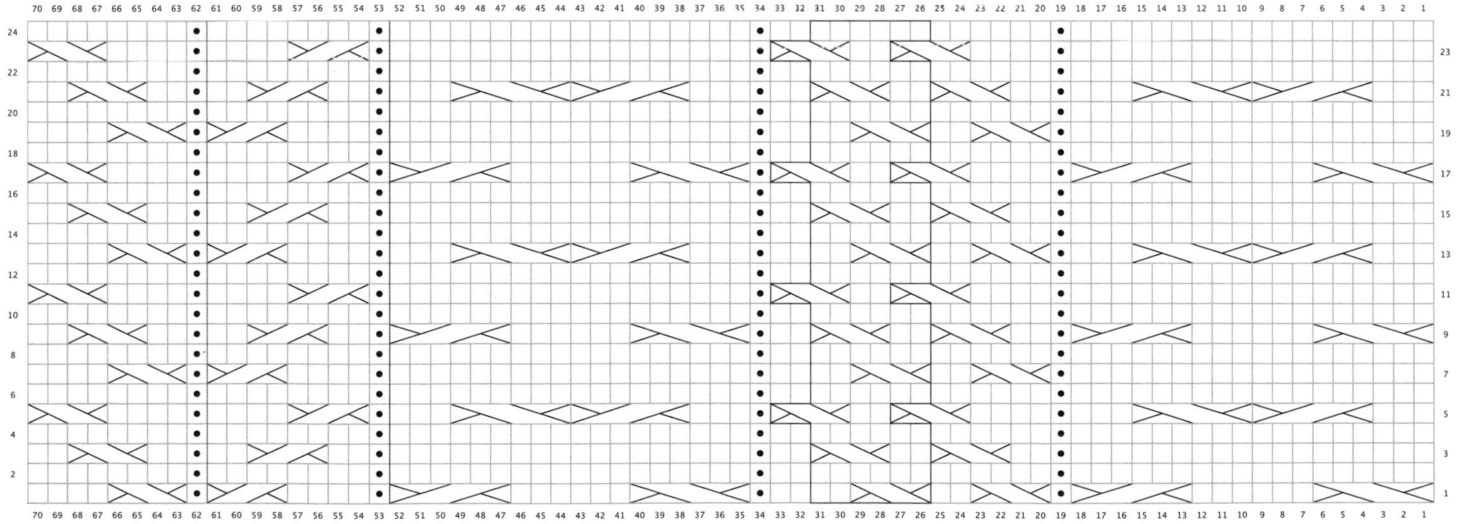

MAD LIBS

EXERCISE TWO

As we've seen thus far, mash-ups are a great way to explore your creativity while working within the framework of visual imagery that we already know. By using images as our starting point, we guarantee ourselves some degree of security with the finished product. Perhaps we already have an existing representation of what the garment shape looks like, or what the stitch pattern looks like when it's placed, or how two colours work together. It's concrete and solid and easier to envision what could happen next.

However, sometimes mash-ups can be overwhelming. They provide a wealth of information at your feet: so many different options, potentially with no clear delineations as to what the final product will be. You could easily take inspiration from a shawl, for instance, and turn it into a hat, or vice versa. Or you could take the lines and swoops of existing lace and turn them into a colourwork chart. Sometimes this is a liberating feeling, but it can be overwhelming to go straight from inspiration to a blank page with no framework. With our next exercise, mad libs, we'll do the opposite: make the inspiration far more nebulous, but give ourselves a stronger framework with which to create the finished design.

A lot of us here in the States grew up playing the game Mad Libs on long car rides. They were hours of entertainment in paperback form. For those not familiar, a Mad Libs sentence is constructed thus: "The (noun) went walking (adverb) by the (adjective) river with their (noun)". The keeper of the book shouts out the word type, and it's the rest of the car's job to supply them with as many ridiculous answers as possible. These are then slotted into their appropriate spots in the now nonsensical sentence, which is read aloud, and hilarity ensues. I suspect that Mad Libs is the reason I've loved grammar since I was a kid, but it also gave me a great idea for a knitting exercise.

Opposite, there's a list of different attributes, ones that we might have gleaned from some previous mash-ups. They are separated into three categories: garment type, fabric type, and direction of knitting. Write all the attributes on scraps of paper and throw them into a bowl, then pick three attributes out at random. You can also decide which ones to use by a random number generator, rolling a pair of dice, throwing them on the floor and seeing which ones the cat plays with, any method you like. Just pick three at random. These three attributes will be the framework for the design you will go on to brainstorm. But here's the catch: because all three categories are jumbled together, you may get any combination. Two garment types and a

fabric type, two fabric types and a direction of knitting, or even three directions of knitting all together. And you can only trade in a slip if you get two of the exact same thing (two cables, for example, or two short rows). Otherwise, just accept the slips that you have and figure out a way to make them work. This forces you to think on your feet and challenges how you define each of the attributes.

Once you have your three attributes, think of the many different interpretations of the words themselves. When I drew my three attributes for the project for this book (a friend randomly chose numbers and told me whether to read the lists up or down, right or left when counting), I got 'sideways', 'cable', and 'shawl'. I freely admit that I lucked out by getting one of each category! But I also knew each word contained multiple options to play with and explore.

I first started with the most solid framework I had, the garment type. Luckily, this is where past experience gave me some clarity: I've knit a lot of shawls in a lot of different shapes, so I have a good idea of the geometry of the finished pieces. They can be triangular, rectangular, circular, half-circular, crescent-shaped, symmetrical, asymmetrical—many options to work with, but ones with which I was

triangular shawl	short rows	center out
circular shawl	short rows	diagonal
circular shawl	lace	sideways
square shawl	lace	top down
scarf	cables	bottom up
cowl	texture	center out
hat	stripes	diagonal
pullover	cables	sideways
triangular shawl	texture	top down
cowl	stripes	bottom up

familiar and comfortable. I jotted my garment options down on paper and put them aside until I knew more about my stitch pattern and my direction of knitting.

After I went through these potential shapes for my shawl, I got sideways as my direction of knitting. This should be simple to interpret. But, since there isn't always a clear shape or clear up or down to shawls, how do I know which direction is sideways? If the shawl were a triangle it could be worked on the diagonal, from tip to tip or tip to edge. If the shawl were a rectangle, I could work it back and forth lengthwise to move sideways across the fabric. Or I could take it to mean that since lengthwise is the typical orientation of knitting for rectangular shawls, going sideways would actually mean knitting it widthways. Or I could work it on the bias so that the rows themselves moved diagonally. Perhaps, if the shawl was a crescent, sideways meant short rows? Who knows! There is no right answer. The only answer is the project that makes you happy.

This is the crux of mad libs. Now you get to tailor all these options to what you want the finished project to be. To that end, I started thinking about what I love in knitting. I tend to prefer angular, architectural cables to those that are more organic, so I knew that would probably be how I brought cables into play on this shawl. I knew that angular cables on a crescent background could be very striking; the cognitive dissonance of the strict lines against the gently curved shape could be very intriguing. But I haven't yet found a method for constructing crescent shawls that I'm fully enamoured with, so I put that aside. I thought about a rectangular background, but knew that the cables would have to be very complex to make the shape unique and fulfilling enough for me, so I put that aside. With all of this in mind, I decided that a triangular shawl would be the best background. The act of incorporating the stitches into the cables would keep the fabric fluid, and the triangular shape would allow for some structure and rhythm without being boring. I played with a few different ideas—antler cables that fanned out from a single point, cables that grew and shrank along the length of the shawl—but I kept coming back to the idea of incorporating the idea of 'sideways' not just into the direction of knitting but the cables themselves. I love the way all over antler cables look, especially when they're left to run wild across the entire expanse of a fabric. I could visualise the lines moving across the shawl, then at some point breaking and twisting unexpectedly in the other direction.

This is the fun of mad libs: rather than the actual pictures that you take inspiration from in mash-ups, the only pictures here are the ones in your head, either from your memory or imagination. Because we have this personal understanding or interpretation of the given attributes, we have a basic framework for the outcome of the piece. Often when I use this exercise in class, someone will ask me "How is a triangular shawl constructed?" or "How is a hat worked diagonally?" and my answer is always the same: there is no correct answer. It doesn't matter how other people have done these things in the past; it matters how you want to do it now. That is not to say that we can't use our previous experience, as with mash-ups, to tell us how something might work. If we've knit a triangular shawl or worked a hat on the diagonal before, those known constructions could inform our understanding of the piece we're creating now. But those constructions are not the only possibility: there is no one way to create something with knitting. So don't let a lack of knowledge of how other people would create a shape or utilise a construction limit your creativity. Often that's when we truly begin to explore the boundaries of what's possible in knitting!

Mad libs are also a good place to take your inspiration outside of the concrete, as with mash-ups. What if, instead of fabric type, you put song titles into the bowl? Or book characters instead of direction of knitting? Or historical era instead of garment type? Don't limit yourself to visual media and see where the exploration takes you!

The final stage of mad libs is to step back and see if the finished piece is something that you will want to knit and that either you or the recipient will want to wear. This is when you can take a step away from the rigid framework of the three attributes you've pulled; if one of them is clearly something you'd never wear in a million years, don't force it. What could you do to make it more you? Experiment with changing, adding, or removing attributes until it fits your needs or wishes. Again, as with mash-ups, you can tweak and tweak and tweak your idea until it no longer resembles the original attributes, but as long as it's what you want, you've got something good on your hands.

Mad libs are one of my favourite exercises when I'm feeling particularly parched in the inspiration department. They force us to think about combinations that we may not have come up with on our own, or constructions we'd never otherwise try, and they also allow us to interpret our own preferences and interests through a helpful framework. Give them a go!

AUDRE
—
SHAWL

Audre Lorde, American poet

Audre

One size:

144 cm / 56¾" wide x 74 cm / 29¼" deep

Yarn: Miss Babs

Keira (4ply / fingering weight;
100% superwash Merino wool;
512 m / 560 yds per 225 g skein)

Shade: Espresso; 2 skeins

Gauge:

28 sts & 33 rows = 10 cm / 4" over cable
pattern on 3.75 mm needles after blocking.

Needles:

3.75 mm / US 5 circular needle,
minimum 80 cm / 32" length

3.25 mm / US 3 circular needle,
minimum 60 cm / 24" length

Always use a needle size that will result
in the correct gauge after blocking.

Notions:

1 stitch marker, cable needle, tapestry
needle, t-pins and blocking wires

Notes:

Audre is cast on with a small number of
stitches, then increased at a consistent
rate to the cast-off edge.

CHARTS – WRITTEN INSTRUCTIONS

CHART A (SET-UP)

ROW 1 (RS): K1, M1L. *1 st inc*
ROW 2 (WS): P2.
ROW 3: K2, M1L. *1 st inc*
ROW 4: K1, p2.
ROW 5: K2, p1, M1L. *1 st inc*
ROW 6: K2, p2.
ROW 7: K2, p2, M1L. *1 st inc*
ROW 8: P1, k2, p2.
ROW 9: K2, p2, k1, M1L. *1 st inc*
ROW 10: P2, k2, p2.
ROW 11: K2, p2, k2, M1L. *1 st inc*
ROW 12: K1, p2, k2, p2.

ROW 13: 2/2 LC, k2, p1, M1L. *1 st inc*
ROW 14: K2, p6.
ROW 15: K2, 2/2 LPC, p2, M1L. *1 st inc*
ROW 16: P1, [k2, p2] twice.
ROW 17: K2, p2, 2/2 LC, k1, M1L. *1 st inc*
ROW 18: P6, k2, p2.
ROW 19: 2/2 LC, k2, 2/2 LPC, M1L. *1 st inc*
ROW 20: K1, p2, k2, p6.
ROW 21: K2, 2/2 LPC, p2, k2, p1, M1L. *1 st inc*
ROW 22: [K2, p2] 3 times.
ROW 23: K2, p2, 2/2 LC, k2, p2, M1L. *1 st inc*
ROW 24: P1, k2, p6, k2, p2.
ROW 25: 2/2 LC, k2, 2/2 LPC, p2, k1, M1L. *1 st inc*
ROW 26: [P2, k2] twice, p6.
ROW 27: K2, p2, 2/2 LPC, p2, 2/2 LC, k2, M1L. *1 st inc*
ROW 28: K1, p6, [k2, p2] twice.
ROW 29: K2, p2, 2/2 LC, k2, 2/2 LPC, p1,
M1L. *1 st inc*
ROW 30: K2, p2, k2, p6, k2, p2.
ROW 31: 2/2 LC, k2, 2/2 LPC, p2, k2, p2,
M1L. *1 st inc*
ROW 32: P1, [k2, p2] 3 times, p4.
ROW 33: K2, 2/2 LPC, p2, 2/2 LC, k2, p2, k1,
M1L. *1 st inc*
ROW 34: P2, k2, p6, [k2, p2] twice.
ROW 35: K2, p2, 2/2 LC, k2, 2/2 LPC, p2, k2,
M1L. *1 st inc*
ROW 36: K1, [p2, k2] twice, p6, k2, p2.
ROW 37: 2/2 LC, k2, 2/2 LPC, p2, 2/2 LC, k2,
p1, M1L. *1 st inc*
ROW 38: K2, p6, [k2, p2] twice, p4.
ROW 39: K2, 2/2 LPC, p2, 2/2 LC, k2,
2/2 LPC, p2, M1L. *1 st inc*
ROW 40: P1, k2, p2, k2, p6, [k2, p2] twice.
ROW 41: K2, p2, 2/2 LC, k2, 2/2 LPC, p2,
2/2 LC, k1, M1L. *1 st inc*
ROW 42: P6, k2, p2, k2, p6, k2, p2.

CHART B (BODY PATTERN)

The section marked in square brackets is
worked once on the first repeat, twice on
the second repeat, 3 times on the third
repeat and so on. Rows 1-24 are worked as
written, but when you work row 1 for the
second time it will be: [2/2 LC, k2, 2/2 LPC,
p2] twice, 2/2 LC, k2, 2/2 LPC, M1L. And the

third time will be worked: [2/2 LC, k2, 2/2
LPC, p2] 3 times, 2/2 LC, k2, 2/2 LPC, M1L.

ROW 1 (RS): [2/2 LC, k2, 2/2 LPC, p2], 2/2 LC,
k2, 2/2 LPC, M1L. *1 st inc*
ROW 2 (WS): K1, p2, k2, p6, [k2, p2, k2, p6].
ROW 3: [K2, 2/2 LPC, p2, 2/2 LC], k2,
2/2 LPC, p2, k2, p1, M1L. *1 st inc*
ROW 4: [k2, p2] 3 times, p4, [p4, (k2, p2) twice].
ROW 5: K2, [p2, 2/2 LC, k2, 2/2 LPC], p2,
2/2 LC, k2, p2, M1L. *1 st inc*
ROW 6: P1, k2, p6, k2, p2, [k2, p6, k2, p2].
ROW 7: [2/2 LC, k2, 2/2 LPC, p2], 2/2 LC, k2,
2/2 LPC, p2, k1, M1L. *1 st inc*
ROW 8: (P2, k2) twice, p6, [k2, p2, k2, p6].
ROW 9: [K2, 2/2 LPC, p2, 2/2 LC], k2,
2/2 LPC, p2, 2/2 LC, k2, M1L. *1 st inc*
ROW 10: K1, p6, (k2, p2) twice, [p4, (k2, p2) twice].
ROW 11: K2, [p2, 2/2 LC, k2, 2/2 LPC],
p2, 2/2 LC, k2, 2/2 LPC, p1, M1L. *1 st inc*
ROW 12: K2, p2, k2, p6, k2, p2, [k2, p6, k2, p2].
ROW 13: [2/2 LC, k2, 2/2 LPC, p2], 2/2 LC, k2,
2/2 LPC, p2, k2, p2, M1L. *1 st inc*
ROW 14: P1, (k2, p2) twice, k2, p6,
[k2, p2, k2, p6].
ROW 15: [K2, 2/2 LPC, p2, 2/2 LC], k2,
2/2 LPC, p2, 2/2 LC, k2, p1, M1L. *1 st inc*
ROW 16: P2, k2, p6, (k2, p2) twice,
[p4, (k2, p2) twice].
ROW 17: K2, [p2, 2/2 LC, k2, 2/2 LPC], p2,
2/2 LC, k2, 2/2 LPC, p2, k2, M1L. *1 st inc*
ROW 18: K1, (p2, k2) twice, p6, k2, p2,
[k2, p6, k2, p2].
ROW 19: [2/2 LC, k2, 2/2 LPC, p2], 2/2 LC,
k2, 2/2 LPC, p2, 2/2 LC, k2, p1, M1L. *1 st inc*
ROW 20: K2, p6, k2, p2, k2, p6, [k2, p2, k2, p6].
ROW 21: [K2, 2/2 LPC, p2, 2/2 LC], k2, 2/2
LPC, p2, 2/2 LC, k2, 2/2 LPC, p2, M1L. *1 st inc*
ROW 22: P1, k2, p2, k2, p6, (k2, p2) twice,
[p4, (k2, p2) twice].
ROW 23: K2, [p2, 2/2 LC, k2, 2/2 LPC], p2,
2/2 LC, k2, 2/2 LPC, p2, 2/2 LC, k1, M1L.
1 st inc
ROW 24: P6, k2, p2, k2, p6, k2, p2,
[k2, p6, k2, p2].

Chart C (Transition)

ROW 1 (RS): (K2, p2) 3 times, [2/2 LC, k2, 2/2 LPC, p2] 9 times, 2/2 LC, k2, 2/2 LPC, M1L. *1 st inc*

ROW 2 (WS): K1, p2, k2, p6, [k2, p2, k2, p6] 9 times, (k2, p2) 3 times.

ROW 3: (K2, p2) 3 times, [k2, 2/2 LPC, p2, 2/2 LC] 9 times, k2, 2/2 LPC, p2, k2, p1, M1L. *1 st inc*

ROW 4: (K2, p2) 3 times, [p4, (k2, p2) twice] 9 times, (k2, p2) 3 times.

ROW 5: (K2, p2) 3 times, k2, [p2, 2/2 LC, k2, 2/2 LPC] 9 times, p2, 2/2 LC, k2, p2, M1L. *1 st inc*

ROW 6: P1, k2, p6, k2, p2, [k2, p6, k2, p2] 9 times, (k2, p2) 3 times.

ROW 7: (K2, p2) 3 times, [2/2 LC, k2, 2/2 LPC, p2] 9 times, 2/2 LC, k2, 2/2 LPC, p2, k1, M1L. *1 st inc*

ROW 8: (P2, k2) twice, p6, [k2, p2, k2, p6] 9 times, (k2, p2) 3 times.

ROW 9: (K2, p2) 3 times [k2, 2/2 LPC, p2, 2/2 LC] 9 times, k2, 2/2 LPC, p2, 2/2 LC, k2, M1L. *1 st inc*

ROW 10: K1, p6, (k2, p2) twice, [p4, (k2, p2) twice] 9 times, (k2, p2) 3 times.

ROW 11: (K2, p2) 3 times, k2, [p2, 2/2 LC, k2, 2/2 LPC] 9 times, p2, 2/2 LC, k2, 2/2 LPC, p1, M1L. *1 st inc*

ROW 12: K2, p2, k2, p6, k2, p2, [k2, p6, k2, p2] 9 times, (k2, p2) 3 times.

ROW 13: (K2, p2) 3 times, [2/2 LC, k2, 2/2 LPC, p2] 9 times, 2/2 LC, k2, 2/2 LPC, p2, k2, p2, M1L. *1 st inc*

ROW 14: P1, (k2, p2) twice, k2, p6, [k2, p2, k2, p6] 9 times, (k2, p2) 3 times.

ROW 15: (K2, p2) 3 times, [k2, 2/2 LPC, p2, 2/2 LC] 9 times, k2, 2/2 LPC, p2, 2/2 LC, k2, p2, k1, M1L. *1 st inc*

ROW 16: P2, k2, p6, (k2, p2) twice, [p4, (k2, p2) twice] 9 times, (k2, p2) 3 times.

ROW 17: (K2, p2) 3 times, k2, [p2, 2/2 LC, k2, 2/2 LPC] 9 times, p2, 2/2 LC, k2, 2/2 LPC, p2, k2, M1L. *1 st inc*

ROW 18: K1, (p2, k2) twice, p6, k2, p2, [k2, p6, k2, p2] 9 times, (k2, p2) 3 times.

ROW 19: (K2, p2) 3 times, [2/2 LC, k2, 2/2 LPC, p2] 9 times, 2/2 LC, k2, 2/2 LPC, p2, 2/2 LC, k2, p1, M1L. *1 st inc*

ROW 20: K2, p6, k2, p2, k2, p6, [k2, p2, k2, p6] 9 times, (k2, p2) 3 times.

ROW 21: (K2, p2) 3 times, [k2, 2/2 LPC, p2, 2/2 LC] 9 times, k2, 2/2 LPC, p2, 2/2 LC, k2, 2/2 LPC, p2, M1L. *1 st inc*

ROW 22: P1, k2, p2, k2, p6, (k2, p2) twice, [p4, (k2, p2) twice] 9 times, (k2, p2) 3 times.

ROW 23: (K2, p2) 3 times, k2, [p2, 2/2 LC, k2, 2/2 LPC] 9 times, p2, 2/2 LC, k2, 2/2 LPC, p2, 2/2 LC, k1, M1L. *1 st inc*

ROW 24: P6, k2, p2, k2, p6, k2, p2, [k2, p6, k2, p2] 9 times, (k2, p2) 3 times.

Chart D (Second Body Pattern)

The section marked in square brackets is worked 10 times on the first repeat, 11 times on the second repeat, 12 times on the third repeat and so on. Row 1 is worked as foll: 2/2 RPC, k2, 2/2 RC, p2, [2/2 LC, k2, 2/2 LPC, p2] 10 times, 2/2 LC, k2, 2/2 LPC, M1L.

But when you work row 1 for the second time it will be 2/2 RPC, k2, 2/2 RC, p2, [v2/2 LC, k2, 2/2 LPC, p2] 11 times, 2/2 LC, k2, 2/2 LPC, M1L.

ROW 1 (RS): 2/2 RPC, k2, 2/2 RC, p2, [2/2 LC, k2, 2/2 LPC, p2], 2/2 LC, k2, 2/2 LPC, M1L. *1 st inc*

ROW 2 (WS): K1, p2, k2, p6, [k2, p2, k2, p6], k2, p6, k2, p2.

ROW 3: K2, p2, 2/2 RPC, k2, p2, [k2, 2/2 LPC, p2, 2/2 LC], k2, 2/2 LPC, p2, k2, p1, M1L. *1 st inc*

ROW 4: (K2, p2) 3 times, [p4, (k2, p2) twice], (k2, p2) 3 times.

ROW 5: K2, 2/2 RC, (p2, k2) twice, [p2, 2/2 LC, k2, 2/2 LPC], p2, 2/2 LC, k2, p2, M1L. *1 st inc*

ROW 6: P1, k2, p6, k2, p2, [k2, p6, k2, p2], k2, p2, k2, p6.

ROW 7: 2/2 RPC, k2, 2/2 RC, p2, [2/2 LC, k2, 2/2 LPC, p2], 2/2 LC, k2, 2/2 LPC, p2, k1, M1L. *1 st inc*

ROW 8: (P2, k2) twice, p6, [k2, p2, k2, p6], k2, p6, k2, p2.

ROW 9: K2, p2, 2/2 RPC, k2, p2, [k2, 2/2 LPC, p2, 2/2 LC], k2, 2/2 LPC, p2, 2/2 LC, k2, M1L. *1 st inc*

ROW 10: K1, p6, (k2, p2) twice, [p4, (k2, p2) twice], (k2, p2) 3 times.

ROW 11: K2, 2/2 RC, (p2, k2) twice, [p2, 2/2 LC, k2, 2/2 LPC], p2, 2/2 LC, k2, 2/2 LPC, p1, M1L. *1 st inc*

ROW 12: K2, p2, k2, p6, k2, p2, [k2, p6, k2, p2], k2, p2, k2, p6.

ROW 13: 2/2 RPC, k2, 2/2 RC, p2, [2/2 LC, k2, 2/2 LPC, p2], 2/2 LC, k2, 2/2 LPC, p2, k2, p2, M1L. *1 st inc*

ROW 14: P1, (k2, p2) twice, k2, p6, [k2, p2, k2, p6], k2, p6, k2, p2.

ROW 15: K2, p2, 2/2 RPC, k2, p2, [k2, 2/2 LPC, p2, 2/2 LC], k2, 2/2 LPC, p2, 2/2 LC, k2, p2, k1, M1L. *1 st inc*

ROW 16: P2, k2, p6, (k2, p2) twice, [p4, (k2, p2) twice], (k2, p2) 3 times.

ROW 17: K2, 2/2 RC, (p2, k2) twice, [p2, 2/2 LC, k2, 2/2 LPC], p2, 2/2 LC, k2, 2/2 LPC, p2, k2, M1L. *1 st inc*

ROW 18: K1, (p2, k2) twice, p6, k2, p2, [k2, p6, k2, p2], k2, p2, k2, p6.

ROW 19: 2/2 RPC, k2, 2/2 RC, p2, [2/2 LC, k2, 2/2 LPC, p2], 2/2 LC, k2, 2/2 LPC, p2, 2/2 LC, k2, p1, M1L. *1 st inc*

ROW 20: K2, p6, k2, p2, k2, p6, [k2, p2, k2, p6], k2, p6, k2, p2.

ROW 21: K2, p2, 2/2 RPC, k2, p2, [k2, 2/2 LPC, p2, 2/2 LC], k2, 2/2 LPC, p2, 2/2 LC, k2, 2/2 LPC, p2, M1L. *1 st inc*

ROW 22: P1, k2, p2, k2, p6, (k2, p2) twice, [p4, (k2, p2) twice], (k2, p2) 3 times.

ROW 23: K2, 2/2 RC, (p2, k2) twice, [p2, 2/2 LC, k2, 2/2 LPC], p2, 2/2 LC, k2, 2/2 LPC, p2, 2/2 LC, k1, M1L. *1 st inc*

ROW 24: P6, k2, p2, k2, p6, k2, p2, [k2, p6, k2, p2], k2, p2, k2, p6.

PATTERN BEGINS

Using smaller needles and the long-tail method, cast on 3 sts.
SET-UP ROW (WS): P2, PM, p1.

Reading from the Charts or Written Instructions, work as foll:
NEXT ROW (RS): Work row 1 of Chart A to marker, SM, k2. *4 sts*
NEXT ROW: P2, SM, work row 2 of Chart A to end.

Continue in patt as set to end of row 12 of Chart A. *9 sts*

Change to larger needles.

Continue in patt as set to end of row 42 of Chart A. *24 sts*

NEXT ROW (RS): Work row 1 of Chart B to marker, working bracketed rep once, SM, k2. *1 st inc*

NEXT ROW (WS): P2, SM, work row 2 of Chart B to end, working bracketed rep once. Continue in patt as set to end of row 24 of Chart B. *36 sts*

Rep rows 1–24 of Chart B once more, working bracketed rep on Chart B twice. *48 sts*

Rep rows 1–24 of Chart B once more, working bracketed rep on Chart B 3 times. *60 sts*

Rep rows 1–24 of Chart B once more, working bracketed rep on Chart B 4 times. *72 sts*

Work a further 5 reps of rows 1–24 of Chart B, working an extra bracketed rep each time. *132 sts*

NEXT ROW (RS): Work row 1 of Chart C to marker, working bracketed rep 9 times, SM, k2. *133 sts*

NEXT ROW (WS): P2, SM, work row 2 of Chart C to end, working bracketed rep 9 times.

Continue in patt as set to end of row 24 of Chart C. *144 sts*

NEXT ROW (RS): Work row 1 of Chart D to marker, working bracketed rep 10 times, SM, k2. *1 st inc*

NEXT ROW (WS): P2, SM, work row 2 of Chart D to end, working bracketed rep 10 times.

Continue in patt as set to end of row 24 of Chart D. *156 sts*

Rep rows 1–24 of Chart D once more, working bracketed rep on Chart D 11 times. *168 sts*

Rep rows 1–24 of Chart D once more, working bracketed rep on Chart D 12 times. *180 sts*

Rep rows 1–24 of Chart D once more, working bracketed rep on Chart D 13 times. *192 sts*

Rep rows 1–24 of Chart D once more, working bracketed rep on Chart D 14 times. *204 sts*

Cast off using a sewn or stretchy method.

FINISHING

Weave in all ends and block to measurements.

AUDRE SCHEMATIC KEY

a. Depth: 74 cm / 29¼"
b. Length: 124 cm / 48¾"
c. Wingspan: 154 cm / 56¾"

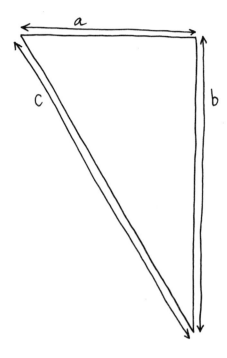

Chart A (Set-up)

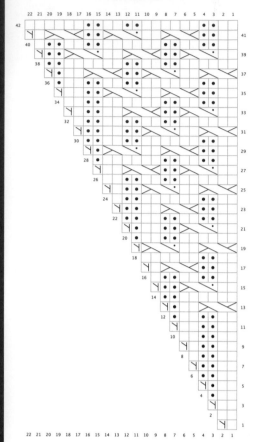

Chart B (Body Pattern)

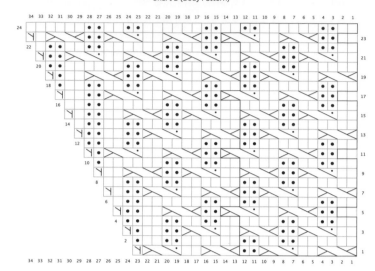

Chart C (Transition)

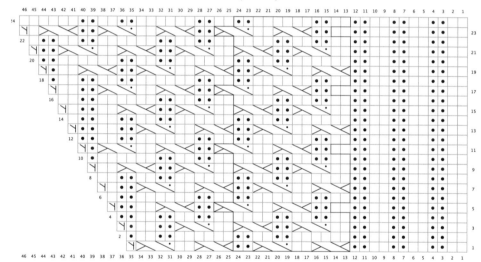

Chart D (Second Body Pattern)

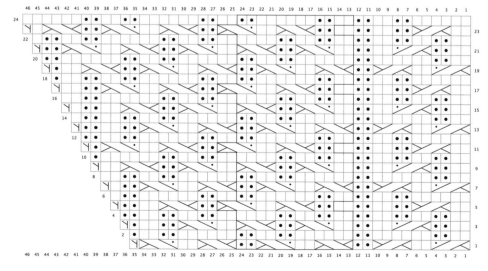

Legend

(empty box)	RS: knit / WS: purl
(dot)	RS: knit / WS: purl
(m1L symbol)	RS: m1L
(cable symbol)	2/2 LC
(cable symbol)	2/2 RC
(cable symbol)	2/2 LPC
(cable symbol)	2/2 RPC
(box)	Repeat

COLOURING INSIDE THE LINES

EXERCISE THREE

As ive said before one commonly... held belief about knitting is that the way things have always been done is the way things must be done. Consequently, there are a few traditional ways we think about creating a knitted piece of fabric: from the top down, from the bottom up, maybe sideways or on the bias if we're feeling particularly spicy. In each of these cases, the direction of knitting is typically worked in isolation, with only one direction governing the entire garment. These directions and these tenets are the default ways to think about constructing a piece of knitted fabric, but they are not the only ways. In this exercise, we'll explore one simple concept: knitting is a shape, and you can fill it from any direction you like, move in any direction you like, and combine as many of directions in a single piece of fabric.

The first step in this exercise is creating the structure for your finished piece. I've given you three different shawl and stole shapes to trace and play with, but this exercise can be performed on any shape you like: a 2D rendering of a sweater, a circular shawl, a cowl—there's no limit. Just make sure to create clear outlines that delineate the shape and give it structure.

Once you choose a shape (or multiple shapes—I find it more interesting to do the exercise over multiple shapes and then pick my favourite), grab a few friends. Take a quick look at your shapes and draw a line in each of them. Curved lines, angled lines, straight lines—I would stay away from wavy lines or closed shapes like circles or dots, but otherwise it's entirely up to you. Don't think about it too hard though! We often get stuck in over-analysis and limit what's possible with our creativity to what we already know and understand. Don't worry about the hows yet—just draw a line quickly and keep moving.

Once you've drawn your line on each shape, pass the drawings over to your first friend. Have them draw a line or lines that interact with your line. Again, the key is not to think about it too long—I've found that five seconds is plenty of time to get multiple lines down on paper before the analysis kicks in. Then, once your first friend has drawn their line or lines, have them pass it on. Keep going until each friend has drawn at least one line. You can keep going with this as long as you'd like—I've done it with two people passing the sheet back and forth (how the examples for this book occurred), to five people going around in a circle twice, to a room full of 25 people drawing lines in assembly-line fashion. I generally like to keep it to around six to ten lines total, but it can be fun to play with more and see what happens!

Now that you have your drawing back in your hands, take a look. Start to analyse your pieces in terms of what resonates with you. Are there particular juxtapositions of shapes and lines that speak to you in one piece or another? Is one shape more linear and another more organic? Which do you prefer? In the three shapes that we made, the juxtaposition of the curved and straight lines in the rectangular and crescent shapes felt like the most interesting and dynamic, and the triangle felt more muddy and chaotic so I steered away from that one. I liked the shapes that were created within both the crescent and the rectangle. But I also loved the one vertical line on the right side of the rectangular shape; that little bit of boldness and structure against the otherwise more random and organic lines sold me on the shape.

After picking a shape, it is time to start trying to figure out the hows. How would you construct this piece? How would you create the individual shapes that make up the whole? When I play with this exercise, I give myself certain parameters. To keep myself on my toes, the big one is that the lines that divide the larger structure into smaller

Below left
Simple Shapes

Below right
Sketch

Opposite
Mapping

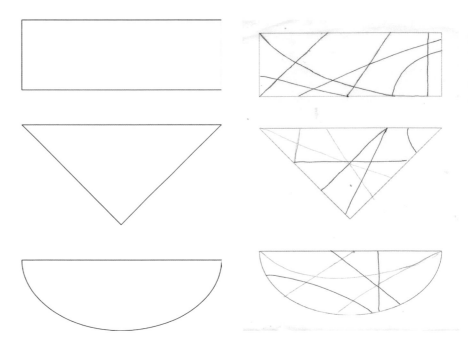

pieces cannot be created simply by changing a colour or switching up the stitch pattern and then continuing to knit in the same direction. Someday I will experiment with those options—I'm particularly interested in the idea of intarsia in one of these pieces to create a garment that almost mimics stained glass—but thinking in these terms tends to keep us oriented within the construction parameters we already know. Instead, I restrict myself to the following tools: increasing, decreasing, casting on, binding off, picking up, joining as for a knitted-on edging or entrelac, and working short rows. Rather than surface ornamentation like colour or texture on a uni-directional structure, these tools are all about creating the structure of the fabric itself. They enable you to think of the whole piece as a collection of disparate shapes, created in whichever direction works best for you and for the flow of the piece.

With these tools, it's not yet important to know the actual mechanics of the increases, decreases, short rows, and so on that you would be using. Don't worry about calculating how many stitches to increase to create this angle, or how many rows to work the short rows over to create that curve. You can start playing with these things if you decide to go further with it, by working a gauge swatch and calculating from there. But for this exercise, use the techniques in their theoretical form: if the sides of the shape move in as you work the fabric, you could decrease. If the sides of the shape move out as you work the fabric, you could increase. If one edge of your fabric is higher than the other, you could use short rows. If you need to join two pieces together, could you pick one up from the edge of the other? Join them as for a knitted-on edging? You have lots of options, but you don't have to know the nuts and bolts quite yet. You just have to think about how you might use these techniques to get what you want.

But how to know where to start? Let's take a closer look at the shapes themselves. There is one major curve in the rectangle I chose, so I know I could work that using short rows. It does have that one vertical line bifurcating it, though, so I couldn't cast on at the farthest right edge and just short row my way around the curve; I'd have to add another piece on. Could that be a place to start? Could I build out from there? Yes, but it looks like my option would be to pick up along the edge of the short row section and work towards the centre. It looks like the fabric would have to grow at very different rates to fill in that section, with lots of increasing, decreasing, and short rows happening all at once. That's a lot to tackle, so maybe not.

How about starting in the top left corner? There's a clear right angle there, with a strong line going from the bottom left corner to the top, creating a nice bound-off end point for that shape. I could use lines of increases and decreases to create the other divisions in that piece, and that would give me that entire bind off to pick up into or join to as for entrelac. But if I change direction there, I'm left with three shapes stacked on top of each other on the side, and I can't go straight up through all three because the lines dividing them would most likely just be binding off and immediately picking back up again. I'm all for interest and innovation in knitting, but that seems unnecessarily complicated. On to Plan C.

What about starting in the top right corner with short rows to create that wedge? That could work, and would leave a clean decrease edge to pick up into and work out from to create the centre shape along the top edge. I could then knit a separate piece for the triangle along the left edge, and join the two pieces together with the furthermost left piece along the top edge. That leaves us with a piece underneath that would need to pick up from the bottom of one piece and join to the side of another piece, but that's possible. I can continue tracing the path of the construction as it finishes all the way out to the right edge. That's doable!

But let's give it one more try, starting with the triangles at the centre bottom. It could be two separate triangles and a trapezoid, or it could be a larger triangle with increases and decreases shaping the divisions within it. From there, I can pick up and move sideways for the shapes to its left, which gives me a good solid base to start with. What would happen then if I started a completely different piece of fabric, and built the short rows off of that for the curve? That would let me pick up along the entirety of the top of both pieces and work over to the right edge. I could then pick up along the left edge, work out that way, then pick up along the whole thing and work up with increases and decreases shaping the changes within the fabric. Both this and the last few are doable, but this construction and order of operation makes the most sense with how I work. So let's do it!

As you can see from these examples, there is no right way to map out a path around these shapes. Experiment with starting at different points of the piece and figuring out how you'd get from Point A to Point B. If you get stuck, pick a different spot to start. Start at an edge, start at the centre, start in multiple pieces and join it at the very end, build off a single starting block into the whole. Turn your paper upside down and look at the shapes from that direction. The goal here is not to try to find The One and Only Solution; the goal is to find the way that works best for you.

If you do decide to pursue this further and knit your shape as I've done, you can also start thinking in terms of what shapes would be most logical. When I started mapping out the maths for mine, I ran into a couple of angles that would have meant increasing or decreasing at an irregular rate; increasing every other row 3 times, then every four rows twice, for example—all while working another set of increases or decreases on the other edge of the shape at a different irregular angle. To save myself that hassle, I experimented with moving the lines a little bit to

see if I could shift the angles into something that would repeat at a more regular rate. Usually by changing the shapes only slightly (you can see the difference between my original and edited versions below, you can tweak them into something more approachable and knittable.

Colouring inside the lines is a fantastic way to let go of our preconceived notions about how knitted fabric is shaped. There is no set path we must follow to create the fabric we want; instead, there are only shapes for us to make however we wish, moulds for us to fill with the material of our choice. The sky is the limit!

top
Original

Bottom
Edited

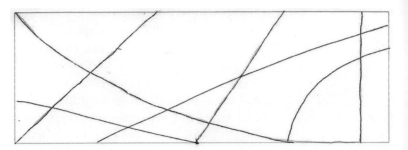

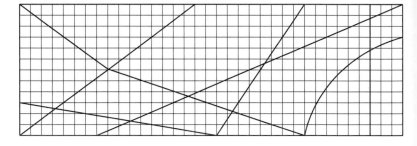

CANADY

SHAWL

Alexa Canady, first African-American female neurosurgeon

Canady

One size:

84 cm / 33" deep x 210 cm / 82¾" long

Yarn: Sweet Fiber

Merino Twist DK (DK weight; 100% superwash Merino wool; 238 m / 260 yds per 115 g skein) Shade: Tea Leaves; 7 skeins

Gauge:

18 sts & 28 rows = 10 cm / 4" over stocking stitch on 4.5 mm needles after blocking.

NOTE: *Due to the construction of Canady the gauge given is an average taken across several sections.*

Needles:

4.5 mm / US 7 circular needle, 80 cm / 32" length

4.5 mm / US 7 circular needle, 150 cm / 60" length

Always use a needle size that will result in the correct gauge after blocking.

Notions:

Stitch markers, locking stitch markers, stitch holders or scrap yarn, tapestry needle, t-pins and blocking wires

Notes:

Canady is constructed modularly and finished with a border worked in the round. Please refer to construction schematic for order
and direction of knitting.

Stitches are referred to as either joining stitches or working stitches; working stitches will include the single stitches to the outsides of the markers defining the working section.

PATTERN BEGINS

SECTION 1

Using the long-tail method, cast on 133 sts.
SET-UP ROW (WS): P69, PM, p2, PM, p62.
ROW 1 (RS): K1, ssk, k to 3 sts before marker, k2tog, k1, SM, yo, k to marker, yo, SM, k1, ssk, k to last 3 sts, k2tog, k1. *2 sts dec*
ROW 2 (WS): P1, p2tog, p to 3 sts before marker, ssp, p1, SM, yo, p to marker, SM, p to last 3 sts, ssp, p1. *2 sts dec*
ROW 3: Rep row 1. *2 sts dec*
ROW 4: P to 3 sts before marker, ssp, p1, SM, yo, p to end.

Rep rows 1-4 a further 8 times. *79 sts*

TRANSITION A

With RS facing, PLM in left edge of fabric.
ROW 1 (RS): K1, ssk, k to 3 sts before marker, k2tog, k1, SM, yo, k to marker, yo, SM, k1, ssk, k2tog, k1. *2 sts dec*
ROW 2 (WS): P1, p2tog, p1, remove marker, p to last 3 sts, ssp, p1. *2 sts dec*
ROW 3: K1, ssk, k to 3 sts before marker, k2tog, k1, SM, yo, k to last 3 sts, k2tog, k1. *2 sts dec*
ROW 4: Purl.
ROW 5: Rep row 3. *2 sts dec*

Rep rows 2-5 once more, then rep row 2 once more. *63 sts*

TRANSITION B

ROW 1 (RS): K1, sk2po, k1, SM, yo, k to last 3 sts, k2tog, k1. *2 sts dec*
ROW 2 (WS): Purl.
ROW 3: K1, ssk, k to last 3 sts, k2tog, k1. *2 sts dec*
ROW 4: P1, p2tog, p to last 3 sts, ssp, p1. *2 sts dec*
ROW 5: Rep row 3. *2 sts dec*
Rep rows 2-5 a further 8 times, then rep rows 2-4 once more. *3 sts*
NEXT ROW (RS): S2kpo. *1 st*

Break yarn and pull through rem st to fasten off.

SECTION 2

With RS of Section 1 facing and cast-on edge at bottom, beg at cast-on edge, pick up and k21 sts to locking stitch marker in left edge, remove locking stitch marker, PM, pick up and k24 sts to end of left edge, using the backwards loop cast on 2 sts. *47 sts total; 2 working sts + 45 joining sts*

Gradually increase within the working sts as directed below and decrease one joining st at the end of every RS row as foll, noting that incs and decs given at the end of a row are changes to working st counts only. Changes to joining st counts are not given until the end of a section.

SET-UP ROW (RS): K1, [yo] twice, PM, ssk, working last cast-on st with first picked-up st, turn. *4 working sts + 44 joining sts*
SET-UP ROW (WS): Sl1, SM, p to end.
ROW 1: K to marker, SM, ssk, turn.
ROW 2: Sl1, SM, p to end.
ROW 3: K1, yo, k to 1 st before marker, yo, k1, SM, ssk, turn. *2 sts inc*
ROW 4: Rep row 2.

Rep rows 1-4 a further 11 times, then rep rows 1-2 once more. *28 working sts + 19 joining sts*

TRANSITION A

SET-UP ROW (RS): K1, yo, k to 3 sts before marker, k2tog, k1, SM, [yo] twice, PM, k1, ssk, turn. *30 working sts + 18 joining sts*
SET-UP ROW (WS): Sl1, p to end.
ROW 1: [K to marker, SM] twice, ssk, turn.
ROW 2: Sl1, p to end.
ROW 3: K1, yo, k to 3 sts before marker, k2tog, k1, SM, yo, k to marker, yo, SM, ssk, turn. *2 sts inc*
ROW 4: Rep row 2.
Rep rows 1-4 a further 4 times, then rep rows 1-2 once more. *40 working sts + 7 joining sts*

With RS facing, PLM in right edge of fabric.

TRANSITION B

ROW 1 (RS): K1, ssk, k to 3 sts before marker, k2tog, k1, SM, yo, k to marker, yo, SM, ssk, turn.
ROW 2 (WS): Sl1, p to end.
ROW 3: K to second marker, SM, ssk, turn.
ROW 4: Sl1, p to last 3 sts, ssp, p1. *1 st dec*
ROW 5: K to 3 sts before marker, k2tog, k1, SM, yo, k to marker, yo, SM, ssk, turn. *1 st inc*
ROW 6: Rep row 2.
ROW 7: K1, ssk, [k to marker, SM] twice, ssk, turn. *1 st dec*
ROW 8: Rep row 2.
ROW 9: Rep row 5. *1 st inc*
ROW 10: Rep row 4. *1 st dec*
ROW 11: Rep row 3.
ROW 12: Rep row 2.

Rep rows 1–2 once more. *39 working sts + 0 joining sts*

TRANSITION C

ROW 1 (RS): K to 3 sts before marker, k2tog, k1, SM, yo, k to end.
ROW 2 (WS): Purl.
ROW 3: K1, ssk, k to end. *1 st dec*
ROW 4: Knit.
ROW 5: Rep row 1.
ROW 6: Purl to last 3 sts, ssp, p1. *1 st dec*
ROW 7: Knit.
ROW 8: Purl.
ROW 9: K1, ssk, k to 3 sts before marker, k2tog, k1, SM, yo, k to end. *1 st dec*
ROW 10: Purl.
ROW 11: Knit.
ROW 12: Rep row 6. *1 st dec*

Rep rows 1–12 once more, then rep rows 1–4 once more. *30 sts*

TRANSITION D

ROW 1 (RS): Knit.
ROW 2 (WS): P to last 3 sts, ssp, p1. *1 st dec*
ROW 3: Knit.
ROW 4: Purl.
ROW 5: K1, ssk, k to end. *1 st dec*
ROW 6: Purl.

Rep rows 1–6 a further 12 times, then rep rows 1–4 once more. *3 sts*

NEXT ROW (RS): Sk2po. *1 st*

Break yarn and pull through rem st to fasten off.

SECTION 3

Using the long-tail method, cast on 3 sts.
ROW 1 (WS): Purl.
ROW 2 (RS): K1, yo, k to last st, yo, k1.
2 sts inc

Rep rows 1–2 a further 8 times, then rep row 1 once more. *21 sts*

NEXT ROW: K1, yo, k to last 3 sts, k2tog, k1.
NEXT ROW: Purl.

Rep last 2 rows a further 59 times.

Work short rows as foll:
SET-UP ROW (RS): K1, yo, k to last 3 sts, k2tog, k1.
SHORT ROW 1 (WS): P to last 4 sts, turn.
SHORT ROW 2 (RS): Yob around RH needle, k to last 3 sts, k2tog, k1. *1 st dec*
Rep short rows 1–2 twice more. *18 sts*

NEXT SHORT ROW: P to last 4 sts, turn.
NEXT SHORT ROW: Yob around RH needle, k to end.
NEXT ROW: P to end resolving all short rows through the back loop as you pass them.
NEXT ROW: Knit.

Break yarn and place all sts on stitch holder or scrap yarn.

SECTION 4

With RS of Section 3 facing and live sts at top, beg at bottom of left edge, pick up and p80 sts in left edge.

Work short rows as foll:
SHORT ROW 1 (RS): K to last 5 sts, turn.
SHORT ROW 2 (WS): Yob around RH needle, p to end.
SHORT ROW 3: K to 20 sts before yob, turn.
SHORT ROW 4: Rep short row 2.
SHORT ROW 5: Rep short row 3.
SHORT ROW 6: Rep short row 2.
SHORT ROW 7: K1, ssk, k to 20 sts before yob, turn. *1 st dec*
SHORT ROW 8: Rep short row 2.
SHORT ROW 9: K to last 10 sts, resolving all short rows as you pass them, turn.

SHORT ROW 10–16: Rep short rows 2–8.
1 st dec
SHORT ROW 17: K to end, resolving all short rows as you pass them.
ROW 18: Sl1, p to end.
SHORT ROW 19: K to 20 sts before end, turn.
SHORT ROW 20–24: Rep short rows 4–8.
1 st dec

Rep rows 1–24 twice more. *71 sts*

TRANSITION A

SHORT ROW 1 (RS): K to last 5 sts, turn.
SHORT ROW 2 (WS): Yob around RH needle, p to end.
SHORT ROW 3: K to 20 sts before yo, turn.
SHORT ROW 4: Rep row 2.
SHORT ROW 5: Rep row 3.
SHORT ROW 6: Rep row 2.
SHORT ROW 7: K1, ssk, k to 20 sts before yob, turn. *1 st dec*
SHORT ROW 8: Rep row 2.
SHORT ROW 9: K to last 10 sts, turn.
SHORT ROW 10: Yob around RH needle, p to end.
SHORT ROW 11: K to 20 sts before yob, turn.
SHORT ROW 12: Rep row 2.
SHORT ROW 13: Rep row 3.
SHORT ROW 14: Rep row 2.
SHORT ROW 15: K1, ssk, turn. *1 st dec*
SHORT ROW 16: Rep row 2.
SHORT ROW 17: Knit.
ROW 18: Sl1, p to end.
SHORT ROW 19: K to 20 sts before end, turn.
SHORT ROWS 20–24: Rep rows 4–8. *1 st dec*

Rep rows 1–24 once more. *65 sts*

TRANSITION B

SHORT ROW 1 (RS): K to last 5 sts, turn.
SHORT ROW 2 (WS): Yob around RH needle, p to end.
SHORT ROW 3: K to 20 sts before yob, turn.
SHORT ROW 4: Rep row 2.
SHORT ROW 5: Rep row 3.
SHORT ROW 6: Rep row 2.
SHORT ROW 7: K1, ssk, turn. *1 st dec*
SHORT ROW 8: Rep row 2.
SHORT ROW 9: K to last 10 sts, turn.
SHORT ROW 10: Yob around RH needle, p to end.

SHORT ROW 11: K to 20 sts before yob, turn.
SHORT ROW 12: Rep row 2.
SHORT ROW 13: Rep row 3.
SHORT ROW 14: Rep row 2.
SHORT ROW 15: K1, ssk, turn. *1 st dec*
SHORT ROW 16: Rep row 2.
SHORT ROW 17: Knit.
ROW 18: Sl1, p to end.
SHORT ROW 19: K to 20 sts before end, turn.
SHORT ROWS 20-24: Rep rows 4-8. *1 st dec*

Rep rows 1-17 once more. *60 sts*

Break yarn and place all sts on stitch holder or scrap yarn.

SECTION 5

With RS of Sections 1 & 2 facing, cast-on edge of Section 1 at the bottom, and Sections 3 & 4 sitting to the right of Section 1 with live sts of Section 4 at the bottom, replace 18 held Section 3 sts on LH needle. Join yarn and work across live sts. Then pick up and k80 sts in curved side of Section 4, and then, starting at cast-on edge of Section 1, pick up and k45, then pick up and k2 sts in cast-on of Section 2. *145 sts total; last 2 picked up are working sts and rem 143 are joining sts*

Gradually increase within the working sts as directed below and decrease one joining st at the end of every WS row as foll:
SET-UP ROW (WS): P1, PM for joining dec position, p2tog, using last working st and first joining st, turn.
SET-UP ROW (RS): Sl1, SM, [yo] twice, k1. *4 working sts + 142 joining sts*
ROW 1: P to joining marker, SM, p2tog, turn.
ROW 2: Sl1, SM, k to end.
ROW 3: Rep row 1.
ROW 4: Sl1, SM, yo, k to last st, yo, k1. *2 working sts inc*

Rep rows 1-4 a further 9 times. *24 working sts + 122 joining sts*

TRANSITION A
SET-UP ROW (WS): P to joining marker, PM, SM, p2tog, turn. *24 working sts + 121 joining sts*
ROW 1 (RS): Sl1, SM, k to marker, yo, SM, k1, ssk, k to end.

ROW 2 (WS): P to 3 sts before marker, ssp, p1, SM, yo, p to joining marker, SM, p2tog, turn.
ROW 3: Sl1, SM, yo, k to marker, yo, SM, k1, ssk, k to last st, yo, k1. *2 sts inc*
ROW 4: Rep row 2.

Rep rows 1-4 a further 6 times. *38 working sts + 107 joining sts rem*

NEXT ROW (RS): Sl1, SM, k to marker, yo, SM, k1, ssk.
NEXT ROW (WS): Ssp, SM, yo, p to joining marker, p2tog, turn.
NEXT ROW: K1, SM, yo, k to final marker, yo, remove marker, k1. *40 working sts + 106 joining sts*
NEXT ROW: P to joining marker, SM, p2tog, turn. *40 working sts + 105 joining sts*
With RS facing, PLM in left edge of fabric.

TRANSITION B
ROW 1 (RS): K1, yo, k to last st, yo, k1. *2 sts inc*
ROW 2 (WS): P to joining marker, SM, p2tog, turn.
ROW 3: Knit.
ROW 4: Rep row 2.

Rep rows 1-4 twice more, then rep rows 1-2. *48 working sts + 98 joining sts*

TRANSITION C
ROW 1 (RS): K1, ssk, k to end. *1 working st dec*
ROW 2 (WS): P to last 2 sts before joining marker, ssp, SM, p2tog, turn. *1 st dec*
ROW 3: K1, ssk, k to last st, yo, k1.
ROW 4: Rep row 2. *1 st dec*

Rep rows 1-4 a further 7 times. *24 working sts + 82 joining sts*

TRANSITION D
ROW 1 (RS): K1, ssk, k to end. *1 st dec*
ROW 2 (WS): Purl to marker, SM, p2tog, turn.
ROW 3: K1, ssk, k to last st, yo, k1.
ROW 4: Rep row 2.

Rep rows 1-4 a further 15 times. *8 working sts + 50 joining sts*

TRANSITION E
ROW 1 (RS): Knit.
ROW 2 (WS): P to 2 sts before marker, ssp, SM, p2tog, turn. *1 st dec*
ROW 3: K to last st, yo, k1. *1 st inc*
ROW 4: P to marker, SM, p2tog, turn.

ROW 5: K1, ssk, k to end. *1 st dec*
ROW 6: Rep row 4.
ROW 7: Rep row 3. *1 st inc*
ROW 8: Rep row 2. *1 st dec*
ROW 9: Rep row 1.
ROW 10: Rep row 4.
ROW 11: K1, ssk, k to last st, yo, k1.
ROW 12: Rep row 4.

Rep rows 1-12 once more. *6 working sts + 38 joining sts*

TRANSITION F
ROW 1 (RS): Knit.
ROW 2 (WS): P to marker, SM, p2tog, turn.
ROW 3: K1, ssk, k to last st, yo, k1.
ROW 4: Rep row 2.

Rep rows 1-4 a further 9 times, then rep rows 1-2. *6 working sts + 18 joining sts*

With RS facing, PLM in left edge of fabric.

TRANSITION G
ROW 1 (RS): Knit.
ROW 2 (WS): P to marker, SM, p3tog using last working st and first 2 joining sts, turn.
ROW 3: K1, ssk, k to last st, yo, k1.
ROW 4: P to marker, SM, p2tog, turn.

Rep rows 1-4 a further 5 times. *6 working sts + 0 joining sts*

Break yarn and place sts on stitch holder or scrap yarn.

SECTION 6

With RS facing and cast-on edge of Section 1 at bottom, beg at locking stitch marker in edge of Section 2, pick up and k31 sts, PM, then pick up and k54 sts to cast off edge of Section 2. *85 sts*

SET-UP ROW (WS): Purl.
ROW 1 (RS): K1, ssk, k to marker, yo, SM, k1, ssk, k to last 3 sts, k2tog, k1. *2 sts dec*
ROW 2 (WS & all following WS ROWS): Purl.
ROW 3: K to last 3 sts, k2tog, k1. *1 st dec*
ROW 5: K to marker, yo, SM, k1, ssk, k to last 3 sts, k2tog, k1. *1 st dec*
ROW 7: Rep row 3. *1 st dec*
ROW 8 (WS): Purl.

Rep rows 1–8 a further 7 times, then rep rows 1–4 once more removing marker on final row. *42 sts*

TRANSITION A

ROW 1 (RS): K to last 3 sts, k2tog, k1. *1 st dec*
ROW 2 (WS & all following WS ROWS): Purl.
ROWS 3–6: Rep rows 1–2 twice more. *2 sts dec*
ROW 7: K1, ssk, k to last 3 sts, k2tog, k1. *2 sts dec*
ROW 8: Purl.

Rep rows 1–8 a further 6 times, then rep rows 1–4 once more. *5 sts*

NEXT ROW (RS): K1, s2kpo, k1. *3 sts*
NEXT ROW (WS): Purl.
NEXT ROW: S2kpo. *1 st*

Break yarn and pull through rem st to fasten off.

SECTION 7

With RS facing, beg at rightmost marker on Section 5, pick up and k88 sts to locking st marker, remove locking st marker, PM, pick up and k38 sts to cast-on of Section 5, PM, pick up and k38 sts to end of Section 2, PM, pick up and k66 sts to end of Section 6. Break yarn, slip sts to centre marker back to LH needle, then slip first st on RH needle to LH needle and join yarn. *230 sts total; 2 working sts in centre (1 either side of centre marker) + 125 joining sts to right of working sts + 103 joining sts to left of working sts*

Gradually increase within the working sts as directed below and decrease one joining st at the end of every RS and every WS row as foll:
SET-UP ROW (RS): K1, PM, [yo] twice, ssk, turn. *4 sts*

NOTE: *What was the centre marker becomes the second joining marker.*

SET-UP ROW (WS): P to joining marker, SM, p2tog, using last working st and first joining st, turn.
ROW 1 (RS): K1, yo, k to joining marker, yo, SM, ssk, turn. *2 sts inc*
ROW 2: P1, SM, yo, p to joining marker, yo, SM, p2tog, turn. *2 sts inc*
ROW 3: Rep row 1. *2 sts inc*
ROW 4: P to joining marker, SM, p2tog, turn.

Rep rows 1–4 a further 16 times, then rep

rows 1–2 once more. *110 working sts + 89 joining sts on right + 67 joining sts on left*

TRANSITION A

SET-UP ROW (RS): K1, SM, yo, k2tog, k1, PM, yo, k to 3 sts before joining marker, k2tog, k1, PM, [yo] twice, SM, ssk, turn. *112 working sts + 89 joining sts on right + 67 joining sts on left*
SET-UP ROW (WS): P to joining marker, SM, p2tog, turn.
ROW 1 (RS): K1, SM, yo, k to marker, k1, SM, k to 3 sts before marker, k2tog, k1, SM, yo, k to joining marker, yo, SM, ssk, turn. *2 sts inc*
ROW 2 (WS): P to marker, yo, SM, p2tog, turn. *1 st inc*
ROW 3: K1, SM, yo, [k to 3 sts before marker, k2tog, k1, SM, yo] twice, k to joining marker, yo, SM, ssk, turn. *2 sts inc*
ROW 4: P to joining marker, p2tog, turn.

Rep rows 1–4 a further 31 times, then rep row 1 once more. *274 working sts + 24 joining sts on right + 1 joining st on left*

NEXT ROW (WS): P to marker, SM, p36, PM, p36, SM, p to marker, p2tog, turn. *23 joining sts on right*

SHORT ROWS

SET-UP ROW (RS): K1, yo, k to marker placed on previous turn, turn. *1 st inc*
SET-UP ROW (WS): Yob around RH needle, p to joining marker, yo, SM, p2tog, turn. *1 st inc*
SHORT ROW 1 (RS): K1, yo, k to 3 before marker, k2tog, k1, SM, yo, k to 3 sts before previous turn, turn. *1 st inc*
SHORT ROW 2 (WS): Yob around RH needle, p to joining marker, SM, p2tog, turn.
SHORT ROW 3: K1, yo, k to 3 sts before previous turn, turn. *1 st inc*
SHORT ROW 4: Yob around RH needle, p to joining marker, yo, SM, p2tog, turn. *1 st inc*

Rep short rows 1–4 a further 6 times. *292 working sts + 8 joining sts on right*

TRANSITION B

SHORT ROW 1 (RS): K1, yo, k to 3 sts before previous turn, turn. *1 st inc*
SHORT ROW 2 (WS): Yob around RH needle, p to joining marker, SM, p2tog, turn.
SHORT ROW 3: Rep row 1. *1 st inc*
SHORT ROW 4: Yob around RH needle,

p to joining marker, yo, SM, p2tog, turn. *1 st inc*
Rep rows 1–4 a further 3 times. *304 working sts + 0 joining sts on right side*

TRANSITION C

SHORT ROW 1 (RS): K to 3 sts before previous turn, turn.

SHORT ROW 2 (WS): Yo around RH needle, p to end.

Rep short rows 1–2 a further 18 times.

NEXT ROW: K to end of all 305 Section 7 sts, resolving short rows as you pass them. Break yarn and place all sts on stitch holder or scrap yarn.

SECTION 8

Pick up and k12 sts along remaining top of Section 5, then pick up and k1 st in the edge of Section 7, PM, pick up and k24 sts along the edge of Section 7. 37 sts total; *25 working sts + 12 joining sts*

SET-UP ROW (WS): P to marker, SM, p2tog using last working st and first joining st, turn.
ROW 1 (RS): K1, SM, ssk, k to end. *1 st dec*
ROW 2 (WS): Purl to marker, SM, p2tog, turn.
ROW 3: Knit.
ROW 4: Rep row 2.

Rep rows 1–4 a further 4 times, then rep rows 1–2 once more. *20 sts*

Break yarn and place all sts on stitch holder or scrap yarn.

BORDER

Pick up and k11 sts along top of Section 8, knit across 305 held sts at top of Section 7, PM, pick up and k106 sts along side of Section 6, PM, pick up and k103 sts along side of Section 2, pick up and k132 sts in bottom of Section 1, knit across 60 live sts of Section 4, pick up and k7 sts in row edge of Section 4 short rows, pick up and k14 sts in bottom of Section 3, PM, pick up and k80 sts along side of Section 3, knit across 6 held sts of Section 5, knit across 20 held sts of Section 8. Join to work in the round and PM for beg of round. *844 sts*

ROUND 1: [K1, yo, k to last st before marker, yo, k1, SM] 4 times. *8 sts inc*

ROUND 2: Knit.

Rep rounds 1–2 once more. *860 sts*

Cast off using Jenny's Suprisingly Stretchy Bind Off.

FINISHING

Weave in all ends and block to measurements.

CANADY SCHEMATIC KEY

a. Width: 210 cm / 82¾"

b. Depth: 84 cm / 33"

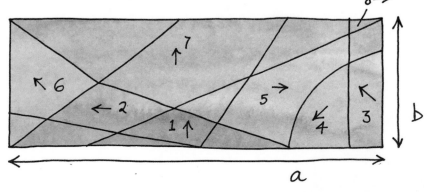

PART II

MAKING YOUR CREATIVITY A REALITY

Once you've got ideas, the next step is to figure out how to execute them. In my knitting experience, I've discovered that there are three major ways to shape and mould fabric: increasing and decreasing, short rows, and stitch patterns that manipulate your fabric.

INCREASES
&
DECREASES

TECHNIQUE ONE

We are all familiar with the basic increases and decreases in knitting. Make 1, yarnover, knit-front-back; knit 2 together, slip, slip, knit, s2kpo. We use them intuitively in all our work, to shape the waist of a sweater, to close the top of a hat, to increase the width of a sleeve, to create the bell and flow of a top-down shawl. But hidden in these simple actions is a concrete and overarching truth that gives increasing and decreasing an understandable structure and rhythm, one that you can use to your advantage.

Knitting, in and of itself, is fundamentally linear. It is the intersection of columns and rows, with stitches lining up on each axis to form a grid. Increasing and decreasing manipulates that grid to create angles that are extensions of the grid themselves: if we were to chart out a set of increases at a regular rate, it would follow a stairstep pattern that adheres to the linear nature of the knitting we know. So, for example, if you increase one stitch every other row, you're following the natural rhythm of up 2 and over 1, up 2 and over 1, up 2 and over 1. . . on and on until you reach the number of stitches or the size you want. This is true of any increase or decrease structure: it follows a natural path and stairstep on the grid of knitting that gives us the angles and the shapes we know and love in knitting. Thanks to this rhythm, this symbiosis with the grid structure, we've got a backstage pass to see how increases and decreases shape our fabric. They are regular, structured, and—what's most exciting—predictable across all gauges.

Now, take a deep breath. This may feel like a lot of unfathomable information, but it is nothing that your hands don't already know. Let's dive deeper into increases and take, as an example, a project you most likely have already knit: a top-down triangular shawl. It has a set increase rate (you will increase four times every right side row), and these increases occur in the same place in the shawl every time (one each at the outside edges, and one each on either side of the spine). I am willing to bet you've knit multiples of these, in all different stitch patterns, different gauges, different yarns. . . but the finished structure is the same no matter what. You will always have a right-angled triangle, with the cast-on edge at the very centre of the wingspan (or, in geometric terms, the hypotenuse of the triangle), and the wingspan measuring a straight horizontal line (or 180 degrees).

Or, for another example, let's look at a typical raglan. Here, the set increase rate is eight increases every other row, and these increases occur at the junctures between the body and the sleeves. As with the shawl, if you look across multiple gauges, multiple stitch patterns, multiple yarns, this ratio gets you the same shape: a flat rectangle with a hole for the neck, whose shorter sides are the circumference of your arms and whose longer sides add up to the circumference of your bust. No matter the changes in the fabric itself, the structure remains the same: a piece of fabric whose increases add up to create a flat, 360 degree rectangle. You've knit this. Your hands know this. But let's look at how and why this works.

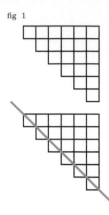

fig 1

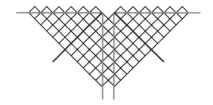

fig 1
Increase decrease illustration

fig 2
Shawl illustration

fig 3
Raglan illustration

Katharine Cobey, in her seminal book *Diagonal Knitting*, discusses how, in garter stitch, you are pretty much guaranteed that the width of a single stitch will be the same as the height of two rows. In other words, a piece of knitted garter stitch fabric that's 1 stitch wide and 2 rows tall will be a square. This makes estimates of the angle of increase or decrease easy and approachable. That ratio we talked about before, up 2 and over 1? With the set and related size of the stitch and rows that we see in garter stitch, this ratio would create a constant and specific stairstep pattern if used as an increase or a decrease (fig. 1).

In this case a square represents 1 stitch wide by 2 rows tall. You can see that concrete angle that we know from the increase or decrease ratio: up 2 and over 1 creates a smooth 45 degree angle.

All well and good, but how does this theoretical concept relate to what we know about knitting? Let's look back at our two examples of familiar projects.

With a top-down shawl, the increase rate is four times every right side row, and these increases occur in the same place in the shawl every time: one each at the outside edges, and one each on either side of the spine as shown below.

fig 2

The number of increases (four every right side row), and placement (at the edges of two mirror-image shapes), show us that this top-down shawl is really just four 45 degree angles put together.

fig 3

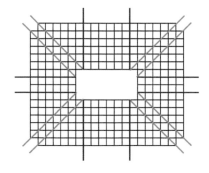

fig 4
Increase vector

a.
1 over 4:
1 increase every 4 rows
2 increases every 8 rows
3 increases every 12 rows
Originating angle:
22.5 degrees
Resultant angles:
67.5 and 90 degrees

b.
1 over 2:
1 increase every 2 rows
2 increases every 4 rows
3 increases every 6 rows
Originating angle:
45 degrees
Resultant angles:
53 and 82 degrees

c.
3 over 4:
3 increases every 4 rows
6 increases every 8 rows
9 increases every 12 rows
Originating angle:
67.5 degrees
Resultant angles:
56.25 and 56.25 degrees

d.
1 over 1:
1 increases every row
2 increases every 2 rows
3 increases every 3 rows
Originating angle:
90 degrees
Resultant angles:
45 and 45 degrees

e.
5 over 4:
5 increases every 4 rows
10 increases every 8 rows
15 increases every 12 rows
Originating angle:
112.5 degrees
Resultant angles:
33.75 and 33.75 degrees

f.
3 over 2:
3 increases every 2 rows
6 increases every 4 rows
9 increases every 6 rows
Originating angle:
135 degrees
Resultant angles:
22.5 and 22.5 degrees

g.
7 over 4:
7 increases every 4 rows
14 increases every 8 rows
21 increases every 12 rows
Originating angle:
157.5 degrees
Resultant angles:
11.25 and 11.25 degrees

h.
2 over 1:
2 increases every row
4 increases every 2 rows
6 increases every 3 rows
Originating angle:
180 degrees

The same is true of a raglan. Here, the increase rate is eight times every other row, and the increases are stacked in the same location every time. Though there are some filler stitches to create enough space for the neck opening, the shapes are the same as with the top-down shawl, and as with the simple up 2 and over 1 triangle. They're all building blocks, and can be used to create any knitted shape you wish.

But this is only the beginning. The most interesting part of these ratios is that they're just that: ratios. This means you can change them to suit your whim: perhaps instead of up 2 and over 1, you go up 4 and over 2, or up 6 and over 3, or up 8 and over 4. While these all mean a different number of increases will happen per increase row, the total number of increases per total number of rows is the same each time: they all simplify down to 1 increase every 2 rows. The ratio is the key, rather than the rate. Even if the increases aren't worked at a frequent rate, as long as they are worked at the same ratio, the shape will be the same. You then get to experiment even further: what does the angle of the fabric do when I place all my increases along one edge? What if I cluster them all in the same place? If I spread them out evenly across the row? Or I place them symmetrically on either edge? When I incorporate them into my lace pattern or my cable? The placement of these increases in the row will dictate the direction your fabric grows in relation

fig 4

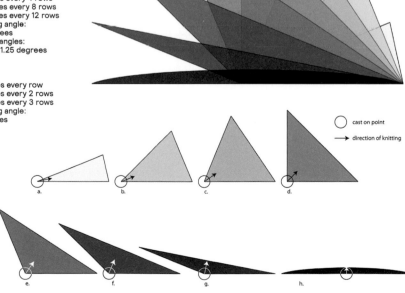

cast on point

→ direction of knitting

to its edges. There is no right answer, only that which helps you achieve your aims.

With that in mind, here's a handy cheat sheet of eight common angles in knitting. To read it, start at the centre, and use the bottom line on the right side of the shape as the bottom line for every angle. These triangles range from one increase every four rows (creating an originating angle, meaning the angle at which you cast on, of 22.5 degrees) to two increases every row (creating an originating angle that's 180 degrees, and which should be familiar—it's that top-down shawl again!). The resultant angles, the angles that are created at the two edges of the cast-off, are also listed. With each shape, there are three different rates given which all distil down to the same ratio, and all three (and many more!) will give you that same transition from originating angle to resultant angles. Try a couple out and see what you think!

Exciting though this may be, it is by no means the be-all and end-all. What might happen if you included increase rates that were spaced further apart, such as one increase every eight rows? Or what might happen if you worked an increase rate that was between those on the cheat sheet, say one increase every three rows? Or what would it look like to take it past 180 degrees? These angles are just a starting point, and I encourage you to play with them to find the shapes that you love and that work to realise your visions.

What does this all mean in terms of your own creativity? It means that you now have reference points with which to either replicate shapes that you see, or to experiment with seeing where you can take those shapes. See if you can match the angles that you see around you to those on the cheat sheet. Or take a look at the knitted shapes of patterns you own, and see if you can guess what increase rate they've used. Once you have these basic ratios, everything can be broken down into these parts.

Think, too, about how you might combine shapes. Let's look at the top-down shawl again. It's comprised of four B triangles mirroring each other, or two D triangles sitting back to back. And the raglan is just eight B triangles or four D triangles. But what would it look like if the shapes weren't symmetrical? What would it look like if, instead of putting two D triangles together, you put one C and one E? It would create the same 180 total angle, but the resulting shape would pull the expected triangular shape a bit left of centre. Or what about B plus F, or even G plus A? You can create myriad complex and interesting shapes just by doing a little bit of mixing and matching. As long as you think of the increase structure as a ratio and therefore something to average out to over a certain number of rows, there's no limit to what you can do.

Here's another thing to think about: there's no reason a shape must adhere to a specific ratio for its entire length. We know this already from our knitting experience; most sleeve shaping instructions will ask you to work an increase or a decrease row every X rows Y times, then every Z rows A times. This means that the ratio changes partway through the sleeve, to accommodate the number of increases or decreases needed to work smoothly in the sleeve length, to accommodate any pattern shaping that might be needed, or to accommodate the body's natural taper from straighter upper arm to quickly narrowing forearm. Changing the ratio also means that you can create the illusion of a curve in your fabric. To understand this, let's look at what might happen if we trace out and approximate the line of a circle onto a grid:

fig 5

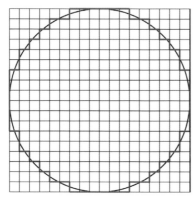

As you can see, we can't follow both the grid AND the circle, but we can get pretty darn close by changing the ratio of increase or decrease to best match the curve. If we were to knit this, or part of this, the changes in the ratio would in theory be angles stacking on top of each other. But due to the malleability of knitted fabric, we'd get very close to a true circle. So this is also something that can be used when you want to play with angles; what might happen if you started out with a B triangle, then switched to a C triangle? Or started with an H and moved to a G?

The same will also be true of any structure involving decreases. With increases, you start from the narrow part of a shape and move towards the wider part; with decreases, you start with the wider part and move towards the shallower. So the same cheat sheet can be used for decreases, by moving from the two outside angles down to the final point at the centre. In this case, you have two originating angles—the two edges at the cast-on of your piece—and one resultant angle at the very end. Here, as with increasing, you also get to play with placement. What happens when you have more decreases placed on one edge than on the other? What does that do to the angle of your fabric within the shape? As with increases, the placement of the decreases will dictate how

your fabric moves in relation to the line of your edges, so that's a whole world of nuance and intention to play with. Knowing these angles, knowing these directions of fabric, you will get to take full control of your fabric and understand not just the how, but the why.

Now, in terms of stitch pattern, so far the nitty gritty maths of the discussion has centred on garter stitch, whose stitch-to-row ratio is, as we know, 1-to-2. But what about stockinette, which is more like 2-to-3 or 3-to-4? Or as we'll see in a later chapter, stitch patterns that might expand or contract your row gauge or stitch gauge, such as brioche, cables, or slip stitches? In these cases, your shape may not adhere exactly to the angle given in the cheat sheet; if the stitches are narrower or the rows are longer, the shape will be a bit narrower; if the stitches are wider or the rows are shorter, the shape will be a bit wider. All of these shapes will exist on a spectrum. But, as we've seen from those top-down shawls and raglans that all block out exactly as they're meant to, knitting is plastic and in most cases the fabric will block out to the proportions and shapes that you desire. You can use those stitch patterns to your advantage (as we'll see) and let them dictate a slight change in shape, or you can let the geometry dictate where the stitch patterns can go. Or you can find a happy medium between the two!

All of the options and ideas above hinge on the idea of a prescribed set of ratios and formulas that will create a shape based on the fundamental understanding of geometry in knitting. But what if you already have a shape in mind, and need to figure out how to fill it? Here is where we run into the two different paths of knitting design: letting technique dictate shape, and letting shape dictate technique. The former is what we've discussed so far in this chapter: we now know how to work the techniques that will get us specific angles in our knitting. But what happens if we have a shape in mind, and need to figure out how to make it real? In that case, we work backwards. We use our stitch and row gauges to calculate how many stitches we need to add or subtract, and over how many rows. Then we can divide the number of rows by the number of increase rows needed (you get to decide how many increases you want to work per row), which will tell us how many rows apart we need to work our shaping. You may need to futz with the numbers a little to get them to divide into a whole number, but you can decide how strictly you want to adhere to the row and stitch counts or whether you're willing to bend and add a little width or length for the sake of knitting ease. In this and any of your other knitting plans, you now have the tools to thoughtfully and intentionally use increases and decreases in your knitting fabric to create angles and fill shapes any way you want to.

fig 5
Circle illustration

HARJO

—

SHAWL

Joy Harjo, *native American poet and musician*

Harjo

The basic triangles of increase and decrease geometry are fascinating and intriguing all on their own. With the Harjo Shawl, I wanted to experiment with taking two of those existing shapes, the B triangle and the F triangle, and combining them together with a simple slipped stitch pattern. The resulting shawl is an unconventional finished shape that hangs and drapes beautifully over your shoulders.

One size:

106 cm / 41¾" wingspan x 46 cm / 18" at deepest point

Yarn: The Fibre Co.

Acadia (sport weight; 60% Merino wool, 20% baby alpaca, 20% silk; 133 m / 145 yds per 50 g skein)
Shade: Yellow Birch; 5 skeins

Gauge:

24 sts & 36 rows = 10 cm / 4" over Chart D pattern on 4.5 mm needles, after blocking.

Needles:

4.5 mm / US 7 circular needle, minimum 80 cm / 32" length
3.5 mm / US 4 circular needle, minimum 80 cm / 32" length

Always use a needle size that will result in the correct gauge after blocking.

Notions:

5 stitch markers, tapestry needle, t-pins and blocking wires

Notes:

Harjo is knit from the centre out, with increases occurring at two different rates: 2 stitches every 4 rows in the B triangles and 6 stitches every 4 rows in the F triangle. The shawl is finished in garter stitch.

In Charts A and B, the make 1 increases are placed next to each other and will be created from the same running thread between stitches. If you are a tight knitter, you can give yourself some extra room by making a yarn over (yo) in that location on the row preceding the increases, then drop the yarn over and work into it as the running thread for the increases themselves.

STITCH GLOSSARY:

CHARTS – WRITTEN INSTRUCTIONS

CHART A (Triangle B Set-Up)

ROW 1 (RS): M1L, M1R. *2 sts*
ROW 2: Purl.
ROW 3: Knit.
ROW 4: Purl.
ROW 5: K1, M1L, M1R, k1. *4 sts*
ROW 6: Sl4 wyib.
ROW 7: Sl1wyif, k2, sl1wyif.
ROW 8: Purl.
ROW 9: K2, M1L, M1R, k2. *6 sts*
ROW 10: P2, sl2wyib, p2.
ROW 11: K1, sl4wyif, k1.
ROW 12: Sl2wyib, p2, sl2wyib.
ROW 13: Sl1wyif, k2, M1L, M1R, k2, sl1wyif. *8 sts*
ROW 14: Purl.
ROW 15: K3, sl2wyif, k3.
ROW 16: P2, sl4wyib, p2.
ROW 17: K1, sl2wyif, k1, M1L, M1R, k1, sl2wyif, k1. *10 sts*
ROW 18: Sl2wyib, p6, sl2wyib.
ROW 19: Sl1wyif, k8, sl1wyif.
ROW 20: P4, sl2wyib, p4.
ROW 21: K3, sl2wyif, M1L, M1R, sl2wyif, k3. *12 sts*
ROW 22: [P2, sl2wyib, p2] twice.
ROW 23: K1, sl2wyif, k6, sl2wyif, k1.
ROW 24: Sl2wyib, p8, sl2wyib.

CHART B (Triangle F Set-Up)

ROW 1 (RS): M1R, M1L. *2 sts*
ROW 2 (WS): M1P, sl2wyib, M1PR. *4 sts*
ROW 3: M1R, sl4wyib, M1L. *6 sts*
ROW 4: Sl2wyib, p2, sl2wyib.
ROW 5: M1R, sl1wyif, k4, sl1wyif, M1L. *8 sts*

ROW 6: M1P, sl1wyib, p6, sl1wyib, M1PR. *10 sts*
ROW 7: M1R, sl1wyif, k8, sl1wyif, M1L. *12 sts*
ROW 8: Sl1wyib, p4, sl2wyib, p4, sl1wyib.
ROW 9: M1R, k4, sl4wyif, k4, M1L. *14 sts*
ROW 10: M1P, p4, sl2wyib, p2, sl2wyib, p4, M1PR. *16 sts*
ROW 11: M1R, [k4, sl2wyif] twice, k4, M1L. *18 sts*
ROW 12: P4, sl2wyib, p6, sl2wyib, p4.
ROW 13: M1R, k3, sl2wyif, k8, sl2wyif, k3, M1L. *20 sts*
ROW 14: M1P, p3, [sl2wyib, p4] twice, sl2wyib, p3, M1PR. *22 sts*
ROW 15: M1R, k3, sl2wyif, k4, sl4wyif, k4, sl2wyif, k3, M1L. *24 sts*
ROW 16: P3, sl2wyib, p4, sl2wyib, p2, sl2wyib, p4, sl2wyib, p3.
ROW 17: M1R, k2, [sl2wyif, k4] 3 times, sl2wyif, k2, M1L. *26 sts*
ROW 18: M1P, p2, sl2wyib, p4, sl2wyib, p6, sl2wyib, p4, sl2wyib, p2, M1PR. *28 sts*
ROW 19: M1R, k2, sl2wyif, k4, sl2wyif, k8, sl2wyif, k4, sl2wyif, k2, M1L. *30 sts*
ROW 20: P2, [sl2wyib, p4] 4 times, sl2wyib, p2.
ROW 21: M1R, k1, [sl2wyif, k4] twice, sl4wyif, [k4, sl2wyif] twice, k1, M1L. *32 sts*
ROW 22: M1P, p1, [sl2wyib, p4] twice, sl2wyib, p2, [sl2wyib, p4] twice, sl2wyib, p1, M1PR. 34 sts
ROW 23: M1R, k1, [sl2wyif , k4] 5 times, sl2wyif, k1, M1L. *36 sts*
ROW 24: P1, [sl2wyib, p4] twice, sl2wyib, p6, [sl2wyib, p4] twice, sl2wyib, p1.

CHART C (Triangle B)

NOTE: *Sections marked by [square brackets] are worked once on the first repeat, twice on the second repeat, 3 times on the third repeat and so on. Rows 1-24 are worked as written, but when working row 1 for the second time it will be: [Sl1wyif, k4, sl1wyif] twice, M1L, M1R, [sl1wyif, k4, sl1wyif] twice. And the third time will be worked: [Sl1wyif, k4, sl1wyif] 3 times, M1L, M1R, [sl1wyif, k4, sl1wyif] 3 times.*

ROW 1 (RS): [Sl1wyif, k4, sl1wyif], M1L, M1R, [sl1wyif, k4, sl1wyif]. *2 sts inc*
ROW 2 (WS): [P4, sl2wyib], p2, [sl2wyib, p4].

ROW 3: [K3, sl2wyif, k1], k2, [k1, sl2wyif, k3].

ROW 4: [P2, sl2wyib, p2], p2, [p2, sl2wyib, p2].

ROW 5: [K1, sl2wyif, k3], k1, M1L, M1R, k1, [k3, sl2wyif, k1]. *2 sts inc*

ROW 6: [Sl2wyib, p4], sl4wyib, [p4, sl2wyib].

ROW 7: [Sl1wyif, k4, sl1wyif], sl1wyif, k2, sl1wyif, [sl1wyif, k4, sl1wyif].

ROW 8: [P4, sl2wyib], p4, [sl2wyib, p4].

ROW 9: [K3, sl2wyif, k1], k2, M1L, M1R, k2, [k1, sl2wyif, k3]. *2 sts inc*

ROW 10: [P2, sl2wyib, p2], p2, sl2wyib, p2, [p2, sl2wyib, p2].

ROW 11: [K1, sl2wyif, k3], k1, sl4wyif, k1, [k3, sl2wyif, k1].

ROW 12: [Sl2wyib, p4], sl2wyib, p2, sl2wyib, [p4, sl2wyib].

ROW 13: [Sl1wyif, k4, sl1wyif], sl1wyif, k2, M1L, M1R, k2, sl1wyif, [sl1wyif, k4, sl1wyif]. *2 sts inc*

ROW 14: [P4, sl2wyib], p8, [sl2wyib, p4].

ROW 15: [K3, sl2wyif, k1], k3, sl2wyif, k3, [k1, sl2wyif, k3].

ROW 16: [P2, sl2wyib, p2], p2, s4wyib, p2, [p2, sl2wyib, p2].

ROW 17: [K1, sl2wyif, k3], k1, sl2wyif, k1, M1L, M1R, k1, sl2wyif, k1, [k3, sl2wyif, k1]. *2 sts inc*

ROW 18: [Sl2wyib, p4], sl2wyib, p6, sl2wyib, [p4, sl2wyib].

ROW 19: [Sl1wyif, k4, sl1wyif], sl1wyif, k8, sl1wyif, [sl1wyif, k4, sl1wyif].

ROW 20: [P4, sl2wyib], p4, sl2wyib, p4, [sl2wyib, p4].

ROW 21: [K3, sl2wyif, k1], k3, sl2wyif, M1L, M1R, sl2wyif, k3, [k1, sl2wyif, k3]. *2 sts inc*

ROW 22: [P2, sl12wyib, p2], p2, sl2wyib, p4, sl2wyib, p2, [p2, sl2wyib, p2].

ROW 23: [K1, sl2wyif, k3], k1, sl2wyif, k6, sl2wyif, k1, [k3, sl2wyif, k1].

ROW 24: [Sl2wyib, p4], sl2wyib, p8, sl2wyib, [p4, sl2wyib].

CHART D (Triangle F)

NOTE: *Sections marked by [square brackets] are worked 3 times on the first repeat, 6 times on the second repeat, 9 times on the third repeat and so on. Row 1 is worked: M1R, [sl2wyif, p4] 3 times, [p4, sl2wyif] 3 times, M1L. Rows 2–24 are worked in the same way. The next time you work row 1 it will be worked: M1R, [sl2wyif, p4] 6 times, [p4, sl2wyif] 6 times, M1L. And the third time*

it will be worked: M1R, [sl2wyif, p4] 9 times, [p4, sl2wyif] 9 times, M1L.

ROW 1 (RS): M1R, [sl2wyif, p4], [p4, sl2wyif], M1L. *2 sts inc*

ROW 2 (WS): M1P, sl1wyib, [sl1wyib, p4, sl1wyib], [sl1wyib, p4, sl1wyib], sl1wyib, M1PR. *2 sts inc*

ROW 3: M1R, sl2wyif, [k4, sl2wyif], [sl2wyif, k4], sl2wyif, M1L. *2 sts inc*

ROW 4: Sl2wyib, p1, [p3, sl2wyib, p1], [p1, sl2wyib, p3], p1, sl2wyib.

ROW 5: M1R, sl1wyif, k2, [k2, sl2wyif, k2], k2, sl2wyif, k2], k2, sl1wyif, M1L. *2 sts inc*

ROW 6: M1P, sl1wyib, p3, [p1, sl2wyib, p3], [p3, sl2wyib, p1], p3, sl1wyib, M1PR. *2 sts inc*

ROW 7: M1R, sl1wyif, k4, [sl2wyif, k4], [k4, sl2wyif], k4, sl1wyif, M1L. *2 sts inc*

ROW 8: Sl1wyib, p4, sl1wyib, [sl1wyib, p4, sl1wyib], [sl1wyib, p4 sl1wyib], sl1wyib, p4, sl1wyib.

ROW 9: M1R, k4, sl2wyif, [k4, sl2wyif], [sl2wyif, k4], sl2wyif, k4, M1L. *2 sts inc*

ROW 10: M1P, p4, sl2wyib, p1, [p3, sl2wyib, p1], [p1, sl2wyib, p3], p1, sl2wyib, p4, M1PR. *2 sts inc*

ROW 11: M1R, k4, sl2wyif, k2, [k2, sl2wyif, k2], [k2, sl2wyif, k2], k2, sl2wyif, k4, M1L. *2 sts inc*

ROW 12: P4, sl2wyib, p3, [p1, sl2wyib, p3], [p3, sl2wyib, p1], p3, sl2wyib, p4.

ROW 13: M1R, k3, sl2wyif, k4, [sl2wyif, k4], [k4, sl2wyif], k4, sl2wyif, k3, M1L. *2 sts inc*

ROW 14: M1P, p3, sl2wyib, p4, sl1wyib, [sl1wyib, p4, sl1wyib], [sl1wyib, p4, sl1wyib], sl1wyib, p4, sl2wyib, p3, M1PR. *2 sts inc*

ROW 15: M1R, k3, sl2wyif, k4, sl2wyif, [k4, sl2wyif], [sl2wyif, k4], sl2wyif, k4, sl2wyif, k3, M1L. *2 sts inc*

ROW 16: P3, sl2wyib, p4, sl2wyib, p1, [p3, sl2wyib, p1], [p1, sl2wyib, p3], p1, sl2wyib, p4, sl2wyib, p3.

ROW 17: M1R, k2, sl2wyif, k4, sl2wyif, k2, [k2, sl2wyif, k2], [k2, sl2wyif, k2], k2, sl2wyif, k4, sl2wyif, k2, M1L. *2 sts inc*

ROW 18: M1P, p2, sl2wyib, p4, sl2wyib, p3, [p1, sl2wyib, p3], [p3, sl2wyib, p1], p3, sl2wyib, p4, sl2wyib, p2, M1PR. *2 sts inc*

ROW 19: M1R, k2, sl2wyif, k4, sl2wyif, k4, [sl2wyif, k4], [k4, sl2wyif], k4, sl2wyif, k4, sl2wyif, k2, M1L. *2 sts inc*

ROW 20: P2, sl2wyib, p4, sl2wyib, p4, sl1wyib, [sl1wyib, p4, sl1wyib], [sl1wyib, p4, sl1wyib], sl1wyib, p4, sl2wyib, p4, sl2wyib, p2.

ROW 21: M1R, k1, sl2wyif, k4, sl2wyif, k4, sl2wyif, [k4, sl2wyif], [sl2wyif, k4], sl2wyif, k4, sl2wyif, k4, sl2wyif, k1, M1L. *2 sts inc*

ROW 22: M1P, p1, sl2wyib, p4, sl2wyib, p4, sl2wyib, p1, [p3, sl2wyib, p1], [p1, sl2wyib, p3], p1, sl2wyib, p4, sl2wyib, p4, sl2wyib, p1, M1PR. *2 sts inc*

ROW 23: M1R, k1, sl2wyif, k4, sl2wyif, k4, sl2wyif, k2, [k2, sl2wyif, k2], [k2, sl2wyif, k2], k2, sl2wyif, k4, sl2wyif, k4, sl2wyif, k1, M1L. *2 sts inc*

ROW 24: P1, sl2wyib, p4, sl2wyib, p4, sl2wyib, p3, [p1, sl2wyib, p3], [p3, sl2wyib, p1], p3, sl2wyib, p4, sl2wyib, p4, sl2wyib, p1.

PATTERN BEGINS

Using larger needles and the long-tail method, cast on 6 sts.

SET-UP ROW (WS): * K1, [PM] twice; rep from * a further 4 times, k1.

Reading from the Charts or Written Instructions, work as foll:

ROW 1 (RS): [P1, SM, work row 1 of Chart A to marker, SM] 4 times, p1, SM, work row 1 of Chart B to marker, SM, p1. *16 sts*

ROW 2 (WS): K1, SM, work row 2 of Chart B to marker, SM, k1, [SM, work row 2 of Chart A to marker, SM, k1] 4 times. *18 sts*

Working the next row of charts each time, continue as set to end of row 24. *90 sts*

Reading from the Charts or Written Instructions, continue as foll:

NEXT ROW (RS): [P1, SM, work row 1 of Chart C to marker, SM] 4 times, p1, SM, work row 1 of Chart D to marker, working each bracketed repeat 3 times (shown in red and blue on the chart), SM, p1. *10 sts inc*

NEXT ROW (WS): K1, SM, work row 2 of Chart D to marker, working each bracketed rep 3 times (shown in blue and red on the chart), SM, k1, [SM, work row 2 of Chart C to marker, SM, k1] 4 times. *2 sts inc*

Continue in patt set to end of row 24. *174 sts*

Rep rows 1–24 of Charts C and D once more, working each Chart C rep twice, and each Chart D rep 6 times. *258 sts*

Rep rows 1–24 of Charts C and D once more, working each Chart C rep 3 times, and each Chart D rep 9 times. *342 sts*

Rep rows 1–24 of Charts C and D once more, working each Chart C rep 4 times, and each Chart D rep 12 times. *426 sts*

Rep rows 1–24 of Charts C and D once more, working each Chart C rep 5 times, and each Chart D rep 15 times. *510 sts*

BORDER

Change to smaller needles.

ROW 1 (RS): [K1, remove marker, k to marker, M1L, SM, k1, remove marker, M1R, k to marker, SM] twice, k1, remove marker, M1R, k to marker, remove marker, M1L, k1. *516 sts; 6 markers removed, 4 markers rem*

ROW 2 (WS): K1, M1P, k to 1 st before marker, M1PR, k1, SM, k to end slipping markers. *2 sts inc*

ROW 3: [K to marker, SM] 4 times, k1, M1R, k to last st, M1L, k1. *2 sts inc*

ROW 4: Knit.

ROW 5: [K to marker, M1L, SM, k1, M1R, k to marker, SM] twice, k1, M1R, k to last st, M1L, k1. *526 sts*

Rep rows 2–4 once more. *530 sts*

Cast off using a sewn or stretchy method.

FINISHING

Weave in all ends and block to measurements.

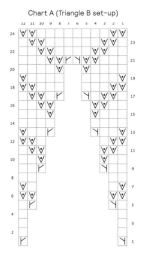

Chart A (Triangle B set-up)

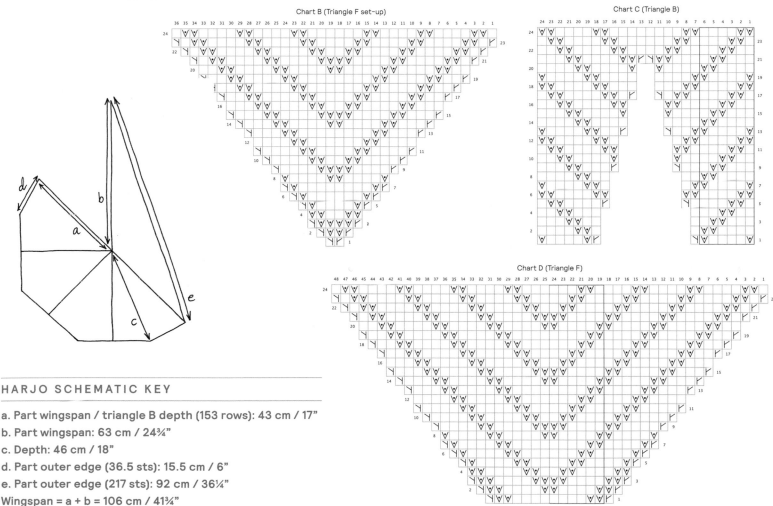

Chart B (Triangle F set-up)

Chart C (Triangle B)

Chart D (Triangle F)

HARJO SCHEMATIC KEY

a. Part wingspan / triangle B depth (153 rows): 43 cm / 17"

b. Part wingspan: 63 cm / 24¾"

c. Depth: 46 cm / 18"

d. Part outer edge (36.5 sts): 15.5 cm / 6"

e. Part outer edge (217 sts): 92 cm / 36¼"

Wingspan = a + b = 106 cm / 41¾"

CARR

——

SHAWL

Emily Carr, *Canadian artist and writer*

Carr

The Carr Shawl came about because I was interested in where I might take a traditional top-down shawl shape if I treated it as a starting point to play with further increasing and decreasing. Here, the traditional shaping veers off into two separate directions, both using increases and decreases at different rates to compensate for opposing angles. The touches of simple lace add delicacy and softness to the graphic garter stitch and linear.

One size:

179 cm / 70½" wide x 43.5 cm / 17¼" deep

Yarn: IndigoDragonfly

Chameleon Sock (4 ply / fingering weight; 63% Merino wool, 20% cashmere, 17% silk; 366 m / 400 yds per 100 g skein)
Shade: Neuralgebra; 2 skeins

Gauge:

24 sts & 39 rows = 10 cm / 4" over garter stitch on 3.5 mm needles after blocking.
24 sts & 32 rows = 10 cm / 4" over lace patterns on 3.5 mm needles after blocking.
Use the following Lace Repeat for your gauge swatch:
ROW 1 (RS): *K1, yo, ssk, k1, k2tog, yo; rep from * to last st, k1.
ROW 2 (WS): Purl.
ROW 3: *K2, yo, s2kpo, yo, k1; rep from * to last st, k1.
ROW 4: Purl.

Needles:

3.5 mm / US 4 circular needle, minimum 80 cm / 32" length

Always use a needle size that will result in the correct gauge after blocking.

Notions:

1 stitch marker, scrap yarn or stitch holder, tapestry needle, T-pins and blocking wires

Notes:

Carr begins from a small number of stitches and is worked with increases at the centre and edges until depth is reached. From there, the sides are split to work individually, with decreases occurring every other row on Side A and every fourth row on Side B.

CHARTS – WRITTEN INSTRUCTIONS

LACE INSET

ROW 1 (RS): K2, yo, [k1, yo, ssk, k1, k2tog, yo] to last 3 sts, k1, yo, k2,
ROW 2 (WS and all following WS rows): Purl.
ROW 3: K2, yo, k1, [k2, yo, s2kpo, yo, k1] to last 4 sts, k2, yo, k2.
ROW 5: K2, yo, k2tog, yo, [k1, yo, ssk, k1, k2tog, yo] to last 5 sts, k1, yo, ssk, yo, k2.
ROW 7: K2, yo, k2tog, yo, k1, [k2, yo, s2kpo, yo, k1] to last 6 sts, k2, yo, ssk, yo, k2.
ROW 9: K2, yo, k2, k2tog, yo, [k1, yo, ssk, k1, k2tog, yo] to last 7 sts, k1, yo, ssk, k2, yo, k2.
ROW 11: K2, yo, k1, yo, s2kpo, yo, k1, [k2, yo, s2kpo, yo, k1] to last 2 sts,, yo, k2.
ROW 12 (WS): Purl.

SIDE A Lace Inset

ROW 1 (RS): K2, yo, [k1, yo, ssk, k1, k2tog, yo] to last 8 sts, k1, yo, ssk, k2, k2tog, k1.
ROW 2 (WS and all following WS rows): P1, p2tog, p to end.
ROW 3: K2, yo, k1, [k2, yo, s2kpo, yo, k1] to last 6 sts, k3, k2tog, k1.
ROW 5: K2, yo, k2, [k1, yo, ssk, k1, k2tog, yo] to last 4 sts, k1, k2tog, k1.
ROW 7: K2, yo, k2tog, yo, k1, [k2, yo, s2kpo, yo, k1] to last 8 sts, k2, yo, s2kpo, yo, k2tog, k1.
ROW 9: K2, yo, k2, k2tog, yo, [k1, yo, ssk, k1, k2tog, yo] to last 6 sts, k1, yo, ssk, k2tog, k1.
ROW 11: K2, yo, k1, yo, s2kpo, yo, k1, [k2, yo, s2kpo, yo, k1] to last 4 sts, k1, k2tog, k1.
ROW 12 (WS): P1, p2tog, p to end.

SIDE B Lace Inset

ROW 1 (RS): K2, yo, [k1, yo, ssk, k1, k2tog, yo] to last 8 sts, k1, yo, ssk, k2, k2tog, k1.

ROW 2 (WS and all following WS rows): Purl.
ROW 3: K2tog, yo, k1, [k2, yo, s2kpo, yo, k1] to last 7 sts, k4, k2tog, k1.
ROW 5: K2, yo, k1, [k1, yo, ssk, k1, k2tog, yo] to last 6 sts, k3, k2tog, k1.
ROW 7: K1, k2tog, yo, k1, [k2, yo, s2kpo, yo, k1] to last 5 sts, k2, k2tog, k1.
ROW 9: K2, yo, k2, [k1, yo, ssk, k1, k2tog, yo] to last 4 sts, k1, k2tog, k1.
ROW 11: K1, yo, s2kpo, yo, k1, [k2, yo, s2kpo, yo, k1] to last 3 sts, k2tog, k1.
ROW 12 (WS): Purl.

PATTERN BEGINS

Using the long-tail method, cast on 6 sts.
SET-UP ROW (WS): K3, PM, k3.
SET-UP ROW (RS): [Kfb] twice, k1, sm, [kfb] twice, k1. *10 sts*
NEXT ROW: Knit.

Commence Main Pattern

NOTE: *Work slip stitches knitwise with yarn in back (Sl1).*

GARTER ROW 1 (RS): Sl1, kfb, k to 2 sts before marker, kfb, k1, SM, kfb, k to last 3 sts, kfb, k2. *4 sts inc*
GARTER ROW 2 (WS): Sl1, k to end.

Rep Garter rows 1-2 a further 23 times. *106 sts; 53 sts either side*

NEXT ROW (RS): Reading from the Chart or Written Instructions, work row 1 of Lace Inset to marker, working 6-st repeat 8 times, SM, reading from the Chart or Written Instructions, work row 1 of Lace Inset to end, working 6 st-repeat 8 times. *110 sts*

NEXT ROW (WS): Work row 2 of Lace Inset to marker, SM, work row 2 of Lace Inset to end.

Continue in patt as set to end of row 12 of Lace Inset. *130 sts; 65 sts either side*

Rep Garter rows 1-2 a further 12 times. *178 sts; 89 sts either side*

NEXT ROW (RS): Work row 1 of Lace Inset to marker, working 6-st repeat 14 times, SM,

work row 1 of Lace Inset to end, working
6 st-repeat 14 times. *182 sts*

NEXT ROW (WS): Work row 2 of Lace Inset
to marker, SM, work row 2 of Lace Inset
to end.

Continue in patt as set to end of row 8
of Lace Inset. *194 sts; 97 sts either side*

Rep Garter rows 1-2 a further 3 times.
206 sts; 103 sts either side

SIDE A

SET-UP ROW (RS): Sl1, kfb, k to 3 sts before
marker, k2tog, k1, remove marker and place
rem sts from LH needle on a stitch holder
or scrap yarn. Turn work.
SET-UP ROW (WS): Sl1, k2tog, k to end.
1 st dec

GARTER ROW 1 (RS): Sl1, kfb, k to 3 sts before
end, k2tog, k1.
GARTER ROW 2 (WS): Sl1, k2tog, k to end.
1 st dec

Rep Garter rows 1-2 a further 7 times. *94 sts*

NEXT ROW (RS): Work row 1 of Side A Lace
Inset to end, working 6-st repeat 13 times.
NEXT ROW (WS): Work row 2 of Side A Lace
Inset to end. *93 sts*

Continue in patt as set to end of row 4
of Side A Lace Inset. *92 sts*

Rep Garter rows 1-2 a further 22 times. *70 sts*

NEXT ROW (RS): Work row 1 of Side A Lace
Inset to end, working 6-st repeat 9 times.
NEXT ROW (WS): Work row 2 of Side A Lace
Inset to end. *69 sts*

Continue in patt as set to end of row 12 of
Side A Lace Inset, then rep Rows 1-4 once
more. *62 sts*

Rep Garter rows 1-2 a further 4 times. *58 sts*

NEXT ROW (RS): Work row 1 of Side A Lace
Inset to end, working 6-st repeat 7 times.
NEXT ROW (WS): Work row 2 of Side A Lace
Inset to end. *57 sts*

Continue in patt as set to end of row 8
of Side A Lace Inset. *54 sts*

Rep Garter rows 1-2 a further 26 times. *28 sts*

NEXT ROW (RS): Work row 1 of Side A Lace
Inset to end, working 6-st repeat twice.
NEXT ROW (WS): Work row 2 of Side A Lace
Inset to end. *27 sts rem*

Continue in patt as set to end of row 4
of Side A Lace Inset. *26 sts*

Rep Garter rows 1-2 a further 22 times. *4 sts*

NEXT ROW (RS): Sl1, k to end.
NEXT ROW (WS): Sl1, k2tog, k to end. 1 st dec
Rep last 2 rows once more. *2 sts*
NEXT ROW: K2tog, break yarn and pull
through rem st to fasten off.

SIDE B

With RS facing, place 103 held sts on needle
and join yarn.

GARTER ROW 1 (RS): Sl1, kfb, k to 3 sts before
end, k2tog, k1.
GARTER ROW 2 (WS): Sl1, k to end.
GARTER ROW 3: Sl1, k to 3 sts before end,
k2tog, k1. *1 st dec*
GARTER ROW 4: Sl1, k to end.

Rep Garter rows 1-4 a further 20 times. 82 sts

NEXT ROW (RS): Work row 1 of Side B Lace
Inset to end, working 6-st repeat 12 times.
NEXT ROW (WS): Work row 2 of Side B Lace
Inset to end.

Continue in patt as set to end of row 4
of Side B Lace Inset. *81 sts*

Rep Garter rows 1-4 once more. *80 sts*

NEXT ROW (RS): Work row 9 of Side B Lace
Inset to end, working 6-st repeat 12 times.
NEXT ROW (WS): Work row 10 of Side B Lace
Inset to end.

Continue in patt as set to end of row 12
of Side B Lace Inset. *79 sts*

Rep Garter Rows 1-4 a further 9 times. *70 sts*

NEXT ROW (RS): Work row 1 of Side B Lace
Inset to end, working 6-st repeat 10 times.
NEXT ROW (WS): Work row 2 of Side B Lace
Inset to end.

Continue in patt as set to end of row 12
of Side B Lace Inset. *67 sts*
Rep Garter rows 1-4 a further 27 times. *40 sts*

NEXT ROW (RS): Work row 1 of Side B Lace
Inset to end, working 6-st repeat 5 times.
NEXT ROW (WS): Work row 2 of Side B Lace
Inset to end.

Continue in patt as set to end of row 12
of Side B Lace Inset. *37 sts*

Rep Garter rows 1-4 a further 3 times. *34 sts*

NEXT ROW (RS): Work row 1 of Side B Lace
Inset to end, working 6-st repeat 4 times.
NEXT ROW (WS): Work row 2 of Side B Lace
Inset to end.

Continue in patt as set to end of row 8
of Side B Lace Inset. *32 sts*

Rep Garter rows 1-4 a further 4 times. *28 sts*

NEXT ROW (RS): Work row 1 of Side B Lace
Inset to end, working 6-st repeat 3 times.
NEXT ROW (WS): Work row 2 of Side B Lace
Inset to end.

Continue in patt as set to end of row 4
of Side B Lace Inset. *27 sts*

Rep Garter rows 1-4 once more.

NEXT ROW (RS): Work row 9 of Side B Lace
Inset to end, working 6-st repeat 3 times.
NEXT ROW (WS): Work row 10 of Side B
Lace Inset to end.

Continue in patt as set to end of row 12
of Side B Lace Inset. *25 sts*

Rep Garter rows 1-4 a further 3 times. *22 sts*

NEXT ROW (RS): Work row 1 of Side B Lace
Inset to end, working 6-st repeat twice.
NEXT ROW (WS): Work row 2 of Side B Lace
Inset to end.

Continue in patt as set to end of row 12
of Side B Lace Inset. *19 sts*

Rep Garter rows 1-4 a further 3 times. *16 sts*

NEXT ROW (RS): Work row 1 of Side B Lace
Inset to end.
NEXT ROW (WS): Work row 2 of Side B Lace
Inset to end.

Continue in patt as set to end of row 4
of Side B Lace Inset. *15 sts*

Rep Garter rows 1–4 a further 11 times. *4 sts*

NEXT ROW (RS): Sl1, k to end.
NEXT ROW (WS): Sl1, k to end.
NEXT ROW: K2tog, k1. 1 st dec
NEXT ROW: Sl1, k to end.

Rep last 4 rows once more. *2 sts*

NEXT ROW: K2tog, break yarn and pull
through rem st to fasten off.

FINISHING

Weave in all ends and block to measurements.

CARR SCHEMATIC KEY

a. Depth: 43.5 cm / 17¼"
b. Wingspan: 179 cm / 70½"

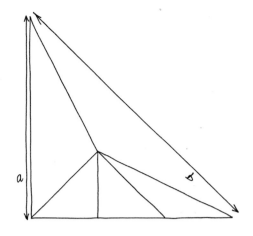

Lace Repeat (for swatching)

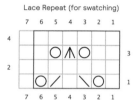

Lace Inset

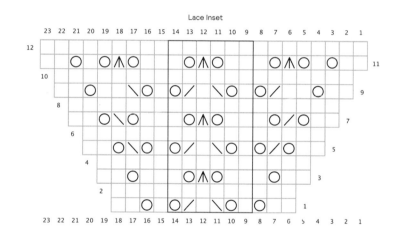

	RS: knit / WS: purl
O	yo
∧	s2kpo
\	ssk
/	k2tog
	Repeat

Side B Lace Inset   Side A Lace Inset

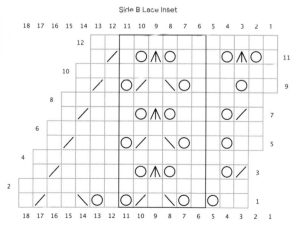
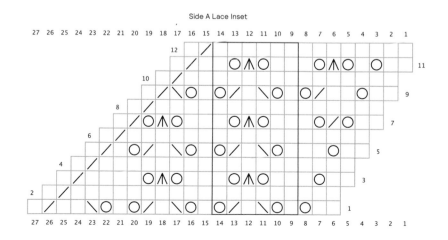

SHARMAN

—

COCOON

Helen Sharman, *first female Briton in space*

Sharman

There is something infinitely wearable and graceful about a top-down shawl, but what might happen if the same shaping were used to create a sweater? Sharman is the result. Worked from the top down with a border and a back panel of architectural and graphic lace, it combines the drape and ease of a shawl with the wearability and structure of a raglan.

Sizes:

1 (2, 3, 4)

Finished back width:

51 (65, 78.5, 92) cm / 20¼ (25½, 30¾, 36¼)" – to fit 76-96.5 (97-117, 117.5-137, 137.5-157.5) cm / 30-38 (38¼-46, 46¼-54, 54¼-62)" bust Model has 86 cm / 34" bust, stands 183 cm / 6' 0" tall and is wearing size 1.

Yarn: Baa Ram Ewe

Dovestone DK (DK weight; 50% Blue-Faced Leicester wool, 25% Masham wool, 25% Wensleydale wool; 230 m / 252 yds per 100 g skein) Shade: Yorkstone; 4 (5, 7, 9) skeins

Gauge:

19 sts and 28 rows = 10 cm / 4" over lace pattern on 3.75 mm needles, after blocking. 24 sts and 28 rows = 10 cm / 4" over stocking stitch on 3.75 mm needles, after blocking.

Needles:

3.75 mm / US 5 circular needle, minimum 80 cm / 32" length

3.5 mm / US 4 circular needle, minimum 80 cm / 32" length **AND** needle suitable for working small circumferences in the round

Always use a needle size that will result in the correct gauge after blocking.

Notions:

Smooth scrap yarn in a similar weight and crochet hook for provisional cast on, 4stitch markers, stitch holders or scrap yarn, tapestry needle, t-pins and blocking wires

Notes:

Sharman is knit from the centre back neck out to the hem. Once the back width is reached, stitches are put on hold for the sleeves and the hem worked across the front band and back stitches. A cuff is then worked onto the sleeves.

Within the stitch pattern the stitch count will fluctuate independent of the regular increases worked to shape the cocoon. Please keep these changes in mind when counting stitches outside of rows where the precise stitch count is given. It is easiest to check stitch counts at the end of each 8-row pattern repeat where there is a regular increase of 4 sts on each sleeve, and 6 sts on the back.

STITCH GLOSSARY:

M3: (K1, yo, kfb) into next st. *3 sts inc*
M6: (K1, yo, k1, yo, k1, yo, k1) into next st. *6 sts inc*

CHARTS – WRITTEN INSTRUCTIONS

CHART A (BAND PATTERN)

Starts with 19 sts.
ROW 1 (RS): M3, [p5, M6] twice, p5, M3. *18 sts inc; 37 sts*
ROW 2 (WS): P4, [k5, p7] twice, k5, p4.
ROW 3: K3, [ssk, p3, k2tog, k5] twice, ssk, p3, k2tog, k3. *6 sts dec; 31 sts*
ROW 4: P4, [k3, p7] twice, k3, p4.
ROW 5: K3, [ssk, p1, k2tog, k5] twice, ssk, p1, k2tog, k3. *6 sts dec; 25 sts*
ROW 6: P4, [k1, p7] twice, k1, p4.
ROW 7: P3, [sk2po, p5] twice, sk2po, p3. *6 sts dec; 19 sts*
ROW 8: K3, [p1tbl, k5] twice, p1tbl, k3.

ROW 9: P3, [M6, p5] twice, M6, p3. *18 sts inc; 37 sts*
ROW 10: K3, [p7, k5] twice, p7, k3.
ROW 11: P2, k2tog, [k5, ssk, p3, k2tog] twice, k5, ssk, p2. *6 sts dec; 31 sts*
ROW 12: K2, [p7, k3] twice, p7, k2.
ROW 13: P1, k2tog, [k5, ssk, p1, k2tog] twice, k5, ssk, p1. *6 sts dec; 25 sts*
ROW 14: [K1, p7] 3 times, k1.
ROW 15: K2tog, [p5, sk2po] twice, p5, ssk. *6 sts dec; 19 sts*
ROW 16: [P1tbl, k5] 3 times, p1tbl.

CHART B (SET-UP BODY)

ROW 1 (RS): Yo, p1, M6, p1, yo. *8 sts inc*
ROW 2 (WS): K2, p7, k2.
ROW 3: Yo, p1, k2tog, k5, ssk, p1, yo.
ROW 4: K2, p7, k2.
ROW 5: Rep Row 3.
ROW 6: P1, k1, p7, k1, p1.
ROW 7: Yo, sk2po, p5, sk2po, yo. *2 sts dec*
ROW 8: K1, p1tbl, k5, p1tbl, k1.

CHART C (BODY PATTERN)

Overall, this pattern increases by 6 sts each repeat. The section marked in [square brackets] is worked once on the first repeat, twice on the second, 3 times on the third and so on. Row 1 will be worked as follows: Yo, p1, M6, p5, M6, p1, yo. The next time you work row 1 it will be: Yo, p1, M6, [p5, M6] twice, p1, yo. And the third time it will be worked: Yo, p1, M6, [p5, M6] 3 times, p1, yo.
ROW 1 (RS): Yo, p1, M6, [p5, M6], p1, yo. *8 sts inc outside repeat, 6 sts inc inside repeat*
ROW 2 (WS): K2, [p7, k5], p7, k2.
ROW 3: Yo, p1, k2tog, k5, [ssk, p3, k2tog, k5], ssk, p1, yo. *2 sts dec inside repeat*
ROW 4: K2, p1, [p6, k3, p1], p6, k2.
ROW 5: Yo, p1, k2tog, k5, [ssk, p1, k2tog, k5], ssk, p1, yo. *2 sts dec inside repeat*
ROW 6: P1, k1, p1, [p6, k1, p1], p6, k1, p1.
ROW 7: Yo, sk2po, p5, [sk2po, p5], sk2po, yo. *2 sts dec outside repeat, 2 sts dec inside repeat*
ROW 8: K1, p1tbl, [k5, p1tbl], k5, p1tbl, k1.

PATTERN BEGINS

Using scrap yarn and the crochet hook, provisionally cast 41 sts onto the larger needle. Join working yarn.

SET-UP ROW (WS): [P1tbl, k5] 3 times, [p1tbl, PM, p1, PM] twice, [p1tbl, k5] 3 times, p1tbl.
SET-UP ROW (RS): [K1tbl, p5] 3 times, k1tbl, SM, yo, k1, SM, yo, k1tbl, yo, SM, k1, yo, SM, [k1tbl, p5] 3 times, k1tbl. *45 sts total; 19 sts before first marker, 2 sts between first and second marker (Sleeve), 3 sts between second and third markers (Back), 2 sts between third and fourth marker (Sleeve), 19 sts after fourth marker*
SET-UP ROW (WS): [P1tbl, k5] 3 times, p1tbl, SM, p to marker, SM, p1, p1tbl, p1 SM, p to marker, SM, [p1tbl, k5] 3 times, p1tbl.

BODY

Reading from the Chart or Written Instructions, work as foll:
ROW 1 (RS): Work row 1 of Chart A to marker, SM, yo, k to marker, SM, work row 1 of Chart B to marker, SM, k to marker, yo, SM, work row 1 of Chart A to end.
ROW 2 (WS): Work row 2 of Chart A to marker, SM, p to marker, SM, work row 2 of Chart B to marker, SM, p to marker, SM, work row 2 of Chart A to end.

Continue in patt as set to end of row 8 of Charts A and B. *59 sts total; 19 sts each Chart A, 6 sts each Sleeve, 9 sts Chart B*

ROW 9 (RS): Work row 9 of Chart A to marker, SM, yo, k to marker, SM, work row 1 of Chart C to marker working bracketed rep once, SM, k to marker, yo, SM, work row 9 of Chart A to end.

ROW 10 (WS): Work row 10 of Chart A to marker, SM, p to marker, SM, work row 2 of Chart C to marker working bracketed rep once, SM, p to marker, SM, work row 10 of Chart A to end.

Work in patt to end of row 8 of Chart C and row 16 of Chart A. *73 sts total; 19 sts each Chart A, 10 sts each Sleeve, 15 sts Chart C*

Continuing in patt as set, rep rows 1-8 of Charts A and C once more but working the Chart C bracketed rep twice. *87 sts; 19 sts in each Chart A, 14 sts in each Sleeve, 21 sts in Chart C*

Continuing patt as set, rep rows 9-16 of Chart A and rows 1-8 of Chart C once more but working the Chart C bracketed rep 3 times. *101 sts total; 19 sts in each Chart A, 18 sts in each Sleeve, 27 sts in Chart C*

Contining patt as set, rep rows 1-8 of Chart C a further 16 (20, 24, 28) times, working an extra rep of the bracketed section each time. *325 (381, 437, 493) sts total; 19 sts in each Chart A, 82 (98, 114, 130) sts each Sleeve, 123 (147, 171, 195) sts in Chart C*

FINISHING

Change to smaller needle.

NEXT ROW (RS): [K1tbl, p1] 9 times, k1tbl, remove marker, place 82 (98, 114, 130) Sleeve sts to next marker on stitch holder or scrap yarn, remove marker, using the backwards loop method cast on 2 sts, [p1, k1tbl] 61 (73, 85, 97) times, p1, remove marker, place 82 (98, 114, 130) Sleeve sts to next marker on stitch holder or scrap yarn, remove marker, using the backwards loop method cast on 2 sts, [k1tbl, p1] 9 times, k1tbl. *165 (189, 213, 237) sts*
RIB ROW (WS): [P1tbl, k1] to last st, p1tbl.
RIB ROW (RS): [K1tbl, p1] to last st, k1tbl.

Work rib as set for 6.5 cm / 2½" ending with a WS row.

Tubular Cast Off

NEXT ROW (RS): [K1, sl1wyif] to last st, k1.
NEXT ROW (WS): Sl1, [k1, sl1wyif] to last 2 sts, k1, p1.

Hold empty needle tip parallel with and behind RH needle. Slip alternating sts to each needle: knit sts to front needle, purl sts to back needle. When all sts are separated, continue to hold needles parallel and graft together using Kitchener stitch.

SLEEVES (BOTH ALIKE)

Using smaller needle, k across 82 (98, 114, 130) held Sleeve sts, pick up and k2 sts in the gap. Join to work in the round and PM for beg of round. *84 (100, 116, 132) sts*

RIB ROUND: [K1tbl, p1] to end.

Work rib as set for 4 cm / 1½".

Tubular Cast Off

Work Tubular Cast Off as for Body.

NECKBAND

Remove scrap yarn from provisional cast-on edge at neck, and place 40 sts on the larger needle. Slip 20 sts to one needle, and, with RSs together and WSs facing out, use 3-needle cast off to join edges of band together.

Weave in all ends and block to measurements.

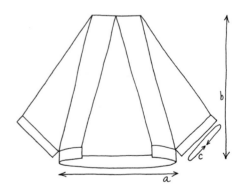

SHARMAN SCHEMATIC KEY

a. Back width: 66 (78.5, 91.5, 104.5) cm / 26 (31, 36, 41)"
b. Total length: 65.5 (77, 88.5, 100.5) cm / 25¾ (30¼, 35, 39½)"
c. Cuff circumference: 35.5 (42.5, 49, 56) cm / 14 (16¾, 19¼, 22)"

Chart A (Band Pattern)

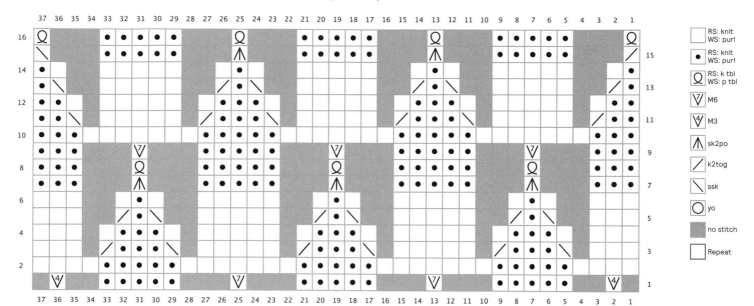

Chart B (Set-up Body Pattern)

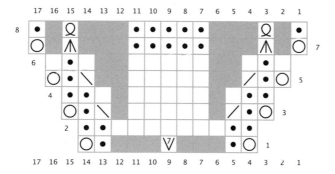

Chart C (Body Pattern)

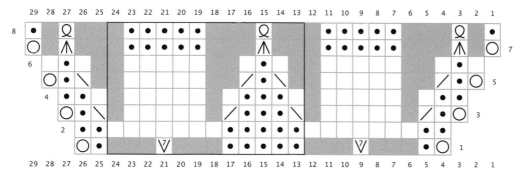

SHORT ROWS

TECHNIQUE TWO

The second method of manipulating fabric turns knitting on its ear, almost literally: short rows. Short rows do exactly what they say on the tin: they create short, or partial, rows of knitting. In essence, part of your row is worked more than the other part or parts. This can be done over two rows (one to work the right side of the partial row, one to work the wrong side), or over as many as you like (typically, by working to a number of stitches before or after the previous turning point, and then repeating that action for each consecutive turning point). This, in turn, enables certain sections of your fabric to gain height, while the rest of the fabric remains at the existing, unworked height. When worked, short rows change the direction of your knitting, building angles and arcs into what we know as a fabric structure built on the horizontal and the vertical.

fig 1

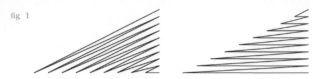

Short rows can work in two directions, starting either with a small number of stitches and adding to the length of the partial rows with every new turning point (small to large), or by starting with the total number of stitches for the longest partial row and subtracting from the length of the partial rows with each new turning point (large to small). So, for example, you could start with a partial row of only two stitches, and then add two more stitches to the row on the next partial row, and the next, ad infinitum. Alternately, you could start with ten stitches on your first partial row, and then work the next partial row with only eight, then only six, and so on. Both options will do different things to your fabric.

With small to large, you will immediately change the direction of your knitting and shift the edge of your fabric in towards the centre, as you can see on the left of fig. 1 above. Once you return to full rows, however, the fabric will follow the new path that you've just created and the edge will continue straight from that point. With large to small, your direction of knitting will stay the same as in your traditional full row knitting, and your edge will stay straight, as you can see on the right of fig. 1 above. However, once your short rows are complete and you go back to working full rows, your fabric will change direction and your edge will curve. Both techniques create the same difference in height and change of direction in your fabric, but they do so at different points. You get to decide how you want your fabric to behave!

While increasing and decreasing are fundamentally linear, short rows are fundamentally arc-based. Rather than creating angled edges, short rows work to turn your knitting on a curve. If you were to work short rows over the same stitches long enough, you'd eventually circle back to where you started and meet your cast-on edge. Because of this proclivity towards organic, curving fabric, often the edges of a short row will meander from the linear path we're most used to with a straight piece of knitted fabric, and create an edge that ripples and curves to mimic the internal structural changes that are occurring.

This doesn't have to be the case, though. You can work short rows in such a way that they don't change the line of your edges, but that will often involve using short rows in combination with increases or decreases to maintain the shape. But let's sit tight on that idea for a little bit!

There are a few different ways that short rows can be added to your fabric. Three of them work on a flat plane, and the fourth works in 3D. One of them brings you back to your original plane and axis of work, and the other three do not. Two work while touching the edges of your fabric while the other two exist in the centre. They can be used alone, in tandem, symmetrically, asymmetrically... As with all other techniques, these will serve to bring your own ideas and visions to life, with no rules or boundaries.

Uncompensated Wedge

fig 2

The simplest of all short rows, the uncompensated wedge is worked by creating a stack of short rows at one edge of your fabric. This can be a lone set of short rows, adding height just once along one edge, or it can be repeated, extending the arc of your edge and changing the direction of your knitting even further. The uncompensated wedge can work in both directions, small to large or large to small, or both can be combined on a single project.

Compensated Wedge

fig 3

A compensated wedge works on the same principle as an uncompensated: it can work from small to large or large to small, and it works at the edges of your fabric. The difference with this one is that the short rows will be performed at opposing edges of the fabric, so that once both sets of short rows are complete, you are returned to your original linear knitting orientation. It also means that these must be performed in sets of two, one on each edge, as opposed to the uncompensated wedge which can be performed any number of times.

Flat Insert

A flat insert is worked away from the edge, with the vast majority of the work happening internally within the fabric itself. Work as normal to the stitches where the partial rows will begin, work the flat insert, and then work to the end of the row, completing it. Flat inserts can touch the edge at its widest point, but the edge isn't integral to the insert's

fig 4
Insert flat

fig 5
3D Insert

structure as it is with the uncompensated and compensated wedges. In addition, the movement of the short rows isn't variable: you must move from small to large and then back to small again to achieve this shape. Depending on the size of your flat insert, this can create a tiny blip of colour (worked over just a few stitches and just a few rows before proceeding to a complete row), to huge sculptural shifts within your fabric (as with the swing knitting technique, where flat inserts are used to fill the fabric with flowing, organic shapes).

fig 4

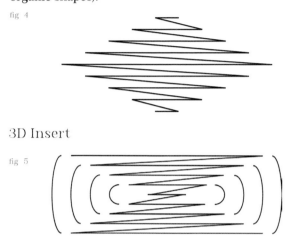

3D Insert

fig 5

There is a reason why the movement of the short rows in a Flat Insert isn't variable. It is due to the fact that, if you move from large to small to large again (rather than small to large to small, as above), the insert that is created folds onto itself, buckling the fabric vertically and creating a 3D shape. This is most commonly used to mould the 2D nature of knitted fabric into the 3D shapes of a human body: short row heels, short row bust shaping, and so on. It is also worked, as with the Flat Insert, internally within the fabric itself. In addition to shaping and moulding the fabric to fit a 3D form, the 3D Insert can be used for decorative effect within a flat fabric, creating peaks and valleys of texture and height on an otherwise homogeneous surface.

Within all of these shapes, short rows follow a similar structure to increases and decreases. The relationship of stitches to rows, that same formula, 1 stitch to 2 rows, that we saw for garter stitch with increases and decreases, remains true here as well. If you create partial rows that shift over one stitch every right side row, you will get the same 45 degree angle as you would by increasing one stitch every right side row. Again, similarly to increasing and decreasing, this remains true across the board with all stitch patterns, with some slight variation when using stitch patterns that vastly manipulate your gauge.

However, unlike with increases and decreases, where a 45 degree angle is one of the smallest you can achieve, with short rows it's the largest you can achieve. In typical short rows, you want to make sure that the difference in height between the unworked and worked stitches—the partial row that's had height added to it and the remaining row that hasn't—is no more than two rows. Indeed, often with some short row techniques, a stitch is slipped at the juncture so that the difference in height is only one row. This means that there is no way to work to the same number of stitches twice in two consecutive partial rows, the short row version of working a larger number of increases per row. Instead, those two consecutive partial rows would equate to four total rows, leaving a massive height difference between the worked and unworked stitches. So with short rows, we can't work any ratio more equal than up 2 and over 1.

Alternatively, what you can do is repeat the sequence of short rows and build to those larger angles by adding multiple smaller angles together. As with increases, I've broken down the angles you can achieve with short rows in this cheat sheet. Unlike increases and decreases, however, short rows don't follow an orderly and even radial progression; instead, they shrink in angle almost exponentially. Because of this, we can't use short rows as building blocks in quite the same way as we can with increases and decreases: A plus B doesn't equal C, and so on. However, we can stack them on themselves to create complex and fascinating shifts in direction, utilising the differences in angle to shape textured and interesting knitted fabric.

As with increases and decreases as well, we also have the capacity to work backwards. Rather than letting the technique dictate the shape, we can let the shape dictate the technique. We can start with the shape we want to achieve, and do the maths to use short rows to fill that space. Using the stitch and row gauges, we can calculate the number of stitches needed to cover the width we wish to short row, and the number of rows needed to cover the height we want to add to part of our fabric. We can then take the number of stitches and divide them by the number of action rows (if a Wedge, half the total rows; if an Insert, the total number of rows) to tell us how many stitches we will need to shift over every short row. As with increasing and decreasing, it may take a bit of finessing of stitch or row count to find an option that divides cleanly into a whole number, but most likely it'll be close enough to your original measurements to call it good.

You can also choose shape over technique by combining short rows with increases or decreases. These are especially useful when you want to mitigate that natural curve and arc of the fabric at the edge of a short row; increases or decreases can work to straighten the edge and keep it in line with the existing fabric. You can check what you might need to do during the sketching or planning process. As an experiment, draw lines in your sketch for the points where you want your short row to start and where you want your short row to end. Use a circle compass (or a pencil with a piece of yarn tied to it, for a low-tech option) to draw an arc with a radius the same length as the point where your short row starts. Take a look at where that arc intersects the line where the short row ends. Does it neatly intersect the end point of the line? Your starting number of stitches and your ending number of stitches are the same. Does the line continue past the intersection with the arc? You'll need to add stitches during the short row process. Does it, on the other hand, end before intersecting with the arc? You'll need to decrease stitches during the short row process. In all cases, you can decide whether to work the increases or decreases at a set rate, or perform calculations to help them fit perfectly into the number of rows worked during your short rows.

Short rows are invaluable tools for changing direction in your knitting, adding height or shaping in certain areas while leaving others untouched, and for adding inserts of colour, texture, or pattern into your fabric while the structure of your full rows bends and waves around them. How might you use them to make your ideas reality?

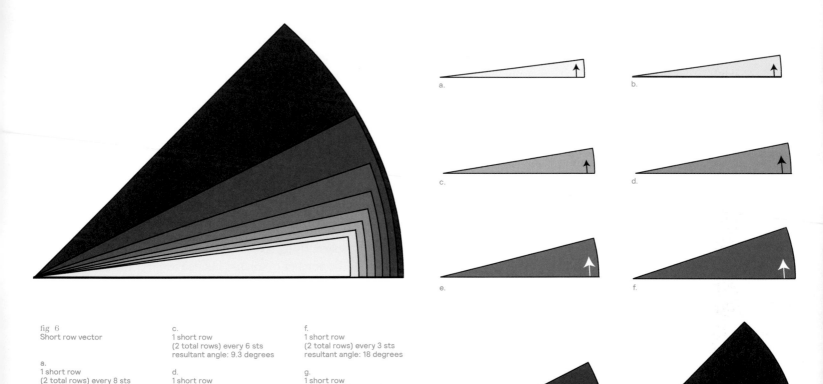

fig 6
Short row vector

a.
1 short row
(2 total rows) every 8 sts
resultant angle: 7.13 degrees

b.
1 short row
(2 total rows) every 7 sts
resultant angle: 8.1 degrees

c.
1 short row
(2 total rows) every 6 sts
resultant angle: 9.3 degrees

d.
1 short row
(2 total rows) every 5 sts
resultant angle: 11.3 degrees

e.
1 short row
(2 total rows) every 4 sts
resultant angle: 14.04 degrees

f.
1 short row
(2 total rows) every 3 sts
resultant angle: 18 degrees

g.
1 short row
(2 total rows) every 2 sts
resultant angle: 26.57 degrees

h.
1 short row
(2 total rows) every 1 sts
resultant angle: 45 degrees

MAILOU
—
MITTS

Loïs Mailou Jones, *American artist and teacher*

Mailou

Short rows on a small scale can often feel gimmicky or overly ostentatious, so my challenge with the Mailou Mitts was to balance the placement and use of the short rows while still keeping the finished pieces wearable. Here, I've used a series of Uncompensated Wedges to help mould the thumb gusset and wrist shaping, and used a combination of short rows and decreasing to turn the cables at the top of the hand 90 degrees so they became a focal panel down the top of the hand.

Sizes:

1 (2, 3)

Finished hand circumference:

19 (20.5, 21.5) cm / 7½ (8, 8½)"
Model wears size 1.

Yarn: Julie Asselin

Leizu DK (DK weight; 90% superwash Merino wool, 10% silk; 238m / 260 yds per 114 g skein)
Shade: London; 1 skein

Gauge:

21 sts & 32 rows = 10 cm / 4" over stocking stitch on 4 mm needles after blocking.

Needles:

4 mm / US 6 needles suitable for working small circumferences in the round

Always use a needle size that will result in the correct gauge after blocking.

Notions:

Smooth scrap yarn and crochet hook for provisional cast on, 2 stitch markers, locking stitch markers, cable needle, spare circular needle in same or smaller size

Notes:

Mailou is worked sideways from a provisional cast on. Short rows are worked to shape the palm, thumb gusset, and to turn the cable 90 degrees before the cable is used to join the live stitches to the provisional cast on.

Stitch Glossary:

Elongated st: For a knit, insert right needle as if to knit, wrap working yarn twice around right needle, pull both loops through as if to knit and drop old stitch off left needle. For a purl, insert right needle as if to purl, wrap working yarn twice around right needle, pull both loops through as if to purl and drop old stitch off left needle.

CABLES

1/3 RC: Slip next 3 sts to cable needle and hold in back, k1 elongated st, dropping second loop as you go, k3 from cable needle.
1/3 LC: Slip next elongated st to cable needle and hold in front, dropping second loop as you go, k3, k1 from cable needle.

CALIPER CABLE – WRITTEN INSTRUCTIONS

(worked over 10 sts and 2 rows)
ROW 1 (RS): P1, 1/3 RC, 1/3LC, p1.
ROW 2 (WS): K1, p3, p2 elongated, p3, k1.

PATTERN BEGINS

LEFT MITT

Using scrap yarn and the crochet hook, provisionally cast on 48 sts. Join working yarn.
SET-UP ROW (WS): P1, k1, p3, p2 elongated, p3, k1, PM, p26, PM, k1, p3, p2 elongated, p3, k1, p1.
ROW 1 (RS): K1, reading from the Chart or Written Instructions, work row 1 of Caliper Cable over next 10 sts, SM, k to marker, SM, work row 1 of Caliper Cable over next 10 sts, k1.
ROW 2 (WS): P1, work row 2 of Caliper Cable, SM, p to marker, SM, work row 2 of Caliper Cable, p1.

Working next row of chart, continue as set for a further 22 (26, 30) more rows. **

PALM SHAPING

Work in short rows as foll:
SHORT ROW 1 (RS): Patt to 1 st before second marker, turn and PLM for JSR.
SHORT ROW 2 (WS): Patt to end.
SHORT ROW 3: Patt to 5 sts before previous turn, turn and PLM for JSR.
SHORT ROW 4: Patt to end.
Rep short rows 3-4 a further 3 times.
NEXT SHORT ROW (RS): Patt to end, resolving all short rows with next st.
NEXT ROW (WS): Patt to end.

THUMB GUSSET

Work in short rows as foll, noting that JSR will only be worked on RS short rows:
SHORT ROW 1 (RS): Patt to 6 sts before second marker, turn and PLM for JSR.
SHORT ROW 2 (WS): Patt to marker, do not SM, then, using the backwards loop method, cast on 1 st, turn. *49 sts*
SHORT ROW 3: Work to 4 sts before previous turn, turn and PLM for JSR.
SHORT ROW 4: Patt to previous turn, turn.
Rep short rows 3-4 a further 3 times.
NEXT SHORT ROW (RS): Patt to end, resolving all short rows with next st.
NEXT ROW (WS): Patt to 2 sts before previous turn, p2tog, patt to end. *48 sts*

HAND SHAPING & BEGINNING OF JOIN

Unzip provisional cast-on and place 47 live sts on spare needle ready to work a WS row. The cast-on edge is joined to live sts as you work the following rows, decrease within the working stitches to finish shaping the thumb gusset, and use short rows to turn the Caliper Cable at the top edge 90 degrees. In the Join sections of the pattern, stitches will be referred to as either joining stitches or working stitches; working stitches include the single stitches to the outsides of the markers defining the working section.
Work in short rows as foll:

SHORT ROW 1 (RS): Patt to first marker, SM, ssk, patt to 1 st before marker, turn and PLM for JSR.

SHORT ROW 2 (WS): Patt to last st, p3tog working last st with first 2 sts of provisional cast-on.

SHORT ROW 3: Patt to marker, SM, ssk, patt to 5 sts before previous turn, turn and PLM for JSR.

SHORT ROW 4: Patt to last st, p3tog working last st with first 2 sts of provisional cast on. Rep short rows 3-4 a further 3 times. *11 joining sts, 32 working sts, 37 provisionally cast-on sts*

JOIN COMPLETION

ROW 1 (RS): Patt to marker, SM, ssk, turn.

ROW 2 (WS): Patt to last working st, p2tog working last st with first st of provisional cast-on, turn.

ROW 3: Patt to marker, SM, sssk, turn.

ROW 4: Pattern to last working st, p3tog working last st with first 2 sts of provisional cast-on, turn.

ROW 5: Rep short row 1.

ROW 6: Rep short row 2.

ROW 7: Patt to marker, SM, sl1 kwise, pick up JSR loop and place on RH needle, sl1 kwise, return these 3 sts to LH needle and k3togtbl, turn.

ROW 8: Rep short row 4.

Rep rows 1-8 a further 5 times. *11 joining sts, 2 working sts, 1 provisionally cast-on st Rep rows 1-2, then rep row 1 once more. 11 joining sts, no working or provisionally cast-on sts*

Cast off pwise.

RIGHT MITT

Work as for Left Mitt to **.

PALM SHAPING

Work in short rows as foll:

SHORT ROW 1 (RS): Patt to end.

SHORT ROW 2 (WS): Patt to 1 st before second marker, turn and PLM for JSR.

SHORT ROW 3: Patt to end.

SHORT ROW 4: Patt to 5 sts before previous turn, turn and PLM for JSR.

Rep short rows 3-4 a further 3 times.

NEXT SHORT ROW (RS): Patt to end, resolving all short rows with next st.

NEXT ROW (RS): Patt to end.

THUMB GUSSET

Work in short rows as foll:

SHORT ROW 1 (WS): Patt to 6 sts before second marker, turn and PLM for JSR.

SHORT ROW 2 (RS): Work in pattern as est to marker, do not SM, then, using the backwards loop method, cast on 1 st, turn. *49 sts*

SHORT ROW 3: Work to 4 sts before previous turn, turn and PLM for JSR.

SHORT ROW 4: Patt to previous turn, turn. Rep short rows 3-4 a further 3 times.

NEXT SHORT ROW (WS): Patt to end, resolving all short rows with next st through the back loop.

NEXT ROW (RS): Patt to 2 sts before previous turn, ssk, patt to end. *48 sts*

HAND SHAPING & BEGINNING OF JOIN

Unzip provisional cast-on and place 47 live sts on spare needle ready to work a WS row. The cast-on edge is joined to live sts as you work the following rows, decrease within the working stitches to finish shaping the thumb gusset, and use short rows to turn the Caliper Cable at the top edge 90 degrees. In the Join sections of the pattern, stitches will be referred to as either joining stitches or working stitches; working stitches include the single stitches to the outsides of the markers defining the working section.

Work in short rows as foll:

SHORT ROW 1 (WS): Patt to 1 st before second marker, turn and PLM for JSR.

SHORT ROW 2 (RS): Patt to 2 sts before second marker, k2tog, SM, patt to last st, sssk working last st with first 2 sts of provisional cast-on, turn.

SHORT ROW 3: Patt to 5 sts before previous turn, turn and PLM for JSR.

SHORT ROW 4: Patt to 2 sts before second marker, k2tog, SM, patt to last st, sssk working last st with first 2 sts of provisional cast-on.

Rep short rows 3-4 a further 3 times. *11 joining sts, 32 working sts, 37 provisionally cast-on sts*

JOIN COMPLETION

ROW 1 (WS): Patt to last working st, p2tog working last st with first st of provisional cast on, turn.

ROW 2 (RS): Patt to marker, SM, ssk, turn.

ROW 3: Patt to last working st, p3tog working last st with first 2 sts of provisional cast-on, turn.

ROW 4: Patt to marker, SM, sssk, turn.

ROWS 5-6: Rep rows 1-2.

ROW 7: Patt to marker, SM, p3tog working first st, JSR and next st, turn.

ROW 8: Rep row 4.

Rep rows 1-8 a further 5 times. *11 joining sts, 2 working sts, 1 provisionally cast-on st*

Rep rows 1-2, then rep row 1 once more. *11 joining sts, no working or provisionally cast-on sts*

Cast off pwise.

FINISHING

Weave in all ends and block to measurements.

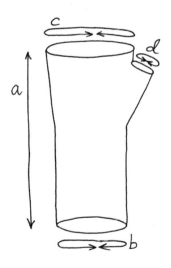

Caliper Cable

	10	9	8	7	6	5	4	3	2	1	
2	●				0̃0̃	0̃0̃				●	
	●									●	1

10 9 8 7 6 5 4 3 2 1

☐ RS: knit
WS: purl

● RS: knit
WS: purl

◺ 1/3 RC

◹ 1/3 LC

0̃0̃ WS: e–p (elongated purl):
Purl, wrapping yarn twice
around needle

MAILOU SCHEMATIC KEY

a. Length: 19.5 cm / 7¾"

b. Wrist circumference: 12.5 (14, 15) cm / 5 (5½, 6)"

c. Hand circumference: 19 (20.5, 21.5) cm / 7½ (8, 8½)"

d. Thumb circumference: 4 cm / 1½"

WISLAWA

—

COWL

Wislawa

Graphic, bold lace interjects into light, delicate fabric with the use of flat insert short rows. In Wislawa, I've set up the short row inserts to spiral through a body of garter ridge, shifting the fabric subtly on the bias to create effortless fold and drape.

One size:

61 cm / 24" circumference x 35 cm / 13¾" deep

Yarn: Shibui Knits

Pebble (light fingering weight/4 ply; 48% recycled silk, 36% fine merino, 16% cashmere; 205 m / 224 yds per 25 g skein) Shade: Cove; 2 skeins

Gauge:

25 sts & 45 rounds = 10 cm / 4" over garter ridge pattern on 3.25 mm needles after blocking.

Needles:

3.25 mm / US 3 circular needle, 40 cm / 16" length

Always use a needle size that will result in the correct gauge after blocking.

Notions:

1 stitch marker, tapestry needle

Notes:

Wislawa is worked in the round from the bottom up. Short row inserts are worked back and forth in a spiraling pattern throughout the fabric.

Stitch Glossary:

GARTER STITCH IN THE ROUND
ROUND 1: Purl.
ROUND 2: Knit.

Rep rounds 1-2 for pattern.

GARTER RIDGE PATTERN
ROUND 1: Purl.
ROUNDS 2-4: Knit.
ROUND 5: Purl.
ROUND 6: Knit.

Rep rounds 1-6 for pattern.
For swatching, rep rounds 1-4 **only**.

Short Row Pattern

SHORT ROW 1 (RS): K1, yo, ssk, yo, s2kpo, yo, k2tog, yo, k1, w&t.
SHORT ROW 2 (WS): P12, w&t.
SHORT ROW 3: K1, [yo, ssk] 3 times, k1, [k2tog, yo] 3 times, k1, w&t.
SHORT ROW 4: P18, w&t.
SHORT ROW 5: K1, [yo, ssk] 4 times, yo, s2kpo, [yo, k2tog] 4 times, yo, k1, w&t.
SHORT ROW 6: P26, w&t;
SHORT ROW 7: K1, [yo, ssk] 7 times, k1, [k2tog, yo] 7 times, k1, w&t.
SHORT ROW 8: P26, w&t.
SHORT ROW 9: [K2tog, yo] 5 times, k1, [yo, ssk] 5 times, w&t.
SHORT ROW 10: P18, w&t.
SHORT ROW 11: [K2tog, yo] 3 times, k3, [yo, ssk] 3 times, w&t.
SHORT ROW 12: P12, w&t.
ROW 13: [K2tog, yo] twice, k1, [yo, ssk] twice.

PATTERN BEGINS

SET-UP
Using the long-tail method, cast on 150 sts. Join for working in the round being careful not to twist. PM to indicate beg of round.

Beg with a purl round, work 14 rounds in G st (see Stitch Glossary).

SECTION A

Work rounds 1-6 of Garter Ridge Pattern (see Stitch Glossary).

NEXT ROUND: K11, reading from the Chart or Written Instructions, work 13 rows of Short Row Pattern, k to end of round, resolving short rows as you pass them.

** Work 2 rounds in St st (knit every round), resolving rem short rows as you pass them. Work rounds 1-6 of Garter Ridge Pattern. **

NEXT ROUND: K26, work 13 rows of Short Row Pattern, k to end of round, resolving short rows as you pass them.

Rep from ** to **.

NEXT ROUND: K41, work 13 rows of Short Row Pattern, k to end of round, resolving short rows as you pass them.

Rep from ** to **.

NEXT ROUND: K56, work 13 rows of Short Row Pattern, k to end of round, resolving short rows as you pass them.

Rep from ** to **.

SECTION B

NEXT ROUND: K71, work 13 rows of Short Row Pattern, k to end of round, resolving short rows as you pass them.

Rep from ** to **.

NEXT ROUND: K86, work 13 rows of Short Row Pattern, k to end of round, resolving short rows as you pass them.

Rep from ** to **.

NEXT ROUND: K101, work 13 rows of Short Row Pattern, k to end of round, resolving short rows as you pass them.

Rep from ** to **.

NEXT ROUND: K116, work 13 rows of Short Row Pattern, k to end of round, resolving short rows as you pass them.

Rep from ** to **.

NEXT ROUND: K131, work 13 rows of Short Row Pattern, k to end of round, resolving short rows as you pass them.

Rep from ** to **.

NEXT ROUND: K146, work 13 rows of Short Row Pattern, k to end of round, resolving short rows as you pass them.

NOTE: *On this round Short Row Pattern will occur over beg of round.*

Work 1 round in St st resolving rem short rows as you pass them.

SECTION C

Rep **SECTION A.**

Beg with a purl round, work 15 rounds in G st.

Cast off using the SSK Cast Off method.

FINISHING

Weave in ends and block to measurements.

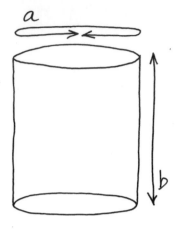

WISLAWA SCHEMATIC KEY

a. Circumference: 61 cm / 24"

b. Depth: 35 cm / 13¾"

Short Row Pattern

□	RS: knit / WS: purl
O	yo
╱	k2tog
╲	ssk
⋀	sk2po
C	RS: w&t
⊃	WS: w&t

ARBUS
—
PULLOVER

Diane Arbus, *American photographer*

Arbus

Short rows go for a field day in this pullover, with the clean lines of garter stitch stripes showing off the angles and changes of Uncompensated Wedges and Compensated Wedges. In Arbus, I wanted to see if it was possible to create graphic intersections of stripes that also served to help shape the sweater. Here, the yoke is partly shaped with short rows and partly shaped as a typical raglan, and the body is shaped with a combination of knitted-on short rows and clean stockinette.

Sizes:

1 (2, 3, 4, 5, 6, 7, 8)

Finished bust circumference:

90 (101, 112, 123, 134, 145, 156, 167) cm / 35½ (39¾, 44, 48½, 52¾, 57, 61½, 65¾)" – to be worn with 7.5-12.5 cm / 3-5" positive ease

Model has 92 cm / 36" bust, stands 183 cm / 6'0" tall, and is wearing size 2.

Yarn: Magpie Fibers

Solstice (DK weight; 50% domestic merino wool, 25% cotton, 25% silk; 274 m / 300 yds per 100 g skein)

Yarn A: Driftwood; 3 (3, 4, 4, 4, 5, 5, 5) skeins

Yarn B: Harpoon; 1 (1, 1, 1, 2, 2, 2) skeins

Gauge:

18.5 sts & 31 rows/rounds = 10 cm / 4" over stocking stitch on 4.5 mm needles after blocking.

15 sts & 36 rows/rounds = 10 cm / 4" over garter stitch on 4.5 mm needles after blocking.

Needles:

4.5 mm / US 7 circular needle, 60-80 cm / 24-32" length **AND** needles suitable for working small circumferences in the round

3.75 mm / US 5 circular needle, 60-80 cm / 24-32" length **AND** needles suitable for working small circumferences in the round

Always use a needle size that will result in the correct gauge after blocking.

Notions:

4 stitch markers, locking stitch markers for Japanese Short Rows (JSR), scrap yarn and crochet hook for provisional cast on, spare needle in same size as larger needle, stitch holders or waste yarn, tapestry needle, t-pins and blocking wires

Notes:

Arbus begins at the neckline and is worked sideways with short row shaping to create the top half of the yoke, which is then grafted together and stitches are picked up and worked down with traditional raglan shaping. After the yoke is split for body and sleeves, a panel is worked sideways at the centre front and two short row triangles are created to join the panel to the remaining front stitches. Once those panels are complete, further short rows are worked to fill in the angles and join the work to the live stitches on the back. Work is then picked up and knit down again in the round to the hem. Sleeves are picked up and knit in the round to the cuff.

Where only one number is given, this applies to all sizes.

Stitch Glossary:

STRIPE SEQUENCE (FLAT IN ROWS)
ROWS 1-2: Using yarn A, knit.
ROWS 3-4: Using yarn B, knit.

STRIPE SEQUENCE (IN THE ROUND)
ROUND 1: Using yarn A, knit.
ROUND 2: Using yarn A, purl.
ROUND 3: Using yarn B, knit.
ROUND 4: Using yarn B purl.

SPECIAL TECHNIQUES
Modified Kitchener stitch for g st:
With needles held parallel, live sts on front needle, provisional cast-on sts on back needle, and RS facing out:

Set-Up 1: Insert tapestry needle pwise through first st on front needle.

Set-Up 2: Insert tapestry needle pwise through first st on back needle.

Step 1: Insert tapestry needle kwise through first st on front needle, drop st off LH needle, insert tapestry needle pwise through new first st on LH needle.

Step 2: Insert tapestry needle kwise through first st on back needle, drop st off LH needle, insert tapestry needle pwise through new first st on LH needle.

Rep steps 1 & 2 until 1 st remains on either needle.

Step 3: Insert tapestry needle kwise through first st on front needle, drop st off LH needle.

Step 4: Insert tapestry needle kwise through first st on back needle, drop st off LH needle.

PATTERN BEGINS

YOKE

RIGHT BACK
Using larger needle scrap yarn, and the crochet hook, provisionally cast on 16 (16, 18, 18, 20, 22, 22, 24) sts. Working in rows, work Stripe Sequence (see Stitch Glossary) for 20 (22, 24, 24, 26, 26, 28, 28) rows.

Yoke Short Rows

Continuing in Stripe Sequence, work short rows as foll:

BODY RAGLAN 1
SHORT ROW 1 (RS): K to last st, turn and PLM for JSR.
SHORT ROW 2 (WS): Knit to end.
SHORT ROW 3: K to 1 st before last turn, turn and PLM for JSR.
SHORT ROW 4: Knit to end.

Rep short rows 3-4 a further 3 (5, 5, 9, 11, 13, 15, 17) times.

NEXT SHORT ROW (RS): K to 2 sts before last turn, turn and PLM for JSR.
NEXT SHORT ROW (WS): Knit to end.

Rep last 2 short rows a further 4 (3, 4, 2, 2, 2, 1, 1) times.

NEXT SHORT ROW (RS): Knit to end, resolving short rows as you go.
NEXT SHORT ROW (WS): Knit to end.

Sleeve Short Row Section 1

SHORT ROW 1 (RS): K3 (3, 3, 2, 2, 2, 2, 2), turn and PLM for JSR.
SHORT ROW 2 (WS): Knit to end.
SHORT ROW 3: K to previous turn, resolve short row with next st, k1, turn and PLM for JSR.
SHORT ROW 4: Knit to end.

Rep short rows 3-4 a further 5 (5, 6, 6, 7, 8, 7, 8) times.

SIZES 4, 5, 6, 7 & 8 ONLY:
NEXT SHORT ROW (RS): K to previous turn, resolve short row with next st, turn and PLM for JSR.
NEXT ROW (WS): Knit to end.

Rep last 2 short rows a further – (–, –, 0, 0, 0, 2, 2) times.

ALL SIZES AGAIN:
NEXT SHORT ROW (RS): Knit to end, resolving final short row.
NEXT SHORT ROW (WS): Knit to end.
Work straight in Stripe Sequence for a further 30 (30, 32, 32, 34, 36, 38, 38) rows.

Sleeve Short Row Section 2

Continuing in Stripe Sequence, work short rows as foll:
SHORT ROW 1 (RS): K to 1 st before end, turn and PLM for JSR.
SHORT ROW 2 (WS): Knit to end.
SHORT ROW 3: K to 2 (2, 2, 1, 1, 1, 1, 1) sts before last turn, turn and PLM for JSR.
SHORT ROW 4: Knit to end.

Rep short rows 3-4 a further 5 (5, 6, 0, 0, 0, 2, 2) times.

SIZES 4, 5, 6, 7 & 8 ONLY:
NEXT SHORT ROW (RS): K to 2 sts before last turn, turn and PLM for JSR.
NEXT SHORT ROW (WS): Knit to end.

Rep last 2 rows a further – (–, –, 6, 7, 8, 7, 8) times.

ALL SIZES AGAIN:
NEXT SHORT ROW (RS): Knit to end, resolving short rows as you go.
NEXT SHORT ROW (WS): Knit to end.

BODY RAGLAN 2
SHORT ROW 1 (RS): K1, turn and PLM for JSR.
SHORT ROW 2 (WS): Knit to end.
SHORT ROW 3: K to previous turn, resolve short row with next st, k1, turn and PLM for JSR.
SHORT ROW 4: Knit to end.

Rep short rows 3-4 a further 4 (3, 4, 2, 2, 2, 1, 1) times.

NEXT SHORT ROW (RS): K to previous turn, resolve short row with next st, turn and PLM for JSR.
NEXT SHORT ROW (WS): Knit to end.

Rep last 2 rows a further 3 (5, 5, 9, 11, 13, 15, 17) times.

NEXT SHORT ROW (RS): Knit to end, resolving short rows as you go.
NEXT SHORT ROW (WS): Knit to end.

Yoke Short Rows now complete.

CENTRE FRONT

Work straight in Stripe Sequence for a further 38 (44, 48, 48, 52, 54, 56, 56) rows.

Work Yoke Short Rows once more.

LEFT BACK

Work straight in Stripe Sequence for a further 17 (21, 23, 23, 25, 27, 27, 27) rows, ending with a RS row in yarn B.

Unzip provisional cast-on and place sts on spare needle. With RSs together and WSs facing out, using yarn B and garter stitch, graft tog with garter Kitchener stitch (see Stitch Glossary). Graft will sit at centre back.

RAGLAN

With RS facing, using yarn A and starting to the right of short row resolution row at the left back raglan line, pick up and k56 (62, 70, 74, 80, 86, 92, 96) in back to right back raglan line, PM, pick up and k40 (42, 44, 48, 52, 56, 60, 62) sts to right front raglan line, PM, pick up and k56 (62, 70, 74, 80, 86, 92, 96) sts to left front raglan line, PM, pick up and k40 (42, 44, 48, 52, 56, 60, 62) sts to left back raglan line, join to work in the round and PM to indicate beg of round. *192 (208, 228, 244, 264, 284, 304, 316) sts*

Continuing in yarn A only, work as foll:
SET-UP ROUND: Knit.
NEXT ROUND (INC): [K1, M1R, k to 1 st before marker, M1L, k1, SM, M1R, k to marker, M1L, SM] twice. *8 sts inc*

Rep Inc round every other round a further 8 (8, 9, 8, 8, 8, 8, 7) times, then every round 0 (1, 1, 3, 4, 6, 7, 10) times. *264 (288, 316, 340, 368, 404, 432, 460) sts*

NEXT ROUND (BODY ONLY INC): [K1, M1R, k to 1 st before marker, M1L, k1, SM, k to marker, SM] twice. *4 sts inc*

Rep Body Only Inc round every round a further 3 (4, 4, 6, 7, 7, 8, 9) times. *280 (308, 336, 368, 400, 436, 468, 500) sts*

SEPARATE FOR BODY AND SLEEVES

NOTE: *After separating the body and sleeves as you would for a typical raglan, the centre body motifs are worked. The first is a striped panel that will sit at the centre front, and will be joined to the live stitches as for a knitted-on edging. This panel will consume the centre 12 (16, 20, 28, 36, 44, 52, 60) sts, and after separating for the sleeves, you will reorient your stitches to make these central stitches available to join. After the striped panel is complete, you will break yarn, and work short rows over the remaining stitches in the right front. You'll break yarn again, work short rows over the remaining stitches in the left front, work across the back stitches, and work a final set of short rows to join with the short rows on the right front.*

NEXT ROUND: [K to marker, SM, slip next 58 (62, 66, 72, 78, 86, 92, 98) sts onto stitch holder or scrap yarn, remove marker] twice.

Beginning of round now sits at left underarm. *164 (184, 204, 224, 244, 264, 284, 304) sts* Break yarn and slip previous 47 (54, 61, 70, 79, 88, 97, 106) sts to LH needle – this positions the first available stitch at centre front.

STRIPED PANEL

Using short, larger size needle, scrap yarn, and crochet hook, provisionally cast on 35 (38, 41, 42, 43, 44, 45, 46) sts.

ROW 1 (RS): Using yarn A, knit. These sts form the Panel.
ROW 2 (WS): Work row 2 of Stripe Sequence.
ROW 3: Continuing in Stripe Sequence, k to final st of Panel, ssk working last panel st with first st of body.
ROW 4: P1, work Stripe Sequence to end.
ROWS 5-6: Rep rows 3-4.
ROW 7: Continuing in Stripe Sequence, k to final st of Panel, sk2po working last panel st with first 2 sts of body.
ROW 8: P1, work Stripe Sequence to end.

Rep rows 3-8 a further 2 (3, 4, 6, 8, 10, 12, 14) times.

Break yarns and place Panel sts on stitch holder or scrap yarn. *35 (38, 41, 42, 43, 44, 45, 46) sts rem in Front on either side of Striped Panel*

RIGHT BODY TRIANGLE

Unzip provisional cast on and place 35 (38, 41, 42, 43, 44, 45, 46) sts on spare needle. Rejoin yarns at junction of RH needle and spare needle. You will be positioned with RS facing so that Body sts are on the right-hand side, and provisionally cast-on Panel sts are on the left-hand side.

Continuing in Stripe Sequence, work short rows as foll:
SHORT ROW 1 (RS): K1 from striped Panel, turn and PLM for JSR.
SHORT ROW 2 (WS): K1, k1 from Body, turn and PLM for JSR.
SHORT ROW 3: K to previous turn, resolve with next st, turn and PLM for JSR.
SHORT ROW 4: K to previous turn, resolve with next st, turn and PLM for JSR.

Rep short rows 3-4 a further 33 (36, 39, 40, 41, 42, 43, 44) times, until you have worked all sts of Body and Panel. *70 (76, 82, 84, 86, 88, 90, 92) sts*

Break yarns and place all right triangle sts on stitch holder or scrap yarn.

LEFT BODY TRIANGLES

Place held Panel sts on spare needle. Rejoin yarns at junction of LH needle and spare needle. You will be positioned with RS facing so that Body sts are on the left-hand side, and Panel sts are on the right-hand side.

Continuing in Stripe Sequence, work short rows as foll:
SHORT ROW 1 (RS): K1 from Body, turn and PLM for JSR.
SHORT ROW 2 (WS): K1, k1 from striped Panel, turn and PLM for JSR.
SHORT ROW 3: K to previous turn, resolve with next st, turn and PLM for JSR.
SHORT ROW 4: K to previous turn, resolve with next st, turn and PLM for JSR.

Rep short rows 3-4 a further 33 (36, 39, 40, 41, 42, 43, 44) times, until you have worked all sts of Body and Panel. *70 (76, 82, 84, 86, 88, 90, 92) sts*

NEXT SHORT ROW (RS): K2tog, turn and PLM for JSR.
NEXT SHORT ROW (WS): Knit to end.
NEXT SHORT ROW: K to previous turn, k3tog, working JSR loop with next 2 sts, turn and PLM for JSR.
NEXT SHORT ROW: Knit to end.

Rep last 2 short rows a further 33 (36, 39, 40, 41, 42, 43, 44) times. *35 (38, 41, 42, 43, 44, 45, 46) sts*

Work is now at beg of round marker. PLM at right edge of fabric for left side seam.

BACK

SIZES 2, 4, 6, & 8 ONLY:
NEXT ROW (RS): Continuing in Stripe Sequence, k to final st of Panel, ssk, working last panel st tog with first st on LH needle of Body.
NEXT ROW (WS): Work Stripe Sequence to end.

Rep last 2 rows once more.

ALL SIZES AGAIN:
** **NEXT ROW (RS):** Continuing in Stripe Sequence, k to final st of Panel, ssk, working last panel st tog with first st on LH needle of Body.
NEXT ROW (WS): Work Stripe Sequence to end.
Rep last 2 rows once more.
NEXT ROW (RS): Continuing in Stripe Sequence, k to final st of Panel, sk2po, working last Panel st tog with first 2 sts on LH needle of Body.
NEXT ROW (WS): Work Stripe Sequence to end. **

Rep from ** to ** a further 19 (21, 24, 26, 29, 31, 34, 36) times.

NEXT ROW (RS): Continuing in Stripe Sequence, k to final st of Panel, ssk working last Panel st tog with first st on LH needle of Body.

NEXT ROW (WS): Work Stripe Sequence to end.

Rep last 2 rows once more.

PLM to indicate right side seam.

All Body sts have been consumed.
35 (38, 41, 42, 43, 44, 45, 46) Panel sts rem

RIGHT JOINING TRIANGLE

ROW 1 (RS): Continuing in Stripe Sequence, k to last 2 Panel sts, k2tog, replace held right triangle sts on needle ready to work RS row, k2tog, working first 2 right triangle sts, turn and PLM for JSR.
ROW 2 (WS): Ssk, k to end. *1 st dec*
ROW 3: K to 2 sts before previous turn, k2tog, k3tog, working JSR loop tog with next 2 right triangle sts, turn and PLM for JSR.
ROW 4: Ssk, k to end. *1 st dec*
Rep rows 3-4 a further
31 (34, 37, 38, 39, 40, 41, 42) times. *2 sts*

NEXT ROW (RS): K2tog, k3tog working JSR loop tog with next 2 right triangle sts, turn and PLM for JSR.
NEXT ROW (WS): Ssk. *1 st dec*
NEXT ROW: K1, k3tog, working JSR loop tog with next 2 sts, turn.
NEXT ROW: Ssk. *1 st dec*
Break yarn and pull through rem st to fasten off.

BODY

With RS facing, using yarn A and beg at locking stitch marker at left side seam, pick up and k82 (92, 102, 112, 122, 132, 142, 152) sts to locking stitch marker at right side seam, pick up and k35 (38, 41, 42, 43, 44, 45, 46) sts in Right Joining Triangle, pick up and k12 (16, 20, 28, 36, 44, 52, 60) sts in Striped Panel, pick up and k35 (38, 41, 42, 43, 44, 45, 46) sts in Left Body Triangles, join for working in the round and PM to indicate beg of round.
164 (184, 204, 224, 244, 264, 284, 304) sts

Beg with round 2, work 7 rounds straight in Stripe Sequence.

Break yarn B and continue in yarn A only.

Work straight in St st (knit every round) until work measures 38 cm / 15" from underarm.

Change to smaller needle.

RIB ROUND: [K1, p1] to end.

Rep Rib round until rib measures 4 cm / 1½".

Cast off using SSK Cast Off.

SLEEVES

Place held sleeve sts on larger needle, join to work in the round and PM to indicate beg of round. *58 (62, 66, 72, 78, 86, 92, 98) sts*

Using yarn A, work as foll:
NEXT ROUND (DEC): K1, ssk, k to last 3 sts, k2tog, k1. *2 sts dec*
Continue in St st and rep Dec round every 16 (14, 10, 10, 6, 6, 4, 4) rounds a further 1 (4, 1, 6, 1, 5, 1, 4) times, then every 18 (0, 12, 0, 8, 8, 6, 6) rounds 2 (0, 4, 0, 7, 4, 10, 8) times. *50 (52, 54, 58, 60, 66, 68, 72) sts*

Work straight in St st until work measures 25.5 cm / 10" from underarm.

Beg with round 3, work 10 rounds straight in stripe sequence.

Break yarn B and continue in yarn A only.

Change to smaller needle.
RIB ROUND: [K1, p1] to end.

Rep Rib round until rib measures 3 cm / 1¼".

Cast off using SSK Cast Off.

I-CORD NECKBAND

Using yarn A and larger needle, beg at back right raglan, pick up and k40 (46, 50, 50, 54, 52, 58, 58) sts to back left raglan, PM, pick up and k30 (30, 32, 32, 34, 36, 38, 38) sts to front left raglan, PM, pick up and k40 (46, 50, 50, 54, 52, 58, 58) sts to front right raglan, PM, pick up and k30 (30, 32, 32, 34, 36, 38, 38) sts to back right raglan.
140 (152, 164, 164, 176, 176, 192, 192) sts

Using the Backwards Loop method, cast on 3 sts.

** NEXT ROW: K2, ssk, slip sts back to LH needle.

Rep last row to marker, SM.

NEXT ROW: K2, ssk, slip sts back to LH needle.
NEXT ROW: K2, sssk, slip sts back to LH needle.

Rep last row to 0 (0, 1, 1, 2, 0, 1, 1) sts before next marker.

SIZES 3, 4, 5, 7 & 8 ONLY:
NEXT ROW: K2, ssk, slip sts back to LH needle.

Rep last row a further
– (–, 0, 0, 1, –, 0, 0) times. ******

Rep from ** to ** once more.
3 cast-on sts rem

Cast off rem sts knitwise.

Seam cast-off edge of i-cord to cast-on edge of i-cord.

FINISHING

Weave in all ends and block to measurements.

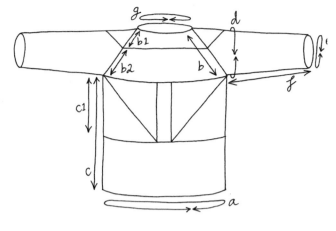

ARBUS SCHEMATIC KEY

a. Bust circumference:
90 (101, 112, 123, 134, 145, 156, 167) cm /
35½ (39¾, 44, 48½, 52¾, 57, 61½, 65¾)"

b. Yoke depth:
18 (18.5, 20.5, 21.5, 23.5, 25.5, 26, 28) cm /
7 (7¼, 8¼, 8½, 9¼, 10, 10¼, 11)"

b1. Yoke depth in short row section:
11 (11, 12, 12, 13.5, 15, 15, 16.5) cm /
4¼ (4¼, 4¾, 4¾, 5¼, 5¾. 5¾, 6½)"

b2. Yoke depth in raglan section:
7 (8, 8.5, 9, 10, 10.5, 11, 12) cm /
2¾ (3, 3¼, 3½, 3¾, 4¼, 4½, 4¾)"

c. Body length: 42 cm / 16½"

c1. Body length in short row section:
23.5 (25.5, 28, 28.5, 29, 30, 30.5, 31) cm /
9¼ (10¼, 11, 11¼, 11½, 11¾, 12, 12¼)"

d. Upper arm circumference:
32 (34, 36, 39.5, 43, 47, 50.5, 54) cm /
12½ (13½, 14¼, 15½, 16¾, 18½, 20, 21¼)"

e. Cuff circumference:
27.5 (28.5, 29.5, 32, 33, 36, 37.5, 39.5) cm /
10¾ (11¼, 11¾, 12½, 13, 14¼, 14¾, 15½)"

f. Sleeve length: 32 cm / 12½"

g. Neck circumference:
39.5 (43, 46.5, 46.5, 49.5, 49.5, 54, 54) cm /
15½ (17, 18¼, 18¼, 19½, 19½, 21¼, 21¼)"

STITCH
PATTERNS

TECHNIQUE THREE

The third method of custom-shaping your fabric is through stitch patterns. Often in patterns the designer will signify a change in needle size when changing stitch pattern—say, going up a needle size between ribbing and stockinette, or going down a needle size between cables and garter stitch. This change in needle size is used to compensate for the fact that different stitch patterns have different gauges. They expand and contract our fabric stitch-wise and row-wise, and it can take a good amount of swatching to figure out how to get multiple stitch patterns to play nicely together in a single pattern. However, when thinking creatively about knitting, we can also take those gauge differences and use them to our advantage.

L et's talk through a couple of examples to illustrate what I mean. Say I want to design a sweater with some waist shaping, but I also want there to be some cables or twisted stitches at the waistline. I can either do the maths to figure out my gauge in stockinette and in the cables, figure out if I need to change needle size to compensate for the difference in gauge, and then figure out how many increases and decreases I might need to work the waist shaping... or... I can accept that cables naturally have a smaller gauge than stockinette, so adding a panel of cables at the waistline will pull my fabric in without all of that kerfuffle. It's clean, it's simple, and it does the shaping for me invisibly, just by taking advantage of what might otherwise be a complication in my project.

Likewise, what if I wanted to make one area of my fabric taller than another, but didn't want to use short rows? In that case, I could think about the stitch patterns I know that compress my row gauge, such as welts, slip stitches, or tuck stitches. Each of these have a larger row to stitch ratio than a typical fabric, and so will get me less height for the same number of rows. Or, I could look at the stitch patterns that expand my row gauge, like elongated stitches or lace. Each of these have a smaller row to stitch ratio than a typical fabric, and so will get me more height for the same number of rows. I could even use both of those in concert, pairing a compressed row gauge pattern on one edge of my fabric with an expanded row gauge pattern on the other. There are endless combinations!

There are some limitations to what you can do with stitch patterns, however. With both increasing and decreasing and short rows, it's possible to get sharp points and clean angles. With stitch patterns, though, no matter how compressed or how expanded other sections are, you will never be able to get down to the finite point you would with the single row of unworked stitches in a short row, or the cast-on edge of a few stitches at the beginning of an angle with increases. While knitted fabric is malleable, it does have limitations, and there's only so far that it can contract or expand. So for places where you want sharp lines and crisp points, your best bet is to combine stitch patterns with either short rows, increases or decreases, or any combination of the three.

Within these combinations, however, there is a lot of room to play. What will happen to the shape of a steadily increasing triangle if you add sections of an expanded stitch gauge pattern? You would get a beautifully billowing, organic wave at the edge, and a 3D ripple to the expanded fabric within. What if you work a compressed row gauge pattern on one edge of your fabric and uncompensated wedge short rows on the other? Your short row edge would bloom and arc at a higher rate than previously possible. Stitch patterns are also, as with the cabled waist shaping example above, a wonderful way to create garments that are thoughtful and couture in their attention to detail. Where else but a knitted garment would you be able to mould and fit fabric to the structure of a body with only a simple change in stitch pattern?

Here too, we can explore the ideas of letting the shape dictate the technique versus letting the technique dictate the shape. Stitch patterns are a prime candidate for the latter. There are basic understandings of how the stitch pattern will affect your fabric, but the exact parameters will boil down to how you knit and how that affects the tension of the yarn in the fabric. So often when using stitch patterns, even if you've done careful swatching and recording of your gauges and the differences between the two, the final relationship of the stitch patterns in your fabric can be unpredictable. But, as I have said, there's no way to define an exact angle or point with stitch patterns alone. So as long as you keep that in mind while letting the technique dictate the shape, the library of stitch pattern manipulation is open for your experimentation. You can let the shape dictate the technique with stitch patterns, but often they take a bit of a back seat to the increasing and decreasing or short rows needed to make those exact lines a reality.

With these characteristics in mind, I've put together a selection of gauge-changing stitch patterns, all worked up in the effortlessly versatile Quince and Co. Lark. They've been separated into categories, and each one is described by its relationship to stockinette—is the stitch gauge larger or smaller, and is the row gauge larger or smaller?—as well as how it works to change the dimensions of the fabric. Experiment, play, and try combining them with each other and with other techniques to see what happens!

STITCH DICTIONARY

This stitch dictionary has been divided into seven sections:
Cables (CA), Elongated (EL), Gathers (GA), Lace (LA),
Slipped (SL), Tucks (TU), and Twists (TW). Each section has
a series of possible characteristics, which I've defined and
explained in the next few pages. Each stitch pattern has
been listed with which of those characteristics are applicable,
as well as which direction it will manipulate your gauge.

CABLES (CA)

Cables, by the act of switching the place of columns of stitches, pull fabric in widthwise. If worked more than every fourth row, they will also pull fabric in lengthwise. In addition, the farther a single column or set of columns is asked to travel, the more the fabric will pull in.

PANEL: A number of stitches, typically bounded on either side with a purl column, discrete and unconnected to the fabric on either side of the purl columns.

ALLOVER: A pattern which has no bounding purl columns on either edge, but is instead worked across the whole width of fabric.

NEGATIVE SPACE: When the cables travel over large distances of reverse stockinette.

NARROW CABLE: When the cable worked is a 1 over 1 cross, which can often pull less on the fabric than more stitches crossed at one time.

GATHERS (GA)

Gathered stitches combine multiple techniques to pull the fabric in widthwise, often with noticeable changes to the structure and direction of the columns of stitches.

INCREASE: When a stitch is created and then used to gather other stitches near it, thereby maintaining the stitch count.

DECREASE: When stitches are worked together, and then worked into, multiple times to compress the fabric and maintain stitch count.

SLIPPED: When stitches are slipped over other nearby stitches. These are often coupled with increases to maintain stitch count.

TWISTED: When the stitches themselves are manipulated, thereby tightening their gauge.

ELONGATED (EL)

Elongated stitches work two ways: when open, they create extra depth or width in the fabric. When closed, they pull across the fabric much like cables do and compress the fabric widthwise.

OPEN: When the elongated stitch is worked normally and remains part of the column in which it originated.

CLOSED: When the elongated stitch switches location, reaching across a number of stitches to a new column.

COMPENSATED: When the elongated stitch pattern is staggered across the row in such a way that all sections of the fabric are affected equally.

UNCOMPENSATED: when the elongated stitch pattern is only worked over a certain part of the row so that section will have a different gauge from other parts of the row.

CROSSED: When the elongated stitch crosses the path of other stitches, either as for a cable or as with passing a stitch over.

LACE (LA)

When traditionally blocked, lace opens up widthwise and compresses slightly lengthwise due to the openness of the yarnovers within the fabric. It can also cause fabric to travel on the diagonal, which will shift the fabric both vertically and horizontally.

FAGGOTING: A constant sequence of increasing and decreasing that creates a very open, mesh-like fabric.

BIAS: When increases and decreases are placed so that the fabric between them travels on the diagonal.

MULTIPLE YARNOVER: When the yarn is wrapped multiple times during a yarnover or multiple stitches are worked into a yarnover, enlarging it.

SLIPPED (SL)

Slipped stitches work to compress both row and stitch gauge, by nature of the fact that they bypass a row of knitting and also replace a stitch's width of knitting with a straight, inflexible line of yarn.

WYIF: Holding the yarn in front while slipping a stitch; creates strong horizontal line.

WYIB: Holding the yarn in back while slipping a stitch; bring focus to the V of the knit stitch as it passes over multiple rows.

COMPENSATED: When the slipped stitch pattern is staggered across the row, often every other stitch or every few stitches in such a way that all sections of the fabric are affected equally.

SPOT: When the slip stitch occurs less frequently across the row, making it more of a highlight and less of an overall fabric.

TUCKS (TU)

Tucks involve working with fabric below that on the needles, either by knitting into the rows below, by slipping multiple stitches in a column, or by dropping stitches and working all the loose threads together.

K1BELOW: Knit 1 below, working both the row on the needle and the row below it together.

SL1-YO: Stacking two strands of yarn from two separate rows on top of each other, ready to be worked together on the next row.

DROP STITCH: When stitches are dropped and laddered down to free loose strands, which are then knit together.

VERTICAL FOCUS: Creates strong vertical lines.

DIAGONAL FOCUS: Creates strong diagonal lines.

COMPENSATED: When the tuck stitch pattern is staggered across the row in such a way that all sections of the fabric are affected equally.

UNCOMPENSATED: When the tuck stitch pattern is only worked over a certain part of the row so that section will have a different gauge from other parts of the row.

TWISTS (TW)

Twisted stitches perform as a synthesis of cables and decrease gathers, by working two stitches together in such a way that two stitches result. These stitches then travel across the fabric, pulling it in both widthwise and lengthwise. As with cables, the more connections a single stitch makes across the fabric and the farther that it is asked to go, the more compressed the gauge.

PANEL: A number of stitches, typically bounded on either side with a purl column, discrete and unconnected to the fabric on either side of the purl columns.

ALLOVER: A pattern which has no bounding purl columns on either edge, but is instead worked across the whole width of fabric.

NEGATIVE SPACE: When the twists travel over large distances of reverse stockinette.

DIAGONAL FOCUS: Creates strong diagonal lines.

CABLES

CA 1

panel, manipulates width

Multiple of 10 + 2

ROW 1 (RS): [P2, 2/2 RC, 2/2 RC] to last 2 sts, p2.
ROW 2 (WS): K2, [p8, k2] to end.
ROW 3: [P2, k2, 2/2 LC, k2] to last 2 sts, p2.
ROW 4: Rep row 2.

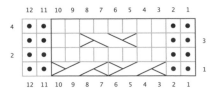
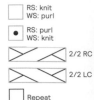

CA 2

panel, narrow cable, manipulates width and depth

Multiple of 10 + 2

ROW 1 (RS): [P2, k2, sl2wyib, k2] to last 2 sts, p2.
ROW 2 (WS): K2, [p2, sl2wyif, p2, k2] to end.
ROW 3: [P2, 1/2 RC, 1/2 LC] to last 2 sts, p2.
ROW 4: K2, [p6, k2] to end.

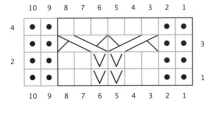
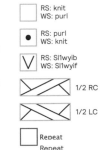

CA 3

allover, manipulates width

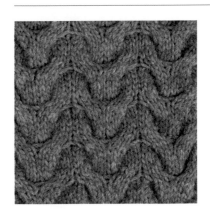

Multiple of 12 + 2

ROW 1 (RS): Knit.
ROW 2 (WS, and all following WS rows): Purl.
ROW 3: K1, [3/3 RC, 3/3 LC] to last st, k1.
ROWS 5 AND 7: Knit.
ROW 8: Purl.

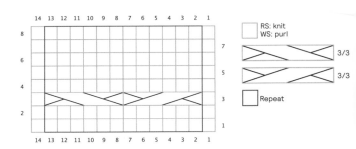

CA 4

allover, manipulates width and depth

Multiple of 8

ROW 1 (RS): Knit.

ROW 2 (WS, and all following WS rows): Purl.

ROW 3: [2/2 RC, 2/2 LC] to end.

ROW 5: Knit.

ROW 7: [2/2 LC, 2/2 RC] to end.

ROW 8: Purl.

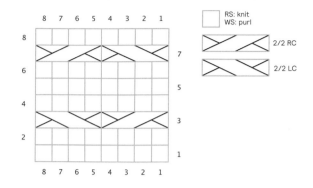

CA 5

allover, manipulates width and depth

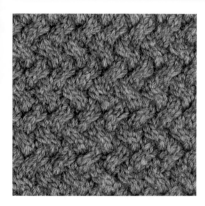

Multiple of 4 + 2

ROW 1 (RS): [2/2 LC] to last 2 sts, k2.

ROW 2 (WS, and all following WS rows): Purl.

ROW 3: Knit.

ROW 5: K2, [2/2 RC] to end.

ROW 7: Knit.

ROW 8: Purl.

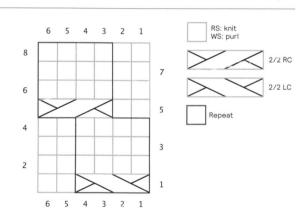

CA 6

allover, manipulates width and depth

Multiple of 12 + 2

ROW 1 (RS): Knit.

ROW 2 (WS, and all following WS rows): Purl.

ROW 3: K1, [2/2 RC, k4, 2/2 LC] to last st, k1.

ROW 5: Knit.

ROW 7: K1, [k2, 2/2 LC, 2/2 RC, k2] to last st, k1.

ROW 8: Purl.

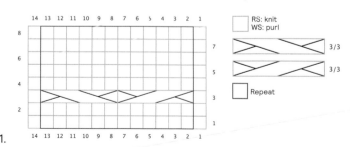

C A 7

Multiple of 16 + 4

ROW 1 (RS): K2, [(k1, 2/1 LC) twice, 2/1 RC, k2, 2/1 LC] to last 2 sts, k2.

ROW 2 (WS, and all following WS Rows): Purl.

ROW 3: [(2/1 LC, k1) twice, k1, 2/1 RC, 2/1 LC, k1] to last 4 sts, 2/1 LC, k1.

ROW 5: K1, [2/1 LC, k1, 2/1 LC, 2/1 RC, k2, 2/1 LC, k1] to last 3 sts, 2/1 LC.

ROW 7: K2, [2/1 LC, k1, (k1, 2/1 RC) twice, 2/1 LC, k1] to last 2 sts, k2.

ROW 9: K2, [k1, 2/1 LC, (2/1 RC, k1) twice, k1, 2/1 LC] to last 2 sts, k2.

ROW 11: [2/1 LC, k1, (k1, 2/1 RC) 3 times] to last 4 sts, 2/1 LC, k1.

ROW 13: K1, [2/1 LC, (2/1 RC, k1) 3 times, k1] to last 3 sts, 2/1 LC.

ROW 15: K2, [2/1 LC, k1, (k1, 2/1 RC) 3 times] to last 2 sts, k2.

ROW 17: K2, [k1, 2/1 LC, (2/1 RC, k1) 3 times] to last 2 sts, k2.

ROW 19: K1, [2/1 RC, 2/1 LC, k2, (2/1 RC, k1) twice] to last 3 sts, 2/1 RC.

ROW 21: [2/1 RC, k2, 2/1 LC, (2/1 RC, k1) twice] to last 4 sts, 2/1 RC, k1.

ROW 23: K2, [(2/1 LC, k1) twice, (k1, 2/1 RC) twice] to last 2 sts, k2.

ROW 25: K2, [(k1, 2/1 LC) twice, (2/1 RC, k1) twice] to last 2 sts, k2.

ROW 27: [(2/1 LC, k1) 3 times, k1, 2/1 RC] to last 4 sts, 2/1 LC, k1.

ROW 29: K1, [(2/1 LC, k1) twice, 2/1 LC, 2/1 RC, k2] to last 3 sts, 2/1 LC.

ROW 31: K2, [(2/1 LC, k1) twice, k1, 2/1 RC, 2/1 LC, k1] to last 2 sts, k2.

ROW 32: Purl.

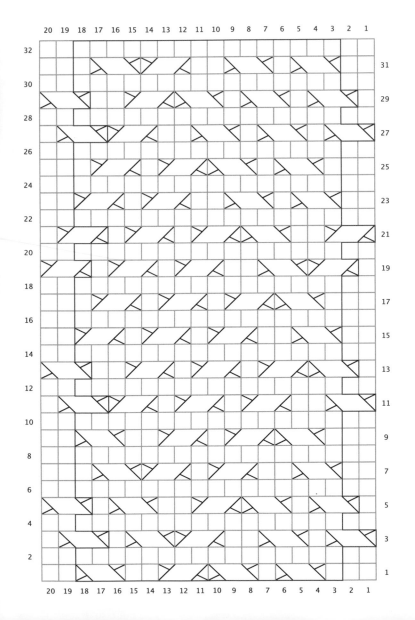

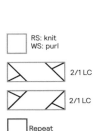

RS: knit
WS: purl

2/1 LC

2/1 LC

Repeat

CA 8

allover, narrow cable, manipulates width and depth

Multiple of 6 + 6
ROW 1 (RS): Knit.
ROW 2 (WS): Purl.
ROW 3: [1/2 RC, 1/2 LC] to end.
ROW 4: P1, [p4, 1/1 WSRC], p5.

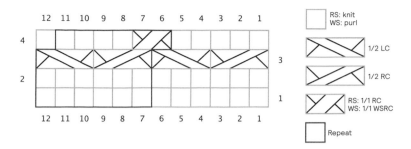
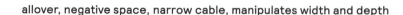

		RS: knit
		WS: purl

1/2 LC

1/2 RC

RS: 1/1 RC
WS: 1/1 WSRC

Repeat

CA 9

allover, negative space, narrow cable, manipulates width and depth

Multiple of 8 + 9
ROW 1 (RS): K1tbl, p1, [p1, s2kpo, p2, k1tbl, p1] to last 7 sts, p1, s2kpo, p2, k1tbl.
ROW 2 (WS): P1tbl, k2, (p1-yo-p1) into next st, k1, [k1, p1tbl, k2, (p1-yo-p1) into next st, k1] to last 2 sts, k1, p1tbl.
ROW 3: K1tbl, p1, [1/1 RPC, k1, 1/1 LPC, p1, k1tbl, p1] to last 7 sts, 1/1 RPC, k1, 1/1 LPC, p1, k1tbl.
ROW 4: P1tbl, k1, p1, k1, p1tbl, k1, p1, [(k1, p1tbl, k1, p1) twice] to last 2 sts, k1, p1tbl.
ROW 5: K1tbl, [1/1 RPC, p1, k1tbl, p1, 1/1 LPC, k1tbl] to last 8 sts, 1/1 RPC, p1, k1tbl, p1, 1/1 LPC, k1tbl.

ROW 6: P1tbl, p1, k2, p1tbl, k2, [p1, p1tbl, p1, k2, p1tbl, k2] to last 2 sts, p1, p1tbl.
ROW 7: K2tog, [p2, k1tbl, p2, s2kpo] to last 7 sts, p2, k1tbl, p2, ssk.
ROW 8: M1p-l, p1, k2, p1tbl, k2, [(p1-yo-p1) in next st, k2, p1tbl, k2] to last st, p1, m1p-r.
ROW 9: K1, [1/1 LPC, p1, k1tbl, p1, 1/1 RPC, k1] to last 8 sts, 1/1 LPC, p1, k1tbl, p1, 1/1 RPC, k1.
ROW 10: Rep row 4.
ROW 11: K1tbl, p1, [1/1 LPC, k1tbl, 1/1 RPC, p1, k1tbl, p1] to last 7 sts, 1/1 LPC, k1tbl, 1/1 RPC, p1, k1tbl.
ROW 12: P1tbl, k2, p1, p1tbl, p1, k1, [k1, p1tbl, k2, p1, p1tbl, p1, k1] to last 2 sts, k1, p1tbl.

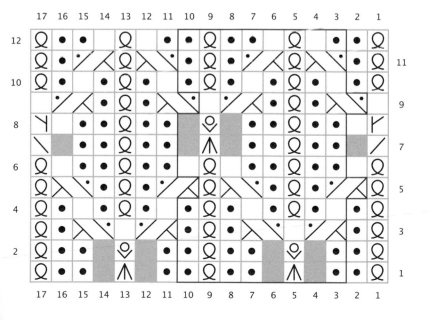
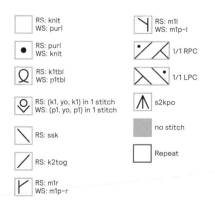

		RS: knit
		WS: purl

RS: purl
WS: knit

RS: k1tbl
WS: p1tbl

RS: (k1, yo, k1) in 1 stitch
WS: (p1, yo, p1) in 1 stitch

RS: ssk

RS: k2tog

RS: m1r
WS: m1p-r

RS: m1l
WS: m1p-l

1/1 RPC

1/1 LPC

s2kpo

no stitch

Repeat

CA 10

allover, negative space, manipulates width and depth

Multiple of 28 + 6

ROW 1 (RS): [3/3 LC, 3/2 LPC, p12, 3/2 RPC]
to last 6 sts, 3/3 RC.
ROW 2 (WS): P3, [p3, k2, p3, k12, p3, k2, p3]
to last 3 sts, p3.
ROW 3: K3, [k3, p2, 3/2 LPC, p8, 3/2 RPC, p2, k3]
to last 3 sts, k3.
ROW 4: P3, [p3, k4, p3, k8, p3, k4, p3]
to last 3 sts, p3.
ROW 5: K3, [k3, p4, 3/2 LPC, p4, 3/2 RPC, p4, k3]
to last 3 sts, k3.

ROW 6: P3, [p3, k6, p3, k4, p3, k6, p3]
to last 3 sts, p3.
ROW 7: [3/3 LPC, p6, 3/2 LPC, 3/2 RPC, p6]
to last 6 sts, 3/3 RPC.
ROW 8: K3, [p3, k8, p6, k8, p3] to last 3 sts, k3.
ROW 9: P3, 3/2 LPC, p6, 3/3 LC, p6, 3/2 RPC]
to last 3 sts, p3.
ROW 10: K3, [k2, p3, k6, p6, k6, p3, k2]
to last 3 sts, k3.
ROW 11: P3, [p2, 3/2 LPC, p4, k6, p4, 3/2 RPC, p2]
to last 3 sts, p3.
ROW 12: K3, [k4, p3, k4, p6, k4, p3, k4]
to last 3 sts, k3.
ROW 13: P3, [p4, 3/2 LPC, p2, k6, p2, 3/2 RPC, p4]
to last 3 sts, p3.
ROW 14: K3, [k6, p3, k2, p6, k2, p3, k6]
to last 3 sts, k3.
ROW 15: P3, [p6, 3/2 LPC, 3/3 LC, 3/2 RPC, p6]
to last 3 sts, p3.
ROW 16: K3, [k8, p12, k8] to last 3 sts, k3.
ROW 17: P3, [p6, 3/3/2 RPC, 3/3/2 LPC, p6]
to last 3 sts, p3.
ROWS 18, 20, AND 22: K3, [k6, p6, k4, p6, k6]
to last 3 sts, k3.
ROWS 19 AND 21: P3, [p6, k6, p4, k6, p6]
to last 3 sts, p3.
ROW 23: P3, [p4, 3/3/2 RPC, p4, 3/3/2 LPC, p4]
to last 3 *sts, p3.*
ROWS 24, 26, AND 28: K3, [k4, p6, k8, p6, k4]
to last 3 sts, k3.
ROWS 25 AND 27: P3, [p4, k6, p8, k6, p4]
to last 3 sts, p3.
ROW 29: P3, [p2, 3/3/2 RPC, p8, 3/3/2 LPC, p2]
to last 3 sts, p3.
ROWS 30, 32, AND 34: K3, [k2, p6, k12, p6, k2]
to last 3 sts, k3.
ROWS 31 AND 33: P3, [p2, k6, p12, k6, p2]
to last 3 sts, p3.
ROW 35: P3, [3/3/2 RPC, p12, 3/3/2 LPC]
to last 3 sts, p3.
ROW 36: K3, [p6, k16, p6] to last 3 sts, k3.

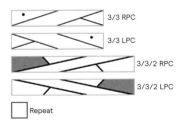

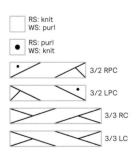

□ RS: knit / WS: purl	
● RS: purl / WS: knit	
⬈ 3/2 RPC	
⬊ 3/2 LPC	
⬡ 3/3 RC	
⬡ 3/3 LC	
	⬈ 3/3 RPC
	⬊ 3/3 LPC
	⬡ 3/3/2 RPC
	⬡ 3/3/2 LPC
	□ Repeat

CA 11

allover, negative space, narrow cable, manipulates width and depth

Multiple of 14 + 14

ROW 1 (RS): P4, k3, [k3, p8, k3] to last 7 sts, k3, p4.

ROW 2 (WS): K4, p3, [p3, k8, p3] to last 7 sts, p3, k4.

ROW 3: P4, [3/3 RC, p8] to last 10 sts, 3/3 RC, p4.

ROWS 4 AND 6: Rep row 2.

ROW 5: Rep row 1.

ROW 7: P2, 1/2 RPC, k2, [k2, 1/2 LPC, p4, 1/2 RPC, k2] to last 7 sts, k2, 1/2 LPC, p2.

ROW 8: K2, p1, k2, p2, [p2, k2, p1, k4, p1, k2, p2] to last 7 sts, p2, k2, p1, k2.

ROW 9: 1/2 RPC, p2, k2, [k2, p2, 1/2 LPC, 1/2 RPC, p2, k2] to last 7 sts, k2, p2, 1/2 LPC.

ROW 10: P1, k4, p2, (p2, k4) twice, to last 7 sts, p2, k4, p1.

ROW 11: K1, p2, 1/2 RPC, k1, [k1, 1/2 LPC, p2, k2, p2, 1/2 RPC, k1] to last 7 sts, k1, 1/2 LPC, p2, k1.

ROW 12: [P1, k2] twice, p1, [(p1, k2) twice, p2, (k2, p1) twice] to last 7 sts, p1, k2, p1, k2, p1.

ROW 13: K1, 1/2 RPC, p2, k1, [k1, p2, 1/2 LPC, k2, 1/2 RPC, p2, k1] to last 7 sts, k1, p2, 1/2 LPC, k1.

ROW 14: P2, k4, p1, [p1, k4, p4, k4, p1] to last 7 sts, p1, k4, p2.

ROW 15: K2, p2, 1/2 RPC, [1/2 LPC, p2, k4, p2, 1/2 RPC] to last 7 sts, 1/2 LPC, p2, k2.

ROW 16: P2, k2, p1, k2, [k2, p1, k2, p4, k2, p1, k2] to last 7 sts, k2, p1, k2, p2.

ROW 17: K2, 1/2 RPC, p2, [p2, 1/2 LPC, k4, 1/2 RPC, p2] to last 7 sts, p2, 1/2 LPC, k2.

ROWS 18 AND 20: P3, k4, [k4, p6, k4] to last 7 sts, k4, p3.

ROW 19: K3, p4, [p4, k6, p4] to last 7 sts, p4, k3.

ROW 21: K3, p4, [p4, 3/3 LC, p4] to last 7 sts, p4, k3.

ROWS 22 AND 24: Rep Row 18.

ROW 23: Rep Row 19.

ROW 25: K2, 1/2 LPC, p2, [p2, 1/2 RPC, k4, 1/2 LPC, p2] to last 7 sts, p2, 1/2 RPC, k2.

ROW 26: Rep Row 16.

ROW 27: K2, p2, 1/2 LPC, [1/2 RPC, p2, k4, p2, 1/2 LPC] to last 7 sts, 1/2 RPC, p2, k2.

ROW 28: Rep Row 14.

ROW 29: K1, 1/2 LPC, p2, k1, [k1, p2, 1/2 RPC, k2, 1/2 LPC, p2, k1] to last 7 sts, k1, p2, 1/2 RPC, k1.

ROW 30: Rep Row 12.

ROW 31: K1, p2, 1/2 LPC, k1, [k1, 1/2 RPC, p2, k2, p2, 1/2 LPC, k1] to last 7 sts, k1, 1/2 RPC, p2, k1.

ROW 32: Rep Row 10.

ROW 33: 1/2 LPC, p2, k2, [k2, p2, 1/2 RPC, 1/2 LPC, p2, k2] to last 7 sts, k2, p2, 1/2 RPC.

ROW 34: Rep Row 8.

ROW 35: P2, 1/2 LPC, k2, [k2, p2, 1/2 RPC, p4, 1/2 LPC, k2] to last 7 sts, k2, 1/2 RPC, p2.

ROW 36: Rep Row 2.

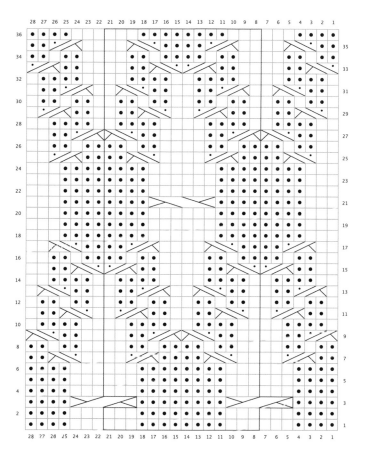

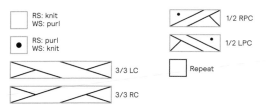

| | RS: knit / WS: purl |
| | RS: purl / WS: knit |

- 3/3 LC
- 3/3 RC
- 1/2 RPC
- 1/2 LPC
- Repeat

ELONGATED

EL 1

open, compensated, manipulates depth

Worked over any number of sts

E-k (elongated knit): Knit, wrapping yarn twice around needle. On following row, drop second wrap from needle.

ROW 1 (RS): E-k to end.
ROW 2 (WS): Purl.
ROW 3: Knit.
ROW 4: Purl.

Rows 3 and 4 can be repeated as many times as desired between elongated rows.

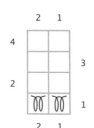

	RS: knit WS: purl
ʘʘ	RS: e-k (elongated knit): Knit, wrapping yarn twice around needle

EL 2

open, compensated, manipulates depth

Multiple of 10 + 6

ROW 1 (RS): Knit.
ROW 2 (WS): Knit.
ROW 3: [K6, (yo) twice, k1, (yo) 3 times, k1, (yo) 4 times, k1, (yo) 3 times, k1, (yo) twice] to last 6 sts, k6.
ROW 4: K6, [drop double yo, k1, drop triple yo, k1, drop quadruple yo, k1, drop triple yo, k1, drop double yo, k6] to end.
ROWS 5-6: Rep rows 1-2.

ROW 7: [K1, (yo) twice, k1, (yo) 3 times, k1, (yo) 4 times, k1, (yo) 3 times, k1, (yo) twice, k5] to last 6 sts, k1, (yo) twice, k1, (yo) 3 times, k1, (yo) 4 times, k1, (yo) 3 times, k1, (yo) twice, k1.
ROW 8: K1, drop double yo, k1, drop triple yo, k1, drop quadruple yo, k1, drop triple yo, k1, drop double yo, k1, [k5, drop double yo, k1, drop triple yo, k1, drop quadruple yo, k1, drop triple yo, k1, drop double yo, k1] to end.

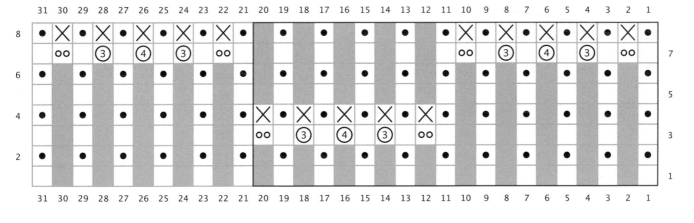

	RS: knit WS: purl
•	RS: purl WS: knit
ʘʘ	(yo) twice
③	(yo) 3 times
④	(yo) 4 times
✕	Drop yos
	no stitch
	Repeat

EL 3

open compensated, manipulates width

Multiple of 8 + 8

SET-UP ROW 1 (RS): K1, [p2, k1, yo, k1, p2, k2] to last 7 sts, p2, k1, yo, k1, p2, k1.

SET-UP ROW 2 (WS): P1, k2, p3, k2, [p2, k2, p3, k2] to last st, p1.

ROWS 1 (RS): K1, [p2, k3, p2, k2] to last 8 sts, p2, k3, p2, k1.

ROWS 2 (WS): P1, k2, p3, k2, [p2, k2, p3, k2] to last st, p1.

ROWS 3–4: Rep rows 1–2.

ROW 5: K1, [p2, k1, drop stitch, unravelling it down to its base, k1, p2, k1, yo, k1] to last 8 sts, p2, k1, drop stitch, unravelling it down to its base, k1, p2, k1.

ROWS 6: P1, k2, p2, k2, [p3, k2, p2, k2] to last st, p1.

ROWS 7: K1, [p2, k2, p2, k3] to last 7 sts, p2, k2, p2, k1.

ROWS 8–9: Rep rows 6–7.

ROW 10: Rep row 6.

ROW 11: K1, [p2, k1, yo, k1, p2, k1, drop stitch, unravelling it down to its base, k1] to last 7 sts, p2, k1, yo, k1, p2, k1.

ROW 12: P1, k2, p3, k2, [p2, k2, p3, k2] to last st, p1.

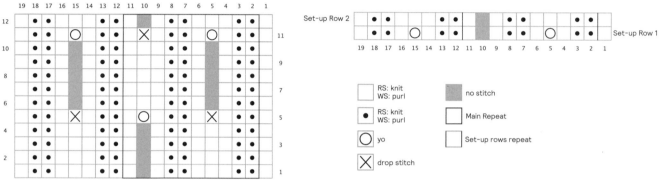

□ RS: knit / WS: purl	▨ no stitch
• RS: knit / WS: purl	□ Main Repeat
○ yo	□ Set-up rows repeat
✕ drop stitch	

EL 4

closed, crossed, manipulates width and depth

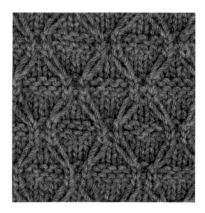

Multiple of 8 + 1

E-p (elongated purl): Purl, wrapping yarn twice around needle. On following row, drop second wrap from needle.

ROW 1 (RS): Knit.

ROW 2 (WS): K1, [e-p1, k5, e-p1, k1] to end.

ROWS 3: [K1, sl1wyib, k5, sl1wyib] to last st, k1.

ROWS 4: P1, [sl1wyif, p5, sl1wyif, p1] to end.

ROWS 5–6: Rep rows 3–4.

ROW 7: [K1, 1/2 LC, k1, 1/2 RC] to last st, k1.

ROW 8: K1, [k2, p1, k1, p1, k3] to end.

ROW 9: Knit.

ROW 10: K1, [k2, e-p1, k1, e-p1, k3] to end.

ROWS 11: [K3, sl1wyib, k1, sl1wyib, k2] to last st, k1.

ROWS 12: P1, [p2, sl1wyif, p1, sl1wyif, p3] to end.

ROWS 13–14: Rep rows 11–12.

ROW 15: [K1, 1/2 RC, k1, 1/2 LC] to last st, k1.

ROW 16: K1, [p1, k5, p1, k1] to end.

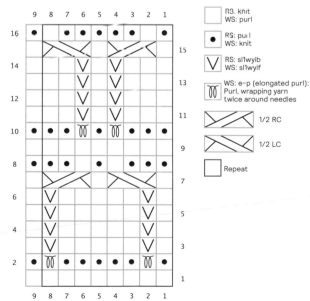

□ RS: knit / WS: purl	
• RS: purl / WS: knit	
V RS: sl1wyib / WS: sl1wyif	
⫼ WS: e-p (elongated purl): Purl, wrapping yarn twice around needles	
⟋⟍ 1/2 RC	
✕ 1/2 LC	
□ Repeat	

EL 5

Multiple of 16 + 1

E-k (elongated knit): Knit, wrapping yarn twice around needle. On following row, drop second wrap from needle.

ROW 1 (RS): E-k1, [e-k4, p7, e-k5] to end.
ROW 2 (WS): [P5, k7, p4] to last st, p1.
ROW 3: E-k1, [e-k3, p9, e-k4] to end.
ROW 4: [P3, k11, p2] to last st, p1.
ROW 5: E-k1, [e-k2, p5, e-k1, p5, e-k3] to end.
ROW 6: [P2, k6, p1, k6, p1] to last st, p1.
ROW 7: E-k1, [e-k1, p5, e-k3, p5, e-k2] to end.
ROW 8: [P1, k6, p3, k6] to last st, p1.
ROW 9: E-k1, [p5, e-k5, p5, e-k1] to end.
ROW 10: [P1, k5, p5, k5] to last st, p1.
ROW 11: P1, [p4, e-k7, p5] to end.
ROW 12: [K5, p7, k4] to last st, k1.
ROW 13: P1, [p3, e-k9, p4] to end.
ROW 14: [K4, p9, k3] to last st, k1.
ROW 15: Rep row 11.
ROW 16: Rep row 12.
ROW 17: Rep row 9.
ROW 18: Rep row 10.
ROW 19: Rep row 7.
ROW 20: [P2, k5, p3, k5, p1] to last st, p1.
ROW 21: Rep row 5.
ROW 22: [P3, k5, p1, k5, p2] to last st, p1.
ROW 23: Rep row 3.
ROW 24: Rep row 2.

Chart (columns 17 → 1, left to right; • = RS purl / WS knit; ꆕ = e-k elongated knit; blank = RS knit / WS purl):

Row	17	16	15	14	13	12	11	10	9	8	7	6	5	4	3	2	1
24						•	•	•	•	•	•	•					
23	ꆕ	ꆕ	ꆕ	ꆕ	•	•	•	•	•	•	•	•	•	ꆕ	ꆕ	ꆕ	ꆕ
22				•	•	•	•	•		•	•	•	•	•			
21	ꆕ	ꆕ	ꆕ	•	•	•	•	•	•	•	•	•	•	ꆕ	ꆕ	ꆕ	ꆕ
20			•	•	•	•	•				•	•	•	•	•		
19	ꆕ	ꆕ	•	•	•	•	•		ꆕ	ꆕ	ꆕ	•	•	•	•	ꆕ	ꆕ
18		•	•	•	•	•				•	•	•	•	•	•		
17	ꆕ	•	•	•	•	•	•	ꆕ	ꆕ	ꆕ	ꆕ	ꆕ	•	•	•	•	ꆕ
16	•	•	•	•	•					•	•	•	•	•			
15	•	•	•	•	•		ꆕ	ꆕ	ꆕ	ꆕ	ꆕ	ꆕ	ꆕ	•	•	•	•
14	•	•	•	•	•						•	•	•	•			
13	•	•	•	•	•	ꆕ	ꆕ	ꆕ	ꆕ	ꆕ	ꆕ	ꆕ	ꆕ	ꆕ	ꆕ	•	•
12	•	•	•	•	•							•	•	•			
11	•	•	•	•	•	ꆕ	ꆕ	ꆕ	ꆕ	ꆕ	ꆕ	ꆕ	ꆕ	•	•	•	•
10		•	•	•	•	•				•	•	•	•	•			
9	ꆕ	•	•	•	•	•	ꆕ	ꆕ	ꆕ	ꆕ	ꆕ	•	•	•	•	•	ꆕ
8		•	•	•	•	•			•			•	•	•	•	•	
7	ꆕ	ꆕ	•	•	•	•		ꆕ	ꆕ	ꆕ	•	•	•	•	•	ꆕ	ꆕ
6			•	•	•	•	•		•		•	•	•	•			
5	ꆕ	ꆕ	ꆕ	•	•	•	•	•	•	•	•	•	•	ꆕ	ꆕ	ꆕ	ꆕ
4				•	•	•	•	•	•	•	•	•	•	•			
3	ꆕ	ꆕ	ꆕ	ꆕ	•	•	•	•	•	•	•	•	•	ꆕ	ꆕ	ꆕ	ꆕ
2						•	•	•	•	•	•	•					
1	ꆕ	ꆕ	ꆕ	ꆕ	ꆕ	•	•	•	•	•	•	•	•	ꆕ	ꆕ	ꆕ	ꆕ

Legend:

- (blank box) RS: knit / WS: purl
- • RS: purl / WS: knit
- ꆕ RS: e-k (elongated knit): Knit, wrapping yarn twice around needle
- (box) Repeat

EL 6

Multiple of 8 + 8

ROWS 1-4: Knit.

ROW 5 (RS): [K1, (k1, wrapping yarn around needle 4 times) 7 times] to last st k1.

ROW 6: [Sl8wyib, dropping all extra wraps, pass first 4 sts over last 4 sts onto left needle, return rem sts to left needle, knit 8 sts in new orientation] to end.

ROWS 7-10: Knit.

ROW 11: K1, (k1, wrapping yarn around needle 4 times) 3 times, [(k1, wrapping yarn around needle 4 times) 8 times] to last 4 sts, (k1, wrapping yarn around needle 4 times) 3 times, k1.

ROW 12: Sl4wyib, dropping all extra wraps, pass first 2 sts over last 2 sts onto left needle, return rem sts to left needle, knit 4 sts in new orientation, [sl8wyib, dropping all extra wraps, pass first 4 sts over last 4 sts onto left needle, return rem sts to left needle, knit 8 sts in new orientation] to last 4 sts, sl4wyib, dropping all extra wraps, pass first 2 sts over last 2 sts onto left needle, return rem sts to left needle, knit 4 sts in new orientation.

ROW 24: Rep row 2.

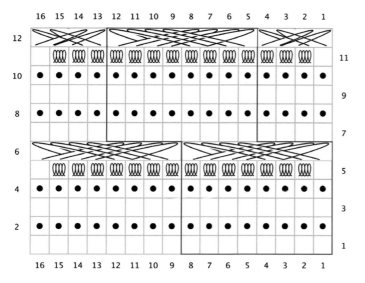

		RS: knit WS: purl
●		RS: purl WS: knit
⦀		k1, wrapping yarn four times
⨯⨯		sl8wyib, dropping all extra wraps, pass first 4sts over last 4 sts onto left needle, return rem sts to left needle. Knit 8 sts in new orientation
⨯⨯		sl4wyib, dropping all extra wraps, pass first 2 sts over last 2 sts onto left needle, return rem sts to left needle. Knit 4 sts in new orientation
		Repeat

EL 7

Multiple of 8 + 2

E-p (elongated purl): Purl, wrapping yarn twice around needle. On following row, drop second wrap from needle.

SET-UP ROW 1 (WS): K1, [k3, e-p2, k3] to last st, k1.

SET-UP ROW 2 (RS): K1, [k3, sl2wyib, k3] to last st, k1.

SET-UP ROW 3 (WS): K1, [k3, sl2wyif, k3] to last st, k1.

ROW 1 (RS): K1, [k3, sl2wyib, k3] to last st, k1.

ROW 2 (WS): K1, [k2, e-p1, sl2wyif, e-p1, k2] to last st, k1.

ROW 3: K1, [1/3 RC, 1/3 LC] to last st, k1.

ROW 4: K1, [k3, sl2wyif, k3] to last st, k1.

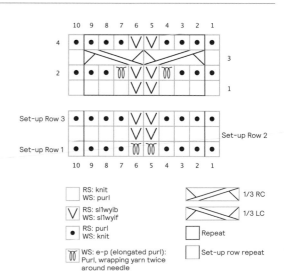

		RS: knit WS: purl			⟋	1/3 RC
V		RS: sl1wyib WS: sl1wyif			⟍	1/3 LC
●		RS: purl WS: knit				Repeat
⦀		WS: e-p (elongated purl): Purl, wrapping yarn twice around needle				Set-up row repeat

GATHERS

GA 1

increase, manipulates width

Worked over any number of sts
ROWS 1 AND 3 (RS): Knit.
ROW 2 (WS, and all following WS rows): Purl.
ROW 5: K1, [kfb] to end.
ROWS 7 AND 9: Knit.
ROW 11: K1, [k2tog] to end.
ROW 12: Purl.
Rows 1–4 or rows 6–10 can be repeated
as many times as desired.

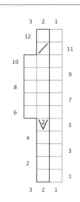

		RS: knit / WS: purl
/		k2tog
V2		kfb
		Repeat

GA 2

increase, manipulates width

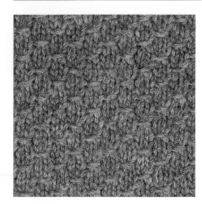

Multiple of 4 + 6
ROW 1 (RS): K2, [yo, k2, pass yo over 2 knit sts, k2]
to last 4 sts, yo, k2, pass yo over 2 knit sts, k2.
ROW 2 (WS): Purl.
ROW 3: K2, [k2, yo, k2, pass yo over 2 knit sts]
to last 4 sts, k4.
ROW 4: Purl.

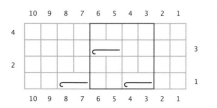

	RS: knit / WS: purl
	yo, k2, pass yo over 2 knit sts
	Repeat

GA 3

slipped, manipulates width

Multiple of 8 + 7
ROW 1 (RS): K1, [sl1, k4, pass slipped st over 4 sts, p3]
to last 6 sts, sl1, k4, pass slipped st over 4 sts, k1.
ROW 2 (WS): K1, p1, k1, m1, k1, p1, [p4, k1, m1, k1, p1]
to last st, k1.
ROW 3: K1, [k1, p3, k4] to last 6 sts, k1, p3, k2.
ROW 4: K1, p1, k3, p1, [p4, k3, p1] to last st, k1.
ROW 5: K2, [p3, sl1, k4, pass slipped st over 4 sts]
to last 5 sts, p3, k2.
ROW 6: K1, p4, [p1, k1, m1, k1, p4] to last 2 sts, p1, k1.
ROW 7: K2, [k4, p3, k1] to last 5 sts, k5.
ROW 8: K1, p4, [p1, k3, p4] to last 2 sts, p1, k1.

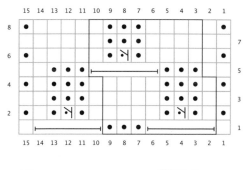

	RS: knit / WS: purl		RS: m1p / WS: m1
•	RS: purl / WS: knit		Repeat
	sl1, k4 pass slipped st over 4sts		

GA 4

decrease, manipulates width and depth

Multiple of 4 + 5
ROW 1 (RS): P1, [k1, p1] to end.
ROW 2 (WS): [K1, p1] to last st, k1.
ROW 3: P1, k1, p1, [k3tog but leave sts on left needle, yo around right needle, k3tog sts on left needle once more, p1] to last 2 sts, k1, p1.
ROW 4: Purl.
ROW 5–6: Rep rows 1 and 2.
ROW 7: P1, k3tog but leave sts on left needle, yo around right needle, k3tog sts on left needle once more, p1, [k3tog but leave sts on left needle, yo around right needle, k3tog sts on left needle once more, p1] to end.
ROW 8: Purl.

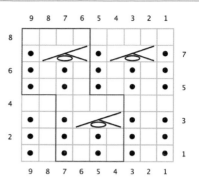

	RS: knit WS: purl
●	RS: purl WS: knit

k3tog but leave sts on left needle, yo around right needle, k3tog sts on left needle once more

Repeat

GA 5

decrease, manipulates width

Multiple of 2 + 3
ROW 1 (RS): K1, [sl1wyib as if to purl tbl, k1] to end.
ROW 2 (WS): [K1, sl1wyif] to last st, k1.
ROW 3: K1, [k1tbl, k1] to end.
ROW 4: Knit.
ROW 5: K1, [k1, sl1wyib as if to purl tbl] to last 2 sts, k2.
ROW 6: K2, [sl1wyif, k1] to last st, k1.
ROW 7: K1, [k1, k1tbl] to last 2 sts, k2.
ROW 8: Knit.

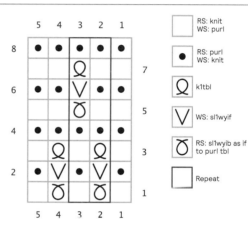

	RS: knit WS: purl
●	RS: purl WS: knit
Ω	k1tbl
V	WS: sl1wyif
ᓂ	RS: sl1wyib as if to purl tbl
	Repeat

GA 6

twisted, slipped, manipulates width and depth

Multiple of 8 + 10
ROW 1 (RS): P2, [k2, p2] to end.
ROW 2 (WS, and all following WS Rows): [K2, p2] to last 2 sts, k2.
ROW 3: P2, [insert needle between 6th and 7th st on left needle, draw loop through, sl st onto left needle and k2tog with first st on left needle, k1, p2, k2, p2] to end.
ROW 5: Rep row 1.
ROW 7: P2, k2, p2, [insert needle between 6th and 7th st on left needle, draw loop through, sl st onto left needle and k2tog with first st on left needle, k1, p2, k2, p2]to last 4 sts, k2, p2.
ROW 8: Rep row 2.

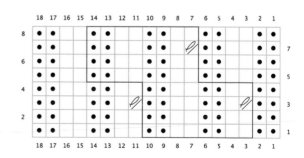

	RS: knit WS: purl
●	RS: purl WS: knit

Insert needle between 6th and 7th st on left needle draw loop through, sl st onto left needle and k2tog with first st on left needle

Repeat

LACE

LA 1

faggoting, manipulates width and depth

Multiple of 2 + 2
ROW 1 (RS): K1, [yo, p2tog] to last st, k1.
ROW 2 (WS): Rep row 1.

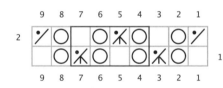

RS: knit / WS: purl
RS: purl / WS: knit — •
yo — ○
RS: k2tog / WS: p2tog — ╱
RS: p2tog / WS: k2tog
Repeat

LA 2

faggoting, manipulates width and depth

Multiple of 4 + 5
ROW 1 (RS): K1, yo, p3tog, [yo, k1, yo, p3tog] to last st, yo, k1.
ROW 2 (WS): K2tog, yo, [p1, yo, k3tog, yo] to last 3 sts, p1, yo, k2tog.

RS: knit / WS: purl
yo — ○
WS: k2tog — ╱
RS: p3tog / WS: k3tog
Repeat

LA 3

faggoting, manipulates width and depth

Multiple of 4 + 5
ROW 1 (RS): [K1, yo, s2kpo, yo] to last 5 sts, k1, yo, s2kpo, yo, k1.
ROW 2 (WS): Purl.
ROW 3: Ssk, yo, [k1, yo, s2kpo, yo] to last 3 sts, k1, yo, k2tog.
ROW 4: Purl.

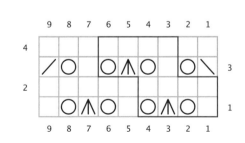

RS: knit / WS: purl
ssk — ╲
k2tog — ╱
s2kpo — ⋀
yo — ○
Repeat

L A 4

bias, manipulates width and depth

Multiple of 2 + 3
ROW 1 (RS): K1, [yo, sl1, k1, yo, pass slipped st over k st and yo] to end.
ROW 2 (WS): [P2, drop yo] to last st, p1.
ROW 3: K2, [yo, sl1, k1, yo, pass slipped st over knit st and yo] to last st, k1.
ROW 4: P1, [p2, drop yo] to last 2 sts, p2.

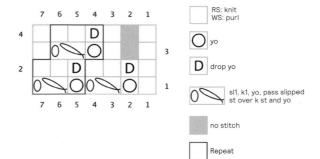

L A 5

bias, manipulates width and depth

Multiple of 10 + 1
ROW 1 (RS): [K1, (yo, ssk) twice, k1, (k2tog, yo) twice]
to last st to last st, k1.
ROW 2 (WS): Purl.
ROW 3: *K2, yo, ssk, yo, s2kpo, yo, k2tog, yo, k1; rep from * to last st, k1.
ROW 4: Purl.

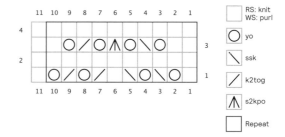

L A 6

bias, manipulates width and depth

Multiple of 4 + 8
ROW 1 (RS): K2, yo, sk2po, [yo, k1, yo, sk2po] to last 3 sts, yo, k3.
ROW 2 (WS, and all following WS rows): Purl.
ROW 3: K3, yo, [sk2po, yo, k1, yo] to last 5 sts, sk2po, yo, k2.
ROW 5: K1, k2tog, yo, k1, [yo, sk2po, yo, k1] to last 4 sts, yo, ssk, k2.
ROW 7: K2, k2tog, yo, [k1, yo, sk2po, yo] to last 4 sts, k1, yo, ssk, k1.
ROW 8: Purl.

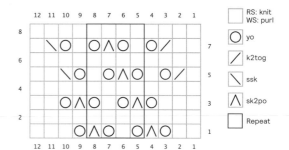

LA 7

bias, manipulates width and depth

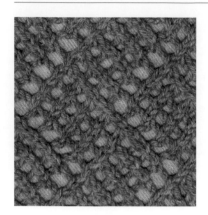

Multiple of 9 + 4

ROW 1 (RS): K1, yo, [(ssk, yo) 3 times, k3tog, (yo) twice] to last 3 sts, ssk, k1.

ROW 2 (WS): P2, [k1, p8] to last 2 sts, p2.

ROW 3: K2tog, yo, [(yo, ssk) twice, yo, k2tog, yo, k2tog, yo] to last 2 sts, k2.

ROW 4: P2, [p8, k1] to last 2 sts, p2.

ROW 5: K1, k2tog, [(yo) twice, ssk, yo, k3tog, (yo, k2tog) twice] to last st, yo, k1.

ROW 6: P2, [p7, k1, p1] to last 2 sts, p2.

ROW 7: K2tog, yo, [k2tog, (yo) twice, sssk, (yo, k2tog) twice, yo] to last 2 sts, k2.

ROW 8: P2, [p6, k1, p2] to last 2 sts, p2.

ROW 9: K1, k2tog, [yo, k2tog, (yo) twice, sssk, (yo, k2tog) twice] to last st, yo, k1.

ROW 10: P2, [p5, k1, p3] to last 2 sts, p2.

ROW 11: K2tog, yo, [k2tog, (yo) twice, ssk, yo, sssk, yo, k2tog, yo] to last 2 sts, k2.

ROW 12: P2, [p6, k1, p2] to last 2 sts, p2.

ROW 13: K1, k2tog, [(yo) twice, (ssk, yo) twice, sssk, yo, k2tog] to last st, yo, k1.

ROW 14: P2, [p7, k1, p1] to last 2 sts, p2.

ROW 15: K2tog, yo, [(yo, ssk) 3 times, yo, k3tog, yo] to last 2 sts, yo, ssk.

ROW 16: P1, k1, [p8, k1] to last 2 sts, p2.

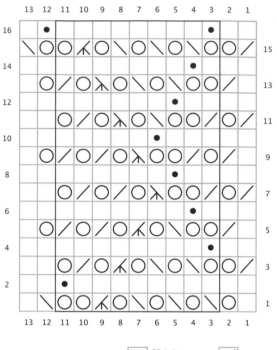

	RS: knit WS: purl		/	k2tog
●	RS: purl WS: knit		⋏	k3tog
○	yo		⋌	sssk
\	yo			Repeat

LA 8

bias, manipulates width and depth

Multiple of 6 + 1

ROW 1 (RS): K1, [k3, k2tog, yo, k1] to end.

ROW 2 (WS): [P1, yo, p1, p2tog, p2] to last st, p1.

ROW 3: K1, [k1, k2tog, k2, yo, k1] to end.

ROW 4: [P1, yo, p3, p2tog] to last st, p1.

ROW 5: P1, [ssk, k3, yo, k1] to end.

ROW 6: [P1, yo, p3, ssp] to last st, p1.

ROW 7: K1, [yo, ssk, k4] to end.

ROW 8: [P3, ssp, p1, yo] to last st, p1.

ROW 9: K1, [yo, k2, ssk, k2] to end.

ROW 10: [P1, ssp, p3, yo] to last st, p1.

ROW 11: K1, [yo, k3, k2tog, k1] to end.

ROW 12: [P1, p2tog, p3, yo] to last st, p1.

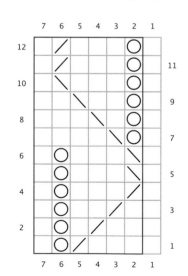

	RS: knit WS: purl
○	yo
/	RS: k2tog WS: p2tog
\	RS: ssk WS: ssp
	Repeat

LA 9

multi yo, manipulates width and depth

Multiple of 4 + 8

ROW 1 (RS): K3, [k1, (yo) twice, k3] to last 5 sts, k1, (yo) twice, k4.

ROW 2 (WS): P2, p2tog, k1, p1, ssp, [p2tog, k1, p1, ssp] to last 2 sts, p2.

ROW 3: K2, yo, [k4, (yo) twice] to last 6 sts, k4, yo, k2.

ROW 4: P3, ssp, p2tog, [k1, p1, ssp, p2tog] to last 3 sts, p3.

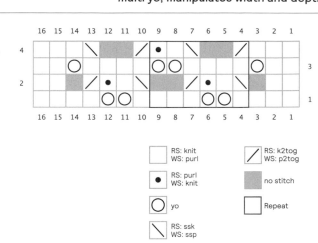

RS: knit / WS: purl

RS: purl / WS: knit

yo

RS: ssk / WS: ssp

RS: k2tog / WS: p2tog

no stitch

Repeat

SLIP

SL 1

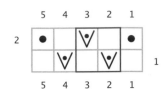

wyif, compensated, manipulates width and depth

Multiple of 2 + 3

ROW 1 (RS): K1, [sl1wyif, k1] to last 2 sts, sl1wyif, k1.

ROW 2 (WS): K1, p1, [sl1wyib, p1] to last st, k1.

Legend:
- RS: knit / WS: purl
- ● RS: purl / WS: knit
- V RS: sl1wyif / WS: sl1wyib
- Repeat

SL 2

wyif, compensated, manipulates width and depth

Multiple of 4 + 2

ROW 1 (RS): [K2, sl2wyif] to last 2 sts, k2.

ROW 2 (WS): P1, [sl2wyib, p2] to last st, p1.

ROW 3: [Sl2wyif, k2] to last 2 sts, sl2wyif.

ROW 4: P2, [p1, sl2wyib, p1] to end.

ROWS 5–12: Rep Rows 1–4 twice.

ROW 13: Rep row 3.

ROW 14: Rep row 2.

ROW 15: Rep row 1.

ROW 16: Rep row 4.

ROWS 17–24: Rep rows 13–16 twice.

Legend:
- RS: knit / WS: purl
- V RS: sl1wyif / WS: sl1wyib
- Repeat

SL 3

wyib, spot, manipulates width and depth

Multiple of 4 + 3

ROW 1 (RS): K1, [k2, sl1wyib, k1] to last 2 sts, k2.
ROW 2 (WS): K2, [k1, sl1wyif, k2] to last st, k1.
ROW 3: K1, [sl1wyib, k3] to last 2 sts, sl1wyib, k1.
ROW 4: K1, sl1wyif, [k3, sl1wyif] to last st, k1.

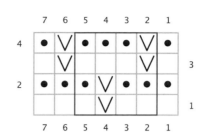
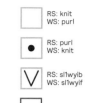

SL 4

wyib, spot, manipulates width and depth

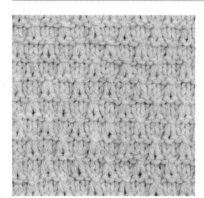

Multiple of 4 + 3

ROW 1 (RS): [K1, sl1wyib, k2] to last 3 sts, k1, sl1wyib, k1.
ROW 2 (WS): P1, sl1wyif, p1, [p2, sl1wyif, p1] to end.
ROW 3: Rep row 1.
ROW 4: Knit.
ROW 5: [K3, sl1wyib] to last 3 sts, k3.
ROW 6: P3, [sl1wyif, p3] to end.
ROW 7: Rep row 5.
ROW 8: Knit.

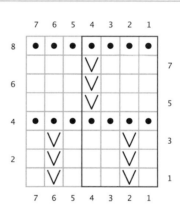

SL 5

wyib, spot, manipulates width and depth

Multiple of 4 + 5

ROW 1 (RS): K1, sl1wyib, k2, [k1, sl1wyib, k2] to last st, k1.
ROW 2 (WS): P1, [p2, sl1wyif, p1] to last 4 sts, p2, sl1wyif, p1.
ROW 3: K1, 1/2 LC, [k1, 1/2 LC] to last st, k1.
ROW 4: Purl.
ROW 5: K2, [k3, sl1wyib] to last 3 sts, k3.
ROW 6: P3, [sl1wyif, p3] to last 2 sts, p2.
ROW 7: K2, [k1, 1/2 RC] to last 3 sts, k3.
ROW 8: Purl.

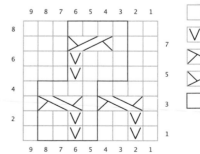
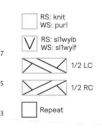

SL 6

wyib, spot, manipulates width and depth

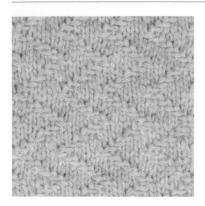

Multiple of 6 + 4

ROW 1 (RS): K1, [sl2wyif, k4] to last 3 sts, sl2wyif, k1.
ROW 2 (WS): P1, sl1wyib, p1, [p3, sl2wyib, p1] to last st, p1.
ROW 3: K1, [k2, sl2wyif, k2] to last 3 sts, k3.
ROW 4: P3, [p1, sl2wyib, p3] to last st, p1.
ROW 5: K1, [k4, sl2wyif] to last 3 sts, k3.
ROW 6: P2, sl1wyib, [sl1wyib, p4, sl1wyib] to last st, p1.
ROW 7: Rep row 1.
ROW 8: Rep row 6.
ROW 9: Rep row 5.
ROW 10: Rep row 4.
ROW 11: Rep row 3.
ROW 12: Rep row 2.

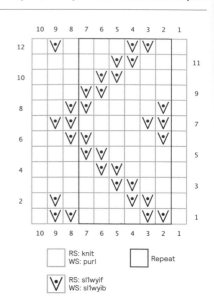

□ RS: knit / WS: purl
□ Repeat
Ⅴ RS: sl1wyif / WS: sl1wyib

TUCK

TU 1

k1below, vertical focus, compensated, manipulates width and depth

Multiple of 2 + 1
SET-UP ROW (WS): P1, [k1, p1] to end.
ROW 1 (RS): [K1 into the stitch below, p1] to last st, k1 into the stitch below.
ROW 2: P1, [k1 into the stitch below, p1].

	RS: knit / WS: purl
•	RS: purl / WS: knit
	WS: k1 in the stitch below
∩	RS: k1 in the stitch below
	Main Repeat
	Set-up row repeat

TU 2

sl1-yo, vertical focus, compensated, manipulates width and depth

Multiple of 2 + 2
SET-UP ROW (RS): Sl1, [sl1yo, k1] to last st, p1.
ROW 1 (WS): Sl1, [sl1yo, brk], p1.
ROW 2: Rep row 1.

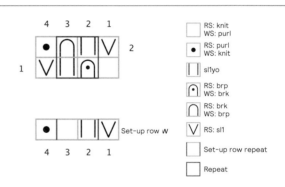

	RS: knit / WS: purl
•	RS: purl / WS: knit
‖	sl1yo
∩•	RS: brp / WS: brk
∩	RS: brk / WS: brp
V	RS: sl1
	Set-up row repeat
	Repeat

TU 3

k1below, diagonal focus, compensated, manipulates width and depth

Multiple of 2 + 3
ROW 1 (RS): K1, k1 into the stitch below, [k1, k1 into the stitch below] to last st, k1.
ROW 2 (WS): K1, [p1, k1] to last 2 sts, p1, k1.
ROW 3: K2, [k1 into the stitch below, k1] to last st, k1.
ROW 4: K1, [k1, p1] to last 2 sts, k2.

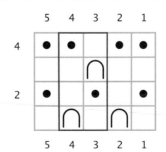

	RS: knit / WS: purl
•	RS: purl / WS: knit
∩	K1 in the stitch below
	Repeat

TU 4

sl1-yo, diagonal focus, compensated, manipulates width and depth

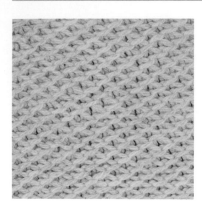

Multiple of 2 + 3

SET-UP ROW (WS): P2, [sl1wyif, yo, p1] to last st, p1.

ROW 1 (RS): Sl1wyib, [p1, sl1wyif knitwise, p1] to last 2 sts, p2.

ROW 2 (WS): P1, sl1wyif, [yo, p2tog, sl1wyif] to last st, yo, p1.

ROW 3: P1, sl1wyif knitwise, [p2, sl1wyif knitwise] to last 2 sts, p2.

ROW 4: Sl1wyif, p2tog, [sl1wyif, yo, p2tog] to last st, sl1wyif.

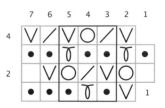

		RS: knit / WS: purl
•		RS: purl / WS: knit
/		RS: k2tog / WS: p2tog
O		yo
V		RS: sl1wyib / WS: sl1wyif
ꙩ		sl1wyif kwise
		Main repeat
		Set-up row repeat

TU 5

sl1-yo, diagonal focus, compensated, manipulates width and depth

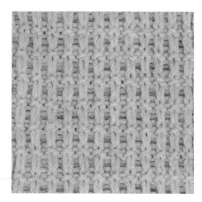

Multiple of 2 + 1

ROW 1 (RS): Purl.

ROW 2 (WS): K1, [p1, k1] to end.

ROW 3: [P1, sl1yo] to last st, p1.

ROW 4: K1, [sl1wyif, dropping yo loop to WS of work, k1] to end.

ROW 5: [P1, sl1wyib] to last st, p1.

ROW 6: K1, [sl1wyif, k1] to end.

		RS: knit / WS: purl
•		RS: purl / WS: knit
V		RS: sl1wyib / WS: sl1wyif
‖		sl1yo (on following row drop the yarnover off the needle to WS of work)
		Repeat

TU 6

drop stitch, vertical focus, compensated, manipulates width and depth

Multiple of 3 + 2

SET-UP ROW (WS): K2, [p1, k2] to end.

ROWS 1 AND 3 (RS): [P2, k1] to last 2 sts, p2.

ROWS 2 AND 4 (WS): K2, [p1, k2] to end.

ROW 5: [P2, drop st off needle and unravel 4 rows, insert right needle kwise into the loose st, then lift loose st and 4 strands above it onto left needle and k them tog] to last 2 sts, p2.

ROW 6: Rep row 2.

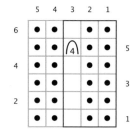
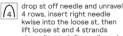

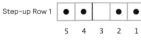

		RS: knit / WS: purl
•		RS: purl / WS: knit
⌂(4)		drop st off needle and unravel 4 rows, insert right needle kwise into the loose st, then lift loose st and 4 strands above it onto left needle and k them tog
		Main repeat
		Step-up row repeat

T U 7

sl1-yo, vertical focus, uncompensated, manipulates depth

Multiple of 6 + 5

ROW 1 (RS): Knit.
ROW 2 (WS): K1, sl3wyif, [p3, sl3wyif] to last st, k1.
ROW 3: K1, [sl3wyib, k3] to last 4 sts, sl3wyib, k1.
ROW 4: Rep row 2.
ROWS 5 AND 7: Knit.
ROW 6: Purl.
ROW 8: K1, p1, insert needle from below under 3 long running threads from slipped sts below, k next st and these 3 strands tog, p1, [p4, insert needle from below under 3 long running threads from slipped sts below, k next st and these 3 strands tog, p1] to last st, k1.
ROW 9: Knit.
ROW 10: K1, p3, [sl3wyif, p3] to last st, k1.
ROW 11: K1, [k3, sl3wyib] to last 4 sts, k4.
ROW 12: Rep row 10.
ROWS 13 AND 15: Knit.
ROW 14: Purl.
ROW 16: K1, p3, [p1, insert needle from below under 3 long running threads from slipped sts below, k next st and these 3 strands tog, p4] to last st, k1.

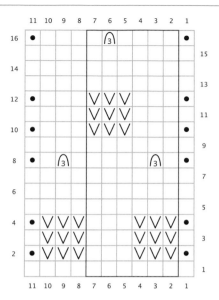

	RS: knit WS: purl
☐	
●	RS: purl WS: knit
V	RS: sl1wyib WS: sl1wyif

Insert needle from below under 3 long running threads from slipped sts below, k next st and these 3 strands tog

☐ Repeat

T U 8

sl1-yo, vertical focus, compensated, manipulates depth

Multiple of 4 + 3

SET-UP ROW (WS): Knit.
ROWS 1 AND 3 (RS): Purl.
ROWS 2 (WS and all following WS rows): Knit.
ROW 5: [P3, drop st off needle and unravel for 5 rows, insert right needle as if to purl into the loose st, then lift loose st and 5 strands above it onto left needle and p them tog] to last 3 sts, p3.
ROWS 7 AND 9: Purl.
ROW 11: [P1, drop st off needle and unravel for 5 rows, insert right needle as if to purl into the loose st, then lift loose st and 5 strands above it onto left needle and p them tog, p2] to last 3 sts, p1, drop st off needle and unravel for 5 rows, insert right needle as if to purl into the loose st, then lift loose st and 5 strands above it onto left needle and p them tog, p1.
ROW 12: Knit.

	7	6	5	4	3	2	1	
12	●	●	●	●	●	●	●	
	●	(5)	●	●	●	(5)	●	11
10	●	●	●	●	●	●	●	
	●	●	●	●	●	●	●	9
8	●	●	●	●	●	●	●	
	●	●	●	●	●	●	●	7
6	●	●	●	●	●	●	●	
	●	●	●	(5)	●	●	●	5
4	●	●	●	●	●	●	●	
	●	●	●	●	●	●	●	3
2	●	●	●	●	●	●	●	
	●	●	●	●	●	●	●	1

Set-Up Row 1: ● ● ● ● ● ● ●

● RS: knit WS: purl

(5) Drop st off needle and unravel for 5 rows, insert right needle as if to purl into the loose st, then lift loose st and 5 strands above it onto left needle and p them tog

☐ Main repeat

☐ Set-up row repeat

TWIST

TW 1

Multiple of 2 + 1
ROW 1 (RS): [LT] to last st, k1.
ROW 2 (WS): [RPT] to last st, p1.

	RS: knit WS: purl
	RS: RT WS: RPT
	RS: LT
	Repeat

TW 2

Multiple of 8 + 10
ROW 1 (RS): RT, LT, [(LT) twice, RT, LT] to last 6 sts, (LT) twice, RT.
ROW 2 (WS and all following WS rows): Purl.
ROW 3: K1, [LT] twice, (LT) twice, [LT, RT, (LT) twice] to last 5 sts, LT, RT, k1.
ROW 5: RT, LT, [LT, (RT) twice, LT] to last 6 sts, LT, (RT) twice.
ROW 7: K1, RT, LT, [(RT) 3 times, LT] to last 5 sts, (RT) twice, k1.
ROW 9: (RT) twice, [LT, (RT) 3 times] to last 6 sts, LT, (RT) twice.
ROW 11: K1, (RT) twice, [LT, (RT) 3 times] to last 5 sts, LT, RT, k1.
ROW 13: (RT) twice, [(LT) twice, (RT) twice] to last 6 sts, (LT) twice, RT twice, RT.
ROW 15: K1, RT, LT, [(LT) twice, RT, LT] to last 5 sts, (LT) twice, k1.
ROW 16: Purl.

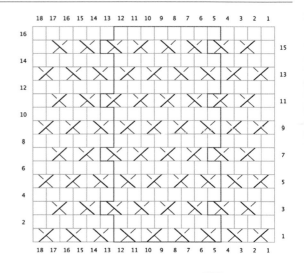

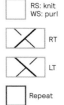

	RS: knit WS: purl
	RT
	LT
	Repeat

T W 3

allover, diagonal focus, manipulates width and depth

Multiple 3 + 6
ROW 1 (RS): K1, p2, [LT, p1] to last 3 sts, LT, k1.
ROW 2 (WS): [K1, sl1wyif, k1] to end.
ROW 3: K1, LT, [p1, LT] to last 3 sts, p1, k2.
ROW 4: K3, sl1wyif, k1, [k1, sl1wyif, k1] to last st, k1.
ROW 5: K1, [p1, LT] to last 2 sts, p1, k1.
ROW 6: P2, [sl1wyif, p2] to last st, p1.

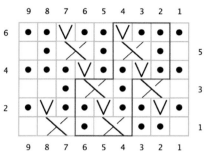

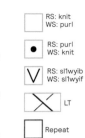

T W 4

allover, negative space, manipulates width

Multiple of 6 + 4
ROW 1 (RS): LT, [(RT) twice, LT] to last 2 sts, RT.
ROW 2 (WS AND all following WS rows): Purl.
ROW 3: K1, LT, [RT, (LT) twice] to last st, k1.
ROW 5: LT, [LT, k2, LT] to last 2 sts, LT.
ROW 7: K1, LT, [LT, RT, LT] to last st, k1.
ROW 9: RT, [LT, (RT) twice] to last 2 sts, LT.
ROW 11: K3, [(LT) twice, k2] to last 2 sts, k2.
ROW 12: Purl.

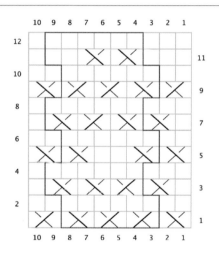

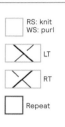

TW 5

Multiple of 8 + 4

ROW 1 (RS): [LT, k1, p5] to last 4 sts, LT, k1, p1.
ROW 2 (WS): K1, p3, [k5, p3] to end.
ROW 3: [K1, LT, p5] to last 4 sts, k1, LT, p1.
ROW 4: Rep row 2.
ROW 5: P1, [k2, p4, RT] to last 3 sts, k2, p1.
ROW 6: K1, p2, [k1, p1, k4, p2] to last st, k1.
ROW 7: P1, [k2, p3, RT, p1] to last 3 sts, k2, p1.
ROW 8: K1, p2, [k2, p1, k3, p2] to last st, k1.a
ROW 9: P1, [k2, p2, RT, p2] to last 3 sts, k2, p1.
ROW 10: K1, p2, [k3, p1, k2, p2] to last st, k1.
ROW 11: P1, [k2, p1, RT, p3] to last 3 sts, k2, p1.
ROW 12: K1, p2, [k4, p1, k1, p2] to last st, k1.
ROW 13: P1, [k2, RT, p4] to last 3 sts, k2, p1.
ROW 14: P3, [k5, p3] to last st, k1.
ROW 15: P1, [k1, RT, p5] to last 3 sts, k1, RT.
ROW 16: Rep row 14.
ROW 17: P1, [RT, k1, p5] to last 3 sts, RT, k1.
ROW 18: K1, p2, [k5, p3] to last st, k1.
ROW 19: P1, [k2, LT, p4] to last 3 sts, k2, p1.
ROW 20: Rep row 12.
ROW 21: P1, [k2, p1, LT, p3] to last 3 sts, k2, p1.
ROW 22: Rep row 10.
ROW 23: P1, [k2, p2, LT, p2] to last 3 sts, k2, p1.
ROW 24: Rep row 8.
ROW 25: P1, [k2, p3, LT, p1] to last 3 sts, k2, p1.
ROW 26: Rep row 6.
ROW 27: P1, [k2, p4, LT] to last 3 sts, k2, p1.
ROW 28: Rep row 2.

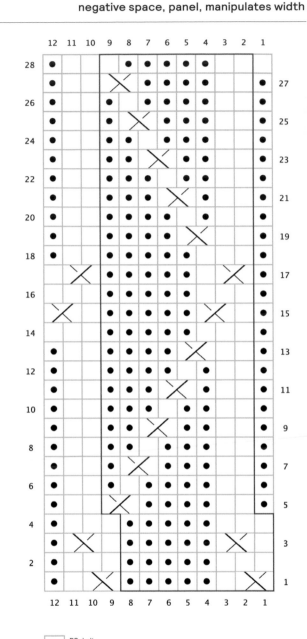

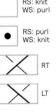

	RS: knit WS: purl
	RS: purl WS: knit (●)
	RT
	LT
	Repeat

JEMISON

—

COWL

Mae Jemison, *first African-American woman in space*

Jemison

I used the contrasting row gauges of brioche and reverse stockinette to create structure and a little bit of volume in this folded loop cowl. With stitch patterns that break up the direction of the single row stripes, it creates a cosy and tailored accessory with graphic interest.

One size:

76.5 cm / 30¼" circumference in brioche pattern, 86 cm / 33¾" circumference in reverse stocking stitch, 20.5 cm / 8" deep

Yarn A: Spincycle Yarns

Dyed in the Wool (sport weight; 100% American wool; 183 m / 200 yds per 56 g skein)
Shade: Deep Bump; 2 skeins

Yarn B: Sincere Sheep

Cormo Sport (sport weight; 100% American Cormo wool; 366 m / 400 yds per 113 g skein)
Shade: Quercus; 1 skein

Gauge:

22 sts & 38 rounds = 10 cm / 4" over brioche pattern on 3.25 mm needles after blocking. 26 sts & 34 rounds = 10 cm / 4" over reverse stocking stitch on 3.25 mm needles after blocking.

Needles:

3.25 mm / US 3 circular needle, 40 cm / 16" length

Always use a needle size that will result in the correct gauge after blocking.

Notions:

2 stitch markers, smooth scrap yarn in a similar weight as working yarn and a 3.25 mm / US D/3 crochet hook (or similar) for provisional cast on, spare needle in same or smaller size, tapestry needle

Notes:

Jemison is worked in the round starting from a provisional cast on which is removed once the cowl is complete and the two ends are grafted together.

Stitch Glossary:

SPECIAL ABBREVIATIONS

sl1yo: Bring yarn to front between needles, slip next st purlwise, bring yarn over needle and slipped stitch. If working a knit afterwards, leave yarn in back ready to work knit stitch; if working a purl afterwards, bring yarn to front between needles ready to work a purl.
brk: Knit slipped st and yo together.
brp: Purl slipped st and yo together.
br-k3tog: Knit next 3 columns together: one brk column, one purl column, and one brk column (5 loops total) (2 columns dec; leans right).
br-sssk: Slip next 3 columns (5 loops total) knitwise individually to right needle, bringing slip stitch and yo together as a single st, then return sts to left needle in new orientation and knit together through the back loop (2 columns dec; leans left).
brkyobrk: Knit 1, keeping brk on left needle, yo around right needle, knit into brk once more and drop from left needle (2 sts inc). On next round, (sl1yo, p1, sl1yo) into three loops of increase.

SPECIAL TECHNIQUES

Modified Kitchener Stitch for rev St-st:
With needles held parallel, live sts on front needle, provisional cast-on sts on back needle, and RS facing out:
Set-Up 1: Insert tapestry needle kwise through first st on front needle.

Set-Up 2: Insert tapestry needle pwise through first st on back needle.

Step 1: Insert tapestry needle pwise through first st on front needle, drop st off LH needle, insert tapestry needle kwise through new first st on LH needle.

Step 2: Insert tapestry needle kwise through first st on back needle, drop st off LH needle, insert tapestry needle pwise through new first st on LH needle.

Rep steps 1 & 2 until 1 st in rev St-st remains on either needle.

TRANSITION TO MODIFIED KITCHENER STITCH FOR BRIOCHE:

Set-Up 1: Insert tapestry needle kwise through first st on front needle, drop st off LH needle, insert tapestry needle pwise through new first st on left needle.

Set-Up 2: Insert tapestry needle pwise through first st on back needle, drop st off LH needle, insert tapestry needle kwise through new first st on LH needle.

Step 1: Insert tapestry needle kwise through first st on front needle, drop st off LH needle, insert tapestry needle kwise through new first st on LH needle.

Step 2: Insert tapestry needle pwise through first st on back needle, drop st off LH needle, insert tapestry needle kwise through new first st on LH needle.

Step 3: Insert tapestry needle pwise through first st on front needle, drop st off LH needle, insert tapestry needle pwise through new first st on LH needle.

Step 4: Rep step 2.

Rep Steps 1-4 until 4 sts rem on front needle and 3 sts rem on back needle, then rep Steps 1-3 once more. 1 st rem on either needle.

Next step: Insert tapestry needle pwise through first st on back needle, drop st off LH needle.

Next step: Insert tapestry needle kwise through first st on front needle, drop st off LH needle.

CHART - WRITTEN INSTRUCTIONS

BRIOCHE PATTERN

(worked over 24 rounds + 2 set-up rounds)

SET-UP (YARN A): [K1, sl1yo] 12 times, k1.

SET-UP (YARN B): [Sl1yo, brp] 12 times, sl1yo.

ROUND 1 (YARN A): Brkyobrk, [sl1yo, brk] twice, sl1yo, br-sssk, sl1yo, br-k3tog, [sl1yo, brk] twice, sl1yo, brkyobrk, [sl1yo, brk] 3 times.

ROUND 2 (YARN B): Sl1yo, p1, [sl1yo, brp] 7 times, sl1yo, p1, [sl1yo, brp] 3 times, sl1yo.

ROUND 3 (YARN A): [Brk, sl1yo] 12 times, brk.

ROUND 4 (YARN B): [Sl1yo, brp] 12 times, sl1yo.

ROUND 5 (YARN A): Brk, sl1yo, brkyobrk, [sl1yo, brk] twice, sl1yo, br-sssk, [sl1yo, brk] 7 times.

ROUND 6 (YARN B): Sl1yo, brp, sl1yo, p1, [sl1yo, brp] 10 times, sl1yo.

ROUND 7 (YARN A): [Brk, sl1yo] 12 times, brk.

ROUND 8 (YARN B): [Sl1yo, brp] 12 times, sl1yo.

ROUND 9 (YARN A): [Brk, sl1yo] twice, brkyobrk, [sl1yo, brk] twice, sl1yo, br-sssk, [sl1yo, brk] 6 times.

ROUND 10 (YARN B): [Sl1yo, brp] twice, sl1yo, p1, [sl1yo, brp] 9 times, sl1yo.

ROUND 11 (YARN A): [Brk, sl1yo] 12 times, brk.

ROUND 12 (YARN B): [Sl1yo, brp] 12 times, sl1yo.

ROUND 13 (YARN A): [Brk, sl1yo] 3 times, brkyobrk, [sl1yo, brk] twice, sl1yo, br-sssk, sl1yo, br-k3tog, [sl1yo, brk] twice, sl1yo, brkyobrk.

ROUND 14 (YARN B): [Sl1yo, brp] 3 times, sl1yo, p1, [sl1yo, brp] 7 times, sl1yo, p1, sl1yo.

ROUND 15 (YARN A): [Brk, sl1yo] 12 times, brk.

ROUND 16 (YARN B): [Sl1yo, brp] 12 times, sl1yo.

ROUND 17 (YARN A): [Brk, sl1yo] 7 times, br-k3tog, [sl1yo, brk] twice, sl1yo, brkyobrk, sl1yo, brk.

ROUND 18 (YARN B): [Sl1yo, brp] 10 times, sl1yo, p1, sl1yo, brp, sl1yo.

ROUND 19 (YARN A): [Brk, sl1yo] 12 times, brk.

ROUND 20 (YARN B): [Sl1yo, brp] 12 times, sl1yo.

ROUND 21 (YARN A): [Brk, sl1yo] 6 times, br-k3tog, [sl1yo, brk] twice, sl1yo, brkyobrk, [sl1yo, brk] twice.

ROUND 22 (YARN B): [Sl1yo, brp] 9 times, sl1yo, p1, sl1yo, [brp, sl1yo] twice.

ROUND 23 (YARN A): [Brk, sl1yo] 12 times, brk.

ROUND 24 (YARN B): [Sl1yo, brp] 12 times, sl1yo.

Rep rounds 1-24 rounds for pattern.

PATTERN BEGINS

Using scrap yarn and crochet hook, provisionally cast 100 sts onto working needle.

Join yarn B and knit 1 row. Join for working in the round being careful not to twist. PM to indicate beg of round.

SET-UP ROUND 1: Using yarn A, p75, PM, reading from the Chart or Written Instructions, work Set-up (yarn A) of Brioche Pattern across next 25 sts.

SET-UP ROUND 2: Using yarn B, p to marker, SM, work Set-up (yarn B) of Brioche Pattern across next 25 sts.

Continue in patt to end of round 24 of Brioche Pattern, then rep rounds 1-24 a further 10 times, then rep rounds 1-21 **only** once more. *285 chart rounds + 2 set-up rounds worked*

Break yarns leaving an 81.5 cm / 32" yarn B tail.

FINISHING

Place all sts on scrap yarn and block cowl to measurements. Tie off or weave in any ends on the inside of the fabric.

Replace held stitches on working needle. Unzip provisional cast-on and place stitches on spare needle. Graft pieces ends together using Modified Kitchener stitch (see Stitch Glossary), taking care to start with stitches at working end of the fabric. Weave in remaining ends and steam graft.

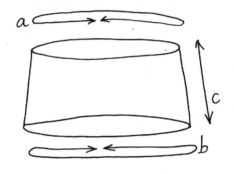

JEMISON SCHEMATIC KEY

a. Brioche circumference: 76.5 cm / 30¼"

b. Reverse stockinette circumference: 86 cm / 33¾"

c. Depth: 20.5 cm / 8"

BRIOCHE PATTERN

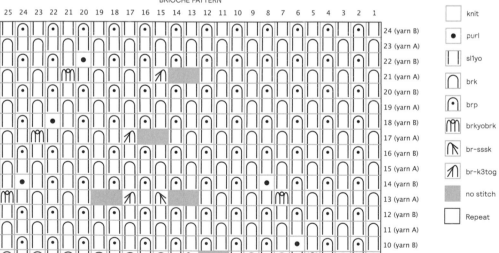

25 24 23 22 21 20 19 18 17 16 15 14 13 12 11 10 9 8 7 6 5 4 3 2 1

Row
24 (yarn B)
23 (yarn A)
22 (yarn B)
21 (yarn A)
20 (yarn B)
19 (yarn A)
18 (yarn B)
17 (yarn A)
16 (yarn B)
15 (yarn A)
14 (yarn B)
13 (yarn A)
12 (yarn B)
11 (yarn A)
10 (yarn B)
9 (yarn A)
8 (yarn B)
7 (yarn A)
6 (yarn B)
5 (yarn A)
4 (yarn B)
3 (yarn A)
2 (yarn B)
1 (yarn A)
Set-up (yarn B)
Set-up (yarn A)

25 24 23 22 21 20 19 18 17 16 15 14 13 12 11 10 9 8 7 6 5 4 3 2 1

Legend

- knit
- • purl
- sl1yo
- brk
- brp
- brkyobrk
- br-sssk
- br-k3tog
- no stitch
- Repeat

YAYOI
— PULLOVER

Yayoi Kusama, *Japanese artist and writer*

Yayoi

Dropping stitches opens up the width of knitted fabric and offers the opportunity for unique shaping on the circular yoke of the Yayoi Pullover. Here, I've worked the dropped stitches in a descending pattern to create sculptural arcs and wedges in the yoke and complement the simple, clean lines of the tailored body and sleeves below.

Sizes:

1 (2, 3, 4, 5, 6, 7, 8)

Finished bust measurement:

82 (88.5, 100, 111, 119, 131, 141.5, 149.5) cm / 32¼ (35, 39¼, 43¾, 47, 51¾, 55 3/4, 59)" – to be worn with 0-7.5 cm / 0-3" positive ease

Model has 92 cm / 36" bust, stands 183 cm / 6'0" tall, and is wearing size 2.

Yarn: The Uncommon Thread

Posh DK (DK weight; 70% superwash Blue-Faced Leicester, 20% silk, 10% cashmere; 230 m / 250 yds per 115 g skein)
Shade: Bois; 5 (5, 6, 6, 7, 7, 8, 8) skeins

Gauge:

22 sts & 32 rounds = 10 cm / 4" over stocking stitch on 4 mm needles after blocking.

15.5 sts & 26 rounds = 10 cm / 4" over drop stitch pattern on 4 mm needles after blocking.

Needles:

4 mm / US 6 circular needles, 40 cm / 16" length AND 80 cm / 32" length AND needles suitable for working small circumferences in the round

3.5 mm / US 4 circular needle, 40 cm / 16" length AND 80 cm / 32" length AND needles suitable for working small circumferences in the round

Always use a needle size that will result in the correct gauge after blocking.

Notions:

8 stitch markers, scrap yarn or stitch holder, spare needle in same or smaller size than smallest needle, tapestry needle, t-pins and blocking wires

Notes:

Yayoi is knit in the round from the top down. Yoke is shaped with a combination of increases and dropped stitches. After the body and sleeves are separated, short rows are worked to lift the back yoke for ease of wearing. Waist shaping is worked on the body, and hem, cuffs, and neckband are all finished with tubular cast offs.

PATTERN BEGINS

YOKE

Using larger needle and the long-tail method, cast on 96 (104, 104, 112, 112, 112, 120, 120) sts. Join for working in the round, being careful not to twist. PM to indicate beg of round.
SET-UP ROUND: [K12 (13, 13, 14, 14, 14, 15, 15), PM] 7 times, k to end.

NEXT ROUND (INC): [K to 2 sts before marker, M1L, k2, SM] 8 times. 8 sts inc
Working in St st, rep Inc round every 4 (4, 4, 4, 2, 2, 2, 2) rounds a further 3 (2, 4, 5, 1, 6, 9, 12) times, then every 0 (0, 0, 0, 4, 4, 4, 0) rounds 0 (0, 0, 0, 6, 3, 1, 0) times. 128 (128, 144, 160, 176, 192, 208, 224) sts

Work 3 (5, 3, 3, 3, 3, 3, 1) rounds straight.

NEXT ROUND (INC): [K to 2 sts before marker, PM, M1L, k to marker, remove marker] 7 times, k to 2 sts before beg of round, PM, M1L, k to end. 8 sts inc

Work 3 (5, 3, 3, 3, 3, 3, 3) rounds straight.

NEXT ROUND (INC): [K to 2 sts before marker, PM, M1L, k to marker, remove marker] 8 times, k to end. 8 sts inc
Rep last Inc round every 4 (6, 4, 4, 4, 4, 4, 4) rounds a further 2 (6, 3, 6, 9, 10, 11, 12) times, then every 6 (0, 6, 6, 0, 0, 0, 0) rounds

4 (0, 4, 2, 0, 0, 0, 0) times. 192 (192, 216, 240, 264, 288, 312, 336) sts
First marker should now be right next to beg of round marker.

NEXT ROUND: Removing all but beg of round marker as you go, * [k2, drop next st, using backward loop method, cast on 3 sts, k2, drop next st, backward loop cast on 2 sts] 3 times, [k2, drop next st, backward loop cast on 3 sts] twice; rep from * a further 6 (6, 7, 8, 9, 10, 11, 12) times, [k2, drop next st, backward loop cast on 3 sts, k2, drop next st, backward loop cast on 2 sts] 3 (3, 4, 3, 4, 3, 4, 3) times, [k2, drop st, backward loop cast on 3 sts] 2 (2, 0, 2, 0, 2, 0, 2) times. 64 (64, 72, 80, 88, 96, 104, 112) sts dropped; 168 (168, 188, 210, 230, 252, 272, 294) sts inc; 296 (296, 332, 370, 406, 444, 480, 518) sts

NEXT ROUND: Knit, unravelling dropped sts back to their base increases.

DIVIDE FOR BODY AND SLEEVES:

Slip next 61 (58, 64, 71, 80, 86, 93, 103) sts to stitch holder or scrap yarn, using backward loop method, cast on 2 (6, 6, 6, 6, 6, 6, 6) sts, k87 (90, 102, 114, 123, 136, 147, 156), slip next 61 (58, 64, 71, 80, 86, 93, 103) sts to stitch holder or scrap yarn, backward loop cast on 1 (3, 3, 3, 3, 3, 3, 3) sts, PM for side, cast on 1 (3, 3, 3, 3, 3, 3, 3) more sts, k to end, remove beg of round marker, k1 (3, 3, 3, 3, 3, 3, 3), PM for new beg of round. 178 (192, 216, 240, 258, 284, 306, 324) sts

Beg of round sits at wearer's left side.

SET-UP ROUND: K to marker, SM (marker 1), k34 (36, 40, 45, 49, 53, 58, 61), PM (marker 2), k21 (24, 28, 30, 31, 36, 37, 40), PM (marker 3), k to end.

Work short rows as foll:
SHORT ROW 1 (RS): K to 3 sts past marker 3, turn and PLM for JSR.
SHORT ROW 2 (WS): P to 3 sts past marker 2, turn and PLM for JSR.

SHORT ROW 3: K to previous turn, resolve JSR with next st, k17 (18, 20, 22, 24, 26, 29, 30), turn and PLM for JSR.

SHORT ROW 4: P to previous turn, resolve JSR with next st through the back loop, p17 (18, 20, 22, 24, 26, 29, 30), turn and PLM for JSR.

Rep short rows 3-4 once more.

NEXT SHORT ROW (RS): K to end, resolving JSR with next st.

NEXT ROUND: K to end, resolving final JSR with next st through the back loop.

Work straight in St as set until work measures 2.5 cm / 1" from yoke split, measured at centre front.

NEXT ROUND (DEC): K1, ssk, [k to 3 sts before marker, k2tog, k1, SM] twice, k to marker, SM, k1, ssk, k to end. *4 sts dec*

Rep Dec round every 6th round a further 3 times. *162 (176, 200, 224, 242, 268, 290, 308) sts*

Work straight in St st for 2.5 cm / 1".

NEXT ROUND (INC): K1, M1L, [k to 1 st before marker, M1R, k1, SM] twice, k to marker, SM, k1, M1L, k to end. *4 sts inc*

Rep Inc round every 8th round a further 5 times. *186 (200, 224, 248, 266, 292, 314, 332) sts*

Work straight in St st until work measures 34.5 cm / 13½" from yoke split.

RIBBING
Change to smaller needle.
RIB ROUND: [K1, p1] to end.

Rep Rib round until rib measures 7.5 cm / 3".

Tubular Cast Off

NEXT ROUND: [K1, sl1wyif] to end.
NEXT ROUND: [Sl1wyib, p1] to end.
Hold spare needle parallel with and behind right needle. Slip alternating sts to each needle: knit sts to front working needle, purl sts to back spare needle. When all stitches are separated, continue to hold needles parallel and graft together using Kitchener stitch.

SLEEVES (BOTH ALIKE)

Place held Sleeve sts on larger needle. Beg at centre of underarm cast-on, pick up and k1 (3, 3, 3, 3, 3, 3, 3) sts, k across 61 (58, 64, 71, 80, 86, 93, 103) sts, pick up and k1 (3, 3, 3, 3, 3, 3, 3) sts in rem underarm cast on. Join for working in the round and PM to indicate beg of round. *63 (64, 70, 77, 86, 92, 99, 109) sts*

Work 2 rounds in St st.

NEXT ROUND (DEC): K1, ssk, k to last 3 sts, k2tog, k1. *2 sts dec*

Continue in St st and rep Dec round every 18 (16, 12, 10, 6, 6, 6, 4) rounds 3 (5, 3, 11, 5, 13, 17, 11) times, then every 20 (18, 14, 12, 8, 8, 8, 6) rounds 3 (2, 6, 1, 12, 6, 3, 14) time(s). *49 (48, 50, 51, 50, 52, 57, 57) sts*

Work straight in St st until Sleeve measures 43 cm / 17" from yoke split.

SIZES 1, 4, 7 & 8 ONLY:
Next round: K to last 3 sts, k2tog, k1. *48 (– , –, 50, –, –, 56, 56) sts*

ALL SIZES AGAIN:
RIBBING
Change to smaller needle.
RIB ROUND: [K1, p1] to end.

Rep Rib round until rib measures 5 cm / 2".

Work Tubular Cast Off as for Body.

FINISHING

NECKBAND
With RS facing, using smaller needle and beg at right back shoulder, pick up and k1 st for every cast-on st. Join for working in the round and PM to indicate beg of round. *96 (104, 104, 112, 112, 112, 120, 120) sts*

Work Ribbing and Tubular Cast Off as for Sleeve.

Weave in all ends and block to measurements.

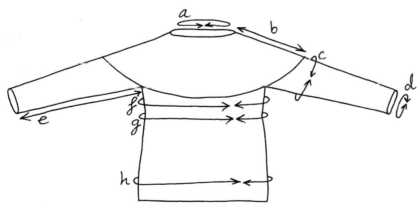

YAIYOI SCHEMATIC KEY

a. Neck circumference:
44.5 (48, 48, 51.5, 51.5, 51.5, 55.5, 55.5) cm /
17½ (19, 19, 20¼, 20¼, 20¼, 21¾, 21¾)"
b. Yoke depth: 21.5 (23.5, 25, 26.5, 29, 29.5, 30.5, 32) cm /
8½ (9¼, 9¾, 10½, 11½, 11¾, 12, 12½)"
c. Upper arm circumference:
29 (29.5, 32.5, 35.5, 39.5, 42.5, 45.5, 50.5) cm /
11½ (11¾, 12¾, 14, 15¾, 16¾, 18, 19¾)"
d. Cuff circumference:
22 (22, 23, 23, 23, 24, 26, 26) cm /
8¾ (8¾, 9, 9, 9, 9½, 10¼, 10¼)"
e. Sleeve length: 48.5 cm / 19"
f. Bust circumference:
82 (88.5, 100, 111, 119, 131, 141.5, 149.5) cm /
32¼ (35, 39¼, 43¾, 47, 51¾, 55¾, 59)"
g. Waist circumference:
75 (81.5, 92.5, 103.5, 112, 124, 134, 142) cm /
29½ (32, 36¼, 40¾, 44, 48¾, 52¾, 56)"
h. Hip circumference:
86 (92.5, 103.5, 114.5, 123, 135, 145, 153.5) cm /
33¾ (36¼, 40¾, 45, 48¼, 53, 57, 60¼)"

O'KEEFFE

—

PULLOVER

Georgia O'Keeffe, *American artist*

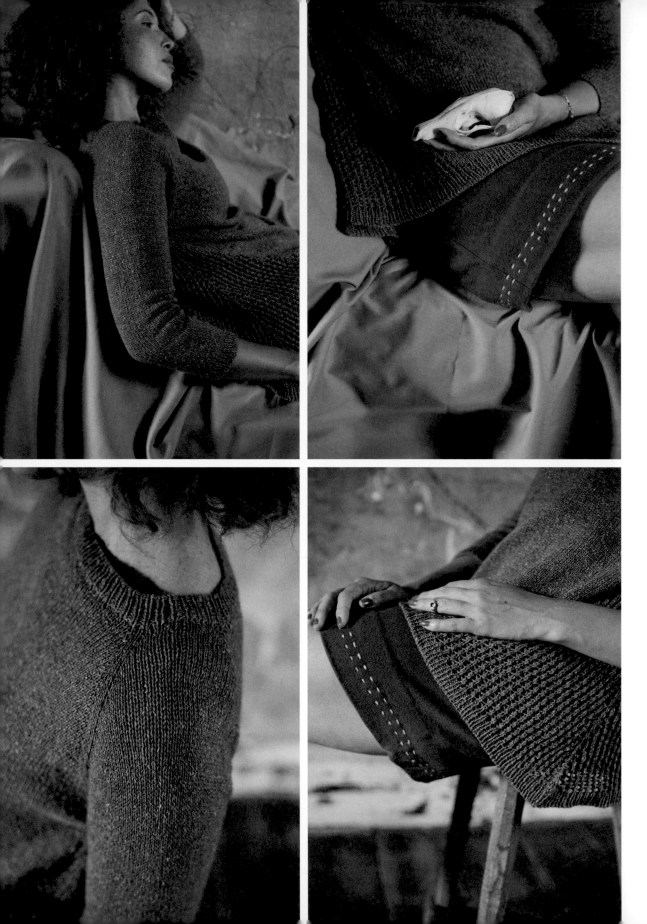

O'Keeffe

The stitch gauge differences between lace mesh and stockinette inspired me to design the O'Keeffe Pullover. With lace that gradually shifts across the body of the fabric and gentle increases at the sides, the change in gauge creates a graceful and feminine trapeze shape that contrasts beautifully with the fitted raglan above.

Sizes:

1 (2, 3, 4, 5, 6, 7, 8)

Finished bust circumference:

89 (99.5, 111, 122, 133, 144, 155, 166.5) cm / 35 (39¼, 43¾, 48, 52¼, 56¾, 61, 65½)" – to be worn with 7.5–15 cm / 3–6" positive ease

Model has 92 cm / 36" bust, stands 183 cm / 6'0" tall, and is wearing size 2

Yarn: Blacker Yarns

Samite (light 4 ply / heavy lace; 40% Shetland wool, 30% Blue-Faced Leicester wool, 10% Gotland wool, 20% Ahimsa silk; 460 m / 503 yds per 100 g skein)
Shade: Iron Hills; 3 (3, 4, 4, 4, 5, 5, 5) skeins

Gauge:

22 sts & 36 rounds = 10 cm / 4" over st st on 3.75 mm needles after blocking.

20 sts & 36 rounds = 10 cm / 4" over lace on 3.75 mm needles after blocking.

Needles:

3.75 mm / US 5 circular needle, 80 cm / 32" length **AND** needles suitable for working small circumferences in the round

3.5 mm / US 4 circular needle, 80 cm / 32" length **AND** 40 cm / 16" length **AND** needles suitable for working small circumferences in the round

Always use a needle size that will result in the correct gauge after blocking.

Notions:

6 stitch markers, stitch holders or scrap yarn, spare needle in same or smaller size than smallest needle, tapestry needle, T-pins and blocking wires

Notes:

O'Keeffe is worked in the round from the top down with raglan shaping. Short rows at the beginning of the raglan shaping add height to the back neck. After the yoke is complete, the body and sleeves are separated and worked down. Lace panels are gradually introduced in the body, which is then finished with ribbing. The sleeves are worked in stocking stitch and finished with ribbing.

CHART A

ROUND 1: K1, yo, s2kpo, [yo] twice, k1, [yo] twice, s2kpo, yo, k1. *2 sts inc*
ROUND 2: K4, p1, k2, p1, k3.
ROUND 3: Ssk, yo, k1, yo, k2tog, k1, ssk, yo, k1, yo, k2tog.
ROUND 4: Knit.
ROUND 5: K1, yo, s2kpo, [yo, k1] 3 times, yo, s2kpo, yo, k1. *2 sts inc*
ROUND 6: Knit.
ROUND 7: Ssk, yo, [k1, yo, s2kpo, yo] twice, k1, yo, k2tog.
ROUND 8: Knit.
ROUND 9: K1, yo, s2kpo, yo, k2, yo, k1, yo, k2, yo, s2kpo, yo, k1. *2 sts inc*
ROUND 10: Knit.
ROUND 11: Ssk, yo, k1, yo, s2kpo, yo, k3, yo, s2kpo, yo, k1, yo, k2tog.
ROUND 12: Knit.
ROUND 13: K1, yo, s2kpo, yo, k1, yo, k2tog, yo, k1, yo, ssk, yo, k1, yo, s2kpo, yo, k1. *2 sts inc*
ROUND 14: Knit.
ROUND 15: Ssk, yo, k1, yo, s2kpo, yo, k5, yo, s2kpo, yo, k1, yo, k2tog.
ROUND 16: Knit.

CHART B

ROUND 1: K1, yo, s2kpo, yo, [k1, yo, s2kpo, yo], yo, k1, yo, [yo, s2kpo, yo, k1], yo, sk2p, yo, k1. *2 sts inc*
ROUND 2: K4, [k4], p1, k1, p1, [k4], k4.
ROUND 3: Ssk, yo, k1, yo, [s2kpo, yo, k1, yo], k2tog, k1, ssk, [yo, k1, yo, s2kpo], yo, k1, yo, k2tog.
ROUND 4: Knit.
ROUND 5: K1, yo, s2kpo, yo, [k1, yo, s2kpo, yo], (k1, yo) twice, k1, [yo, s2kpo, yo, k1], yo, s2kpo, yo, k1. *2 sts inc*
ROUND 6: Knit.
ROUND 7: Ssk, yo, k1, yo, [s2kpo, yo, k1, yo], s2kpo, yo, k1, yo, s2kpo, [yo, k1, yo, sk2p], yo, k1, yo, k2tog.
ROUND 8: Knit.
ROUND 9: K1, yo, s2kpo, yo, [k1, yo, s2kpo, yo], k2, yo, k1, yo, k2, [yo, s2kpo, yo, k1], yo, s2kpo, yo, k1. *2 sts inc*
ROUND 10: Knit.
ROUND 11: Ssk, yo, k1, yo, [s2kpo, yo, k1, yo], s2kpo, yo, k3, yo, s2kpo, [yo, k1, yo, s2kpo], yo, k1, yo, k2tog.
ROUND 12: Knit.
ROUND 13: K1, yo, s2kpo, yo, [k1, yo, s2kpo, yo], k1, yo, k2tog, yo, k1, yo, ssk, yo, k1, [yo, s2kpo, yo, k1], yo, s2kpo, yo, k1. *2 sts inc*
ROUND 14: Knit.
ROUND 15: Ssk, yo, k1, yo, [s2kpo, yo, k1, yo], s2kpo, yo, k5, yo, s2kpo, [yo, k1, yo, s2kpo], yo, k1, yo, k2tog.
ROUND 16: Knit.

PATTERN BEGINS

Using larger needle and the long-tail method, cast on 112 (116, 120, 124, 132, 136, 148, 148) sts. Join for working in the round, being careful not to twist. PM to indicate beg of round.

SET-UP ROUND: K36 (40, 44, 48, 52, 54, 60, 62), PM for right back raglan line, k16 (14, 12, 10, 10, 10, 10, 8), PM for right front raglan line, k44 (48, 52, 56, 60, 62, 68, 70), PM for left front raglan line, k16 (14, 12, 10, 10, 10, 10, 8) to end. Beg of round sits at left back raglan line.

Commence Short Row Shaping

ROW 1 (RS): K1, M1L, k to 1 st before right back raglan line marker, M1R, k1, turn and PLM for JSR. *2 sts inc*

ROW 2 (WS): P to left back raglan line/beg of round marker, turn and PLM for JSR.

ROW 3: K1, M1L, k to 1 st before right back raglan line marker, M1R, k1, SM, resolve JSR with next st, M1L, k7 (6, 5, 4, 4, 4, 4, 3), turn and PLM for JSR. *3 sts inc*

ROW 4: P to left back raglan line/beg of round marker, SM, resolve JSR with next st through the back loop, p7 (6, 5, 4, 4, 4, 4, 3), turn and PLM for JSR.

ROW 5: [K to 1 st before marker, M1R, k1, SM, k1, M1L] twice, k to 2 sts before right front raglan line marker, resolving JSR with next st as you go, turn and PLM for JSR. *4 sts inc*

ROW 6: P to left back raglan line/beg of round marker, SM, p to 2 sts before left front raglan line marker, resolving JSR with next st through the back loop as you go, turn and PLM for JSR.

ROW 7: [K to 1 st before marker, M1R, k1, SM, k1, M1L] 3 times, resolving JSR with next st as you go, (this places you just beyond right front raglan line marker), k7 (6, 5, 4, 4, 4, 3), turn and PLM for JSR. *6 sts inc*

ROW 8: P to left front raglan line marker, resolving JSR with next st through the back loop as you go, SM, p8 (7, 6, 5, 5, 5, 4), turn and PLM for JSR.

ROW 9: [K to 1 st before marker, M1R, k1, SM, k1, M1L] twice, resolving JSR with next st as you go, k to 1 st before right back raglan line marker, M1R, k1. *5 sts inc*

NEXT ROUND: K to end, resolving final JSR through the back loop as you go. *132 (136, 140, 144, 152, 156, 168, 168) sts on needle: 46 (50, 54, 58, 62, 64, 70, 72) sts each Front and Back; 20 (18, 16, 14, 14, 14, 14, 12) sts each Sleeve.*

Commence Raglan Shaping

NEXT ROUND (INC): [K1, M1L, k to 1 st before marker, M1R, k1, sm] 4 times. *8 sts inc*

Continue in St st and rep Inc round every other round a further 13 (19, 23, 29, 33, 38, 40, 39) times, then every round 0 (0, 0, 0, 0, 2, 2, 8) times, then every 4th round 8 (6, 5, 3, 2, 0, 0, 0) times. *308 (344, 372, 408, 440, 484, 512, 552) sts*

Divide for Body and Sleeves:

NEXT ROUND: (K90 (102, 112, 124, 134, 146, 156, 168) to marker, remove marker, slip next 64 (70, 74, 80, 86, 96, 100, 108) Sleeve sts to stitch holder or scrap yarn, using Cable method, cast on 3 (3, 4, 4, 5, 5, 6, 6) sts, PM for side, cable cast on 3 (3, 4, 4, 5, 5, 6, 6)] twice, k45 (51, 56, 62, 67, 73, 78, 84), PM for beg of round. Beg of round now sits at centre back. *192 (216, 240, 264, 288, 312, 336, 360) sts*

Work straight in St st as set until work measures 5 cm / 2" from divide.

NEXT ROUND: [K to 5 sts before side marker, PM (chart marker), reading from the Chart or Written Instructions, work round 1 of Chart A, removing side marker as you go] twice, k to end. *196 (220, 244, 268, 292, 316, 340, 364) sts*

NEXT ROUND: [K to chart marker, work round 2 of Chart A] twice, k to end.

Patt as set to end of round 16 of Chart A. *208 (232, 256, 280, 304, 328, 352, 376) sts*

NEXT ROUND: [K to 4 sts before existing chart marker, PM (new chart marker), work round 1 of Chart B working each 4-st repeat twice and removing previous chart marker as you go] twice, k to end. *212 (236, 260, 284, 308, 332, 356, 380) sts*

NEXT ROUND: [K to chart marker, SM, work round 2 of Chart B] twice, k to end.

Patt as set to end of round 16 of Chart B. *224 (248, 272, 296, 320, 344, 368, 392) sts*

Continue as set until you have worked all 16 rounds of Chart B 6 times total. Each time you start again at round 1, you will place the new chart marker 4 sts before the existing chart marker and add one more repeat of each marked 4-st repeat on the chart.

Count the stitches after completing round 1 of each repeat; there will be 43 sts in lace on either side on the first repeat, 59 sts on second, 75 on third, 91 on fourth, and 107 on fifth. When fifth repeat is complete, 113 sts in lace on either side; 39 (51, 63, 75, 87, 99, 111, 123) sts in St st each Front and Back.

RIBBING
Change to smaller needle.
RIB ROUND: [K1, p1] to end.
Rep Rib Round until rib measures 2.5 cm / 1".

TUBULAR CAST OFF
NEXT ROUND: [K1, sl1wyif] to end.
NEXT ROUND: [Sl1wyib, p1] to end.

Hold spare needle parallel with and behind right needle. Slip alternating sts to each needle: knit sts to front working needle, purl sts to back spare needle. When all stitches are separated, continue to hold needles parallel and graft together using Kitchener stitch.

SLEEVES (BOTH ALIKE)

Place held Sleeve sts on larger needle. Pick up and k3 (3, 4, 4, 5, 5, 6, 6) sts in left half of cabled cast-on, k across 64 (70, 74, 80, 86, 96, 100, 108) held sts, pick up and k3 (3, 4, 4, 5, 5, 6, 6) sts in rem cabled cast-on. Join for working in the round and PM to indicate beg of round. *70 (76, 82, 88, 96, 106, 112, 120) sts*

Work 1 round in St st.
NEXT ROUND (DEC): K1, k2tog, k to last 3 sts, ssk, k1. *2 sts dec*

Continue in St st and rep Dec round every 12 (10, 8, 6, 6, 4, 4, 2) rounds a further 1 (10, 5, 5, 17, 14, 17, 1) times, then every 14 (0, 10, 8, 0, 6, 6, 4) rounds 6 (0, 6, 9, 0, 8, 6, 26) times. *54 (54, 58, 58, 60, 60, 64, 64) sts*

Work straight in St st until Sleeve measures
33 cm / 13" from underarm pick-up.

Change to smaller needle.

Work Ribbing and Tubular Cast Off as for Body.

NECKBAND

Using smaller needle, pick up and k1 st for every
cast-on st in neckline. Join for working in the
round and PM to indicate beg of round. *112 (116,
120, 124, 132, 136, 148, 148) sts*

Work Ribbing and Tubular Cast Off as for Body.

FINISHING

Weave in loose ends and block to measurements.

O'KEEFFE SCHEMATIC KEY

a. Bust circumference: 88.75 (99.75, 110.75, 122, 133, 144, 155.25, 166.25) cm /
35 (39¼, 43¾, 48, 52¼, 56¾, 61, 65½)"
b. Hem circumference: 151 (162, 173, 184, 195, 206, 217.5, 228.5) cm /
59½ (63¾, 68, 72½, 76¾, 81¼, 85½, 90)"
c. Body length: 39 cm / 15½"
d. Yoke depth: 17, (18, 19, 20.5, 21.5, 23, 23.5, 25) cm / 6¾ (7, 7½, 8, 8½, 9, 9¼, 9¾)"
e. Upper arm circumference: 32.5 (35, 38, 40.5, 44.5, 49, 51.5, 55.5) cm /
12¾ (13¾, 15, 16, 17½, 19¼, 20¼, 21¾)"
f. Cuff circumference: 25 (25, 27, 27, 27.5, 27.5, 29.5, 29.5) cm /
9¾ (9¾, 10½, 10½, 11, 11, 11¾, 11¾)"
g. Sleeve length: 35.5 cm / 14"
h. Neck circumference: 51.5 (53.5, 55.5, 57.5, 61, 63, 68.5, 68.5) cm /
20¼ (21, 21¾, 22½, 24, 24¾, 27, 27)"

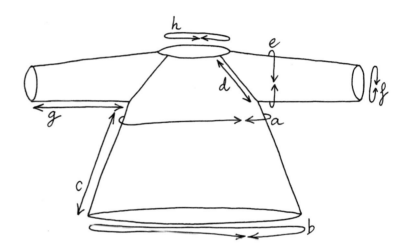

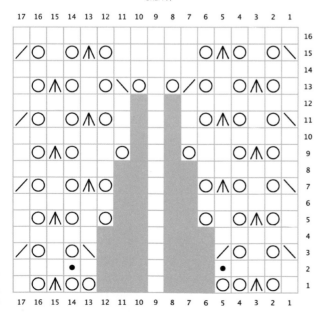

RS: knit
WS: purl

• RS: purl
WS: knit

○ yo

∕ k2tog

∖ ssk

⋀ s2kpo

no stitch

Repeat

Chart A

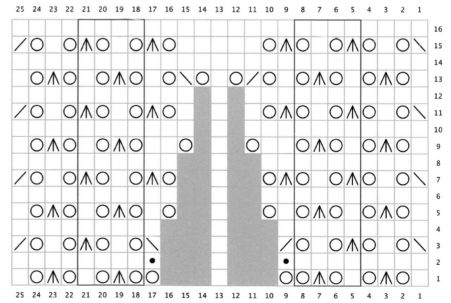

PART 3

GO
FOR
IT!

So. You have your exercises in creativity. You have your technical methods for how to shape fabric. What's next? It's time to make it happen! In this section, I'll break down three designs from start to finish, and talk you through the process.

WOODMAN

—

CARDIGAN

Francesca Woodman, *American photographer*

The first project for this chapter, the Woodman Cardigan, was actually the very last project in the book to coalesce. I knew what inspirations I wanted to pull from—a bit of mash-up, a bit of mad libs, a bit of playing with stitch patterns—but sketch after sketch wasn't exciting me. I finally decided to go back to basics and see if I could put something together that felt the most like me, with details I knew I loved from my previous knitting experience. I pulled down a sketch that I had made while watching a TV show a few years back (*iZombie*, for the record) and looked at it critically. I had always loved the silhouette and the construction, which is what had made me pause the show and record my impressions of it to begin with. But now I began to wonder if I couldn't make some of the shaping occur with the use of a stitch pattern that compressed row gauge: welts.

Welts are one of the stitch patterns that do the most work in compressing your row gauge, by the sheer fact that they actually subtract rows from your fabric. By threading a needle into the heads of the stitches four rows below (in this case; you can also create welts with fewer or more rows) and then knitting these stitches together with the live stitches on the needle, you fold the flat rows into a 3D shape. This takes away their height and adds to their depth, and shrinks the total height of the fabric in which you work them. They're akin to short rows in their placement and function: you can work them at the edge of a fabric and compensate for a welt at one edge with a welt at the other edge; you can build them all along a single edge to really compress and pleat the height of that side; or you can insert them into the centre of the fabric, bringing the rest of the fabric into a pucker around them. They're also akin to short rows in that, if worked over a partial row, they create a fabric in which one part is taller than another part. But, unlike short rows, which add height in certain areas, welts remove height. They're the anti-short row!

In this case, I wondered if I couldn't use that shaping to my advantage in a few key areas: the shoulders and the neckband. My original sketch had epaulettes of fabric that were narrower at the underarm and wider at the top, creating almost the entire width of the shoulder. Could I make that shape happen with welts, thereby using the same number of rows at the heavily-welted underarm as at the lightly-welted top of the shoulder? And could I use welts to create a waterfall shawl collar, whose width at the back neck was wider than at the hem?

The answer, as it almost always is with knitting, was: it's complicated. The neckband? Piece of cake. It behaved exactly as I hoped it would, creating an overflow of soft fabric on the back neck so that the neckband folded and

draped on itself beautifully, while the heavily welted areas at the hem added weight and helped the fabric hang nicely from the body. The shoulders, however, didn't quite work out as planned.

Here's a place where a designer gets to make a judgment call. In this first iteration of the sweater, the shoulders were fully welted at the underarm, and those welts were gradually worked over fewer and fewer stitches at the top of the sleeve until what was left was stockinette. In isolation, on a flat surface, this probably would've worked out very well. But in the 3D planes of a human body, and combined with the other structures of the sweater, what worked on paper and what worked in sketching came up short.

Let's back up a little bit and talk about the structure of the rest of the sweater. The body is knitted flat from the hem up. At the underarm, however, rather than splitting for a traditional front and back, all the front stitches are placed on holders, and the back is continued with a sped-up, more heavily curved version of traditional set-in sleeve shaping. The front stitches are then placed back onto the needle, and stitches are picked up along the side of the back armhole

This page
Original sketch, on whatever spare paper I could find.

Opposite
Sketch reinterpreted with welt shaping.

shaping. These stitches are what are then used to create the shoulder epaulette and the welts.

Within these stitches, we run into some stumbling blocks regarding human anatomy. As you grade out a pattern for different sizes, the bust circumference measurement scales at a much different rate from the yoke depth measurement, the shoulder measurement, or the upper arm circumference measurement, all of which were in play at this point. For some sizes, it worked out well that the number of stitches held for the body related fairly well to the front half of the upper arm circumference, which was the next number of stitches that I'd need to work with. But, for other sizes, they were vastly different, in such a way that if I didn't modify the stitch count somehow, there was no way the sleeves would fit or flatter a human form.

This left me with a few options to consider. I could: a) heavily decrease on the first few rows of the shoulder epaulette, getting me down to the stitch count I needed but potentially leaving me with a good bit of puckering at the pick-up edges; b) decrease during the welts themselves, hiding the changes in stitch count between the 3D ridges;

c) decrease at the front edges of the sweater during the body knitting so that when I arrived at this point, my stitch count would be more appropriate to the upper arm circumference; or d) some combination of all of the above. Since each of these options seemed drastic and could potentially hurt the shape of the sweater on its own, I decided to see if could combine them to create the smoothest and most invisible transition. I went with a combination of decreases at the front edge, at a slow enough rate that it wouldn't make the intersection of front edge and hem too pointy (a personal pet peeve) but fast enough to give me some wiggle room for numbers within the epaulette itself. I left the stitch counts during the pick-up alone, as I knew that would cause the most visual impact if I were to either decrease or change the pick-up rate there. But I calculated out and inserted a decrease structure similar to a bottom-up yoke into the epaulette to narrow the cone of fabric to the stitch count I needed for the short row sleeve cap and the upper arm circumference.

So I had a solution to my fit issue. The decreases would take care of the shaping so that it fit all the sizes in my grading spread, and the welts in the shoulder would shape it in such a way that the underarm would be fully welted and the top of the shoulder would have room to spread, setting up the perfect shoulder width for a top-down short row set-in sleeve. The problem? Man, it was ugly.

I got the sweater back from my lovely sample knitter and it just... wasn't right. The shoulders were too wide; the sleeve cap, which I like to sit over the top of the acromial process (that knobby bone at the top of your shoulder) was sitting much farther out, almost down past the curve of the shoulder itself. The angled line of the welts as they got worked over fewer and fewer stitches was lovely, but it got lost in the fold of the fabric at the underarm. And, on top of that, I had messed up. I had set up the decreases in the epaulette like I might for a circular yoke, equally spaced around the whole decrease round, assuming they would be hidden in the valleys between the welts. Problem was, I had also set up the welts to take up fewer and fewer stitches per round, so that decrease round was now hanging out in the open for everyone to see. In some situations I would've been okay with that, but it felt too conspicuous and clunky here.

This is the moment, as a designer, when you get to decide what's more important: the technique or the finished product. Is it more important that you follow through on exploring the idea, that how the fabric is created is more important than any potential fit issues? Or does the fit override the idea, meaning that you may have to let go of a concept in favour of something more conventional? It's a tricky question to answer, and you're the only one who can.

In my case, I thought about it for a good long while. I could most likely rip back the epaulette and move the decreases closer together each time to be hidden in the valleys between the welts. This might cause a little puckering, especially as the welts got smaller and smaller, but would mean that there would be a clean visual edge along the top of the shoulder. However, that still wouldn't solve the fact that the shoulders themselves were too deep and the change in welt size wasn't that visible. I couldn't think of a way around it while still preserving the original idea of using the welts to create more depth at the top of the shoulder than at the underarm—after all, that extra depth was what was getting me into trouble! So for this sweater, at this time, I kept the decreases as they were and changed the welts so that they were worked across the entire round. It meant that the thickness of the epaulette was the same at the top and underarm, but it meant that the sleeve cap fit much better and showed off the details of the welts themselves much more clearly. Once I re-did the epaulettes with that in mind, I was a million times happier with the fit and the overall aesthetic. So even if I did have to let go of the concept, I was content with the end result. (But I will most definitely revisit the idea of a welt- or short row-shaped shoulder, and will figure out how to make it work if it's the last thing I do!)

Woodman

Sizes:

1 (2, 3, 4, 5, 6, 7, 8)

Finished bust measurement:

106 (114.5, 124.5, 130, 137.5, 141.5, 147.5, 152) cm / 41¾ (45, 49, 51, 54, 55¾, 58, 59¾)" – to be worn with 24-30 cm / 9½-11¾" positive ease

Model has 86 cm / 34" bust, stands 183 cm / 6'" tall and is wearing size 2.

Yarn: Mrs. Crosby Plays

Hat Box (sport weight; 75% Merino wool, 15% silk, 10% cashmere; 290 m / 317 yds per 100 g skein)
Shade: Roasted Chestnut; 5 (6, 6, 7, 7, 7, 8, 8) skeins

Gauge:

24 sts & 32 rows = 10 cm / 4" over stocking stitch on 3.75 mm needles after blocking.

Needles:

3.5 mm / US 4 circular needle, minimum 80 cm / 32" length

3.75 mm / US 5 circular needle, 80 cm / 32" length

3.75 mm / US 5 circular needle, 40 cm / 16" length

3.25 mm / US 3 circular needle, 80 cm / 32" length

3.25 mm / US 3 AND 3 mm / US 2.5 needles suitable for working small circumferences in the round

Always use a needle size that will result in the correct gauge after blocking.

Notions:

2 stitch markers, locking stitch markers, stitch holders or scrap yarn, spare needle in same or smaller size than largest needle, tapestry needle.

Notes:

Woodman is worked flat from the bottom up with shaping at the front neck edges and sides. Once the body is complete, stitches are held for the fronts and the back is worked with exaggerated armhole shaping. Stitches are picked up along the back and the held front stitches, epaulettes are worked using welts, before the sleeves are worked from the top down with a short row sleeve cap. Once the sleeves are complete, a neckband is picked up and worked outwards from the front edges.

Stitch Glossary:

Welt: Insert spare needle in same or smaller size through tops of stitches at back of work and 4 rows down (starting counting with row below that on the needle), for as many stitches as stated in pattern. Hold the needles parallel with one another with working needle in front, * Insert working needle, through first st on LH needle and first st on spare needle, k2tog; rep from * as stated in pattern.

PATTERN BEGINS

POCKET INSERTS (MAKE 2 ALIKE)

Using larger circular needle and the long-tail method, cast on 31 sts.

Beg with a WS purl row, work straight in St st until piece measures 14 cm / 5½" from cast-on edge, ending with a WS row.

NEXT ROW (RS): K2tog, k to last 2 sts, ssk. *29 sts*

Break yarn and place all sts on stitch holder or scrap yarn.

BODY

Using middle-size circular needle and the long-tail method, cast on 200 (220, 244, 260, 284, 304, 328, 352) sts.

RIB ROW 1 (WS): P3, [k2, p2] to last st, p1.
RIB ROW 2 (RS): K3, [p2, k2] to last st, k1.

Last 2 rows set 2x2 rib.

Work in 2x2 rib until piece measures 15 cm / 6" from cast-on edge, ending with a WS row.

POCKET SEPARATION

NEXT ROW (RS): Using longer, large circular needle, patt 18 (18, 21, 21, 24, 27, 30, 33) sts, using SSK method cast off next 29 sts, patt 18 (22, 27, 33, 40, 45, 52, 59) sts (count includes st rem after cast off), PM for side, patt 70 (82, 90, 94, 98, 102, 106, 110) sts, PM for side, patt 18 (22, 27, 33, 40, 45, 52, 59) sts, using SSK method cast off next, patt 18 (18, 21, 21, 24, 27, 30, 33) sts (count includes st rem after cast off).

NEXT ROW (WS): P18 (18, 21, 21, 24, 27, 30, 33), with WS facing place 29 held Pocket Insert sts on LH needle, p across Pocket Insert sts, [p to marker, SM] twice, p18 (22, 27, 33, 40, 45, 52, 59), with WS facing place 29 held Pocket Insert sts on LH needle, p across held Pocket Insert sts, p to end.

Please read to end of this section before beginning, as multiple actions will occur AT THE SAME TIME.

NOTE: From here, garment is worked in St st.
NEXT ROW (RS)(Front Edge Dec): K2, ssk, k to last 4 sts, k2tog, k2. *2 sts dec*

Working in St st throughout, rep Front Edge Dec row every 0 (0, 0, 30, 16, 10, 6, 4) rows a further 0 (0, 0, 2, 3, 1, 13, 22) times, then every 0 (0, 0, 0, 14, 8, 4, 0) rows *0 (0, 0, 0, 2, 9, 2, 0) times. 0 (0, 0, 4, 10, 20, 30, 44) sts dec*

And AT THE SAME TIME, beg after first St st row:
Work straight in St st for a further 22 rows, ending with a WS row.
NEXT ROW (RS)(SIDE DEC ROW): [K to 3 sts before marker, ssk, k1, SM, k1, k2tog] twice, k to end. *4 sts dec*

Rep Side Dec row every 24th row twice more. *8 sts dec*

Work straight in patt as set until piece measures 51 cm / 20" from cast-on edge, ending with a WS row. *186 (206, 230, 242, 260, 270, 284, 294) sts rem after all shaping is complete*

Separate for Fronts and Back

NEXT ROW (RS): [K to 6 (6, 7, 7, 9, 9, 9, 9) sts before marker, cast off next 12 (12, 14, 14, 18, 18, 18, 18) sts knitwise] twice, k to end. *55 (59, 66, 70, 75, 78, 83, 86) sts each Front; 52 (64, 70, 74, 74, 78, 82, 86) Back sts*

Break yarn and place both Fronts on stitch holders or scrap yarn.

BACK

With WS facing, rejoin yarn to 52 (64, 70, 74, 74, 78, 82, 86) Back sts.

NEXT ROW (WS): Purl.
DEC ROW (RS): K1, ssk, k to last 3 sts, k2tog, k1. *2 sts dec*
Rep Dec Row every other row a further 3 (3, 4, 4, 4, 4, 4, 4) times, then every fourth row 2 (2, 2, 2, 4, 4, 4, 4) times. *40 (52, 56, 60, 56, 60, 64, 68) sts*
Work straight in St st until Back measures 21 (22, 24, 25.5, 26, 27.5, 29, 30.5) cm / 8¼ (8¾, 9½, 10, 10¼, 10¾, 11½, 12)" from underarm, ending with a WS row.

Cast off knitwise.

RIGHT EPAULETTE

With RS facing, using short, larger circular needle, rejoin yarn at beg of underarm cast off, pick up and k55 (59, 66, 70, 75, 78, 83, 86) sts along right Back armhole edge, PM, with RS facing place 55 (59, 66, 70, 75, 78, 83, 86) held Right Front sts on LH needle and k across them. Join for working in the round and PM to indicate beg of round. 110 (118, 132, 140, 150, 156, 166, 172) sts

Welt 1

Work 4 rounds in St st (knit every round).
NEXT ROUND: Work Welt (see stitch glossary) across all sts.
DEC ROUND: [K9 (9, 10, 11, 11, 13, 13, 13), k2tog] 10 (4, 11, 4, 3, 1, 5, 2) times, [k0 (8, 0, 10, 10, 12, 14, 14), k2tog] 0 (3, 0, 3, 6, 9, 1, 7) times, [k0

(9, 0, 11, 11, 13, 13, 13), k2tog] 0 (4, 0, 4, 3, 1, 5, 2) times. *100 (107, 121, 129, 138, 145, 155, 161) sts*

Welt 2

Work 4 rounds in St st
NEXT ROUND: Work Welt across all sts.
DEC ROUND: [K8, 8, 9, 10, 10, 12, 12, 12), k2tog] 10 (4, 11, 4, 3, 1, 5, 2) times, [k0 (7, 0, 9, 9, 11, 13, 13), k2tog] 0 (3, 0, 3, 6, 9, 1, 7) times, [k0 (8, 0, 10, 9, 12, 12, 12), k2tog] 0 (4, 0, 4, 3, 1, 5, 2) times. *90 (96, 110, 118, 126, 134, 144, 150) sts*

Welt 3

Work 4 rounds in St st
NEXT ROUND: Work Welt across all sts.
DEC ROUND: [K7, 7, 8, 9, 9, 11, 11, 11), k2tog] 10 (4, 11, 4, 3, 1, 5, 2) times, [k0 (6, 0, 8, 8, 10, 12, 12), k2tog] 0 (3, 0, 3, 6, 9, 1, 7) times, [K0 (7, 0, 9, 8, 11, 11, 11), k2tog] 0 (4, 0, 4, 3, 1, 5, 2) times. *80 (85, 99, 107, 114, 123, 133, 139) sts*

Welt 4

Work 4 rounds in St st
NEXT ROUND: Work Welt across all sts.
DEC ROUND: [K6, 6, 7, 8, 8, 10, 10, 10), k2tog] 10 (4, 11, 4, 3, 1, 5, 2) times, [k0 (5, 0, 7, 7, 9, 11, 11), k2tog] 0 (3, 0, 3, 6, 9, 1, 7) times, [K0 (6, 0, 8, 7, 10, 10, 10), k2tog] 0 (4, 0, 4, 3, 1, 5, 2) times. *70 (74, 88, 96, 102, 112, 122, 128) sts*

SIZES 3, 4, 5, 6, 7 & 8 ONLY
Welt 5

Work 4 rounds in St st
NEXT ROUND: Work Welt across all sts.
DEC ROUND: [K- (-, 6, 7, 6, 9, 9, 9), k2tog] - (-, 11, 4, 3, 1, 5, 2) times, [k- (-, 0, 6, 7, 8, 10, 10), k2tog] - (-, 0, 3, 6, 9, 1, 7) times, [k- (-, 0, 7, 6, 9, 9, 9), k2tog] - (-, 0, 4, 3, 1, 5, 2) times. *- (-, 77, 85, 90, 101, 111, 117) sts*

ALL SIZES AGAIN
RIGHT SLEEVE CAP

SET-UP ROW (RS): Using larger DPNs, k to marker at top of shoulder, k11 (12, 13, 14, 15, 17, 19, 20), turn and PLM for JSR.
NEXT SHORT ROW (WS): P to marker, SM, p11 (12, 12, 13, 15, 16, 18, 19), turn and PLM for JSR.
NEXT SHORT ROW: K to previous turn, resolve short row with next st, turn and PLM for JSR.
NEXT SHORT ROW: P to previous turn, resolve

short row with next st through the back loop, turn and PLM for JSR.
Rep last 2 short rows a further 17 (18, 18, 21, 20, 24, 27, 29) times. 12 (12, 14, 14, 18, 18, 18, 18) sts rem unwrapped at centre of underarm.

RIGHT SLEEVE

NEXT ROW (RS): K to end, resolving short row with next st.
NEXT ROUND: K to end, resolving final short row with next st through the back loop.
DEC ROUND: K1, ssk, k to last 3 sts, k2tog, k1. *2 sts dec*

Continue in St st and rep Dec round every 14 (10, 10, 8, 6, 4, 4, 4) rounds a further 7 (1, 7, 5, 3, 1, 16, 13) times, then every 16 (12, 12, 10, 8, 6, 6, 6) rounds 1 (9, 4, 8, 13, 20, 10, 12) times. *52 (52, 53, 57, 56, 57, 57, 65) sts*

Work straight in St st until Sleeve measures 38 cm / 15" from underarm.

SIZES 3, 4, 6, 7 & 8 ONLY

NEXT ROUND: Using smaller DPNs, [k2, p2] to last 5 sts, k1, k2tog, p2. - (-, 52, 56, -, 56, 56, 64) sts

ALL SIZES AGAIN

Change to smaller DPNs
NEXT ROUND: [k2, p2] to end.

Last round sets 2x2 rib.

Continue as set ribbing measures 10 cm / 4".

Cast off using SSK Cast Off.

LEFT EPAULETTE

Using short, larger circular needle, with RS facing place 55 (59, 66, 70, 75, 78, 83, 86) held Left Front sts on LH needle, rejoin yarn and k across them, PM, pick up and k55 (59, 66, 70, 75, 78, 83, 86) sts along left Back armhole edge. Join for working in the round and PM to indicate beg of round. *110 (118, 132, 140, 150, 156, 166, 172) sts*

Work as for Right Epaulette, Sleeve Cap, and Sleeve.

FRONT BAND

With RS facing, using largest needle and beg
at hem of Right Front, pick up and k97 sts in
edge of Right Front at a rate of approx 3 sts
every 4 rows, pick up and k40 (52, 56, 60, 56,
60, 64, 68) sts in Back neck cast-off edge
at a rate of 1 st for every cast-off st, pick
up and k97 sts in edge of Left Front at a rate
of approx. 3 sts every 4 rows. *234 (246, 250,
254, 250, 254, 258, 262) sts*

Welt 1

Beg with a WS purl row, work 5 rows in St st.
NEXT ROW (RS): Work Welt across all sts.

Welt 2

Work 5 rows in St st.
NEXT ROW (RS): Work Welt across 97 sts, k40
(52, 56, 60, 56, 60, 64, 68), work Welt over
next 97 sts.

Welt 3

Work 5 rows in St st.
NEXT ROW (RS): Work Welt over next 84 sts,
k to last 84 sts, work Welt over next 84 sts.

Welt 4

Work 5 rows in St st.
NEXT ROW (RS): Work Welt over next 72 sts,
k to last 72 sts, work Welt over next 72 sts.

Welt 5

Work 5 rows in St st.
NEXT ROW (RS): Work Welt over next 60 sts,
k to last 60 sts, work Welt over next 60 sts.

Welt 6

Work 5 rows in St st.
NEXT ROW (RS): Work Welt over next 48 sts,
k to last 48 sts, work Welt over next 48 sts.

Welt 7

Work 5 rows in St st.
NEXT ROW (RS): Work Welt over next 36 sts,
k to last 36 sts, work Welt over next 36 sts.

Welt 8

Work 5 rows in St st.
NEXT ROW (RS): Work Welt over next 24 sts,
k to last 24 sts, work Welt over next 24 sts.

Welt 9

Work 5 rows in St st.
NEXT ROW (RS): Work Welt over next 12 sts,
k to last 12 sts, work Welt over next 12 sts.

Change to middle needle.

NEXT ROW (WS): P2, [k2, p2] to end.
NEXT ROW (RS): K2, [p2, k2] to end.

Last two rows sets 2x2 rib.

Work in 2x2 rib for 2.5 cm / 1".

Cast off using SSK Cast Off.

___

FINISHING

Whipstitch pocket inserts to body.

Weave in all ends and block to measurements.

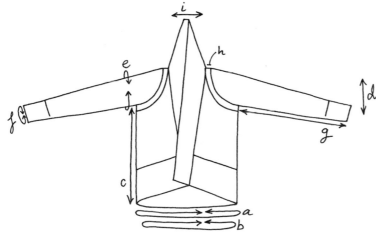

WOODMAN SCHEMATIC KEY

a. Bust circumference:
106 (114.5, 124.5, 130, 137.5, 141.5, 147.5, 152) cm /
41¾ (45, 49, 51, 54, 55¾, 58, 59¾)"

b. Hem circumference: 95.5 (103.5, 114, 119, 126.5, 131, 136.5, 141) cm /
37½ (40¾, 44¾, 46¾, 49¾, 51½, 53¾, 55½)"

c. Body length: 53.5 (53.5, 53.5, 53.5, 53.5, 53.5, 54, 54) cm /
21 (21, 21, 21, 21, 21, 21¼, 21¼)"

d. Back yoke depth: 21 (22, 24, 25.5, 26, 27.5, 29, 30.5) cm /
8¼ (8¾, 9½, 10, 10¼, 10¾, 11½, 12)"

e. Upper arm circumference: 27.5 (29, 30, 33, 35, 39.5, 43.5, 45.5) cm /
10¾ (11½, 11¾, 13, 13¾, 15½, 17, 18)"

f. Cuff circumference: 20.5 (20.5, 20.5, 22, 22, 22, 22, 25) cm /
8 (8, 8, 8½, 8½, 8½, 8½, 9¾)"

g. Sleeve length: 48 cm / 19"

h. Shoulder width: 2.5 (2.5, 2.5, 2.5, 2.5, 2.5 3, 3) cm /
1 (1, 1, 1, 1, 1, 1¼, 1¼)"

i. Back neck width: 17 (22, 23.5, 25.5, 23.5, 25.5, 27, 29) cm /
6¾ (8¾, 9¼, 10, 9¼, 10, 10¾, 11¼)"

DRUYAN

—

SHAWL

Ann Druyan, *creative director of NASA's Voyager Interstellar Message Project*

One of the first projects I wanted to do for this section, the Druyan shawl, was born from a 'what if?'. What if I combined a regular rate of cast-on with a different regular rate of decrease, and then threw short rows into the mix? I had no idea, but I wanted to find out.

For Druyan, I had a couple of variables to put in place to anchor the idea and give it some structure before setting off in search of an unknown result. I knew I wanted to work in chevrons, one of my favourite stitch patterns, and I knew I wanted the short rows within the pattern to turn at the junctures of those chevrons. I knew I wanted to punctuate them with garter ridges, which would help show off the short rows. I knew I wanted to cast on new repeats of the chevrons every few repeats or so, to add width to the whole piece and to give more room for the short rows to work. And I knew I wanted to decrease along the other edge, to give that edge some shape, move the whole piece slightly on the bias, and keep the triangle from getting too deep. I didn't know how wide I wanted the chevrons to be, or how long I wanted the shawl to go. I didn't know if the short rows would cause the whole piece to curve along the decrease edge so that it would become the wingspan, or if the cast-ons would add enough depth that the short row edge would become the wingspan. I didn't even (and this is blasphemy) do a gauge swatch ahead of time. Sometimes, especially when starting with a small number of stitches and increases, it's fun to figure it out as you go along—even (as we'll see) if it means some ripping back.

Okay. So. Once I had my building blocks (chevrons, garter ridge, cast-ons, decreases, short rows), the time came to nail down some details. The beautiful thing about knitting, as I talked about in the very beginning, is that we all see it differently and therefore shape our fabric according to our own individual preferences. In this project, where so much else was nebulous, my preferences came shining through in the things I did have control over.

How many stitches did I want in my chevrons? I'm fond of the number 12 (I have a predilection for numbers with lots of divisors and I don't care if that's strange), and think it makes a pleasantly wide stripe of chevron. So 12 stitches on either side of a centre stitch it was!

How many rows apart did I want my garter ridges? I have endless love for 4-row garter ridge patterns, so I bowed to the inevitable on that front.

How many stitches would I cast on, and how often? It made sense to cast on a full repeat, so 25 total stitches. And, since I like it when numbers line up, I decided that the cast-ons would occur every 24 rows, as 25 rows would make it tough to figure out how to get them all on the same side. An even number made much more sense, and besides, 24 is twice 12, and that's a good enough reason for me. I was aware that casting on too early would lead to a very wide shawl very quickly, so I delayed the first cast-on until the 48th row. And, for ease of pattern writing, I decided to incorporate that extra distance into the later repeats.

How often would I decrease? I put more thorough thought into this one. Ideally, I would decrease away three full chevrons during the length of the shawl, so a total of around 74 stitches, depending on how I would handle the final edge stitch. I had a sneaking suspicion that this one would end up quite large, so I wanted to keep the length of that edge on the conservative side. Therefore, I needed the decrease rate to be brisk but not overwhelming. To go with the 4-row garter ridges, I decided to decrease along the edge every fourth row. This would decrease away all but the edge stitch of the 25-stitch chevron panel every 96 rows.

And finally, how often would I short row? I knew I wanted to tie the number of stitches shifted in the short rows to the chevrons themselves, so I only had a limited number I could perform at one time, especially in the beginning. But I also knew that those short rows were the key to a long side edge, which could result in either a curved hem or a long wingspan, depending on how things turned out. So I set the short rows up to work after the first set of 96 rows, which would give me the width I wanted to make sure the short rows made enough of an impact. Then I set them up to work every 72 rows. This guaranteed that the amount of times short rows were worked increased each time, which increased the length along that edge. And ideally, I could keep going past that point to do something interesting with the border—perhaps decrease down to a smaller point again? I decided to wait and see.

With those details in mind and a bare-bones pattern in hand, my intrepid sample knitter was off and running. So did it work how I thought it would? Nope.

And here's the thing about 'what if?' knitting: sometimes it doesn't behave. You might have a firm grasp of ratios and angles, yet sometimes little things can throw a very large spanner into the works. In this case, it became abundantly clear after a few repeats of the pattern that the chevron cast-on was going much more speedily than I thought it would, and the shawl was growing widthways far more rapidly than I had expected. For all my careful planning of ratios and matching numbers, this wasn't what I wanted, and it soon became apparent that the allotted yarn, that I had intended for a much longer, narrower shawl, was rapidly becoming scarce. I had two options: rip out and start from

the beginning with entirely fresh numbers; or challenge myself to take aspects of what I had and make it work.

With profound apologies to my sample knitter, it turned out as a little bit of both. She ripped back and redid the short rows at a different rate, alternating between the original 72 rows and the new 48 rows. In addition, I rewrote the pattern to start narrowing down at the cast-on edge, hoping that the decreasing size would mitigate the dwindling yarn supply. I crossed my fingers. But still, no dice. There just wasn't enough yarn to get there. So this is the final lesson of 'what if?' knitting exploration: sometimes you have to listen to what the project is telling you, and go with the flow. I rewrote the pattern one more time, this time to finish after the final set of short rows with a simple border. When you ask 'what if?', sometimes you need to recognise that the answer you get might not be the answer you were hoping for.

But do I love the result? Wholeheartedly. What I thought would be the wingspan is now a side angle, and what I thought would be the bottom hem is now the wingspan. What I thought would create a curved, wing-like shape created a top edge that hugs your shoulders. And what I was worried wouldn't be big enough turned out to be *plenty big*.

The most important thing about this project is that I learned something. I learned what fabric would do when cast-ons and short rows were combined on the same edge. I learned that my decrease rate needed to be steeper to get the shape that I had hoped for, or that I needed to cast on less frequently. If I wanted to tie the short row lengths together with the width of the chevron, I needed to make the chevron repeats much narrower and more numerous to have greater visual impact. Finally, I also learned that it's fun to let go and just see what happens. You can rest assured that I'll be trying this construction again, taking all of the above into consideration. And even with this new knowledge, it may surprise me yet.

Druyan

One size:

114.5 cm / 45" wide x 218.5 cm / 86" long

Yarn: Madelinetosh

Tosh Sport (sport weight; 100% Merino wool;
247 m / 270 yds per 100 g skein)
Shade: Hosta Blue; 4 skeins

Gauge:

23.5 sts & 31 rows = 10 cm / 4" over
Repeat Pattern on 4.5 mm needles
after blocking.

Needles:

4.5 mm / US 7 circular needle,
minimum 80 cm / 32" length

Always use a needle size that will result
in the correct gauge after blocking.

Notions:

9 stitch markers, tapestry needle, t-pins
and blocking wires

Notes:

Druyan is worked sideways, with short rows
and cast-ons shaping the top edge and
decreases to shape the bottom edge
before finishing with a garter stitch edging.

Stitch Glossary:

Edge Pattern
ROW 1 (RS): K1, ssk, k8, [kfb] twice, k to last
3 sts, k2tog, k1.
ROW 2 (WS): Purl.
ROW 3: K1, ssk, k8, kfb, k to last 3 sts, k2tog,
k1. *1 st dec*
ROW 4: Knit.
ROWS 5-40: Rep rows 1-4. *9 sts dec*
ROW 41: K1, ssk, k8, kfb, k3.
ROW 42: Purl.
ROW 43: K1, ssk, k8, kfb, k2tog, k1. *1 st dec*
ROW 44: Knit.
ROW 45: Knit.
ROW 46: Purl.
ROW 47: K1, ssk, k to end. *1 st dec*
ROW 48: Knit.

ROWS 49-92: Rep rows 45-48. *11 sts dec*
ROW 93: Knit.
ROW 94: Purl.
ROW 95: K2tog. *1 st dec*
ROW 96: Knit.

Repeat Pattern
ROW 1 (RS): K1, ssk, k8, [kfb] twice, k to last 2
sts, k2tog.
ROW 2 (WS): Purl.
ROW 3: Rep row 1.
ROW 4: Knit.

PATTERN BEGINS

Using the long-tail method, cast on 25 sts.
SET-UP ROW (WS): Knit.
ROW 1 (RS): Work row 1 of Edge Pattern (see
Stitch Glossary).
ROW 2 (WS): Work next row of Edge Pattern.
Continue in patt as set to end of row 24
of Edge Pattern. *19 sts*

At end of final row, turn, PM, using the Cable
Cast On method cast on 24 sts. *43 sts*

CHEVRON SECTION 1

NEXT ROW (RS): Work row 1 of Repeat
Pattern (see Stitch Glossary) to marker,
SM, work row 25 of Edge Pattern.
NEXT ROW (WS): Work row 26 of Edge
Pattern to marker, SM, work row 2
of Repeat Pattern.

Continue in patt as set to end of row 48 of
Edge Pattern and row 4 of Repeat Pattern.
37 sts

At end of final row, turn, PM, using the Cable
Cast On method cast on 24 sts. *61 sts*

CHEVRON SECTION 2

NEXT ROW (RS): [Work row 1 of Repeat
Pattern to marker, SM] twice, work row 49
of Edge Pattern.
NEXT ROW (WS): Work row 50 of Edge
Pattern, [SM, work row 2 of Repeat
Pattern] twice.

Continue in patt as set to end of row 72 of
Edge Pattern and Row 4 of Repeat Pattern.
55 sts

At end of final row, turn, PM, using the
Cable Cast On method cast on 24 sts. *79 sts*

CHEVRON SECTION 3

NEXT ROW (RS): [Work row 1 of Repeat
Pattern to marker, SM] 3 times, work row 73
of Edge Pattern.
NEXT ROW (WS): Work row 74 of Edge
Pattern, [SM, work row 2 of Repeat Pattern]
3 times.

Continue in patt as set to end of row 96 of
Edge Pattern and Row 4 of Repeat Pattern.
73 sts

At beg of final row, remove marker between
Edge Pattern and Repeat Pattern.

At end of final row, turn, PM, using the
Cable Cast On method cast on 24 sts. *97 sts*

SHORT ROW SECTION

SHORT ROW 1 (RS): * Work row 1 of Repeat
Pattern; rep from * to last marker, turn.
SHORT ROW 2 (WS): Yob around RH needle,
patt to end.
SHORT ROW 3 (RS): Patt to 12 sts before
last turn, turn.
SHORT ROW 4 (WS): Yob around RH needle,
patt to end.

Rep short rows 3-4 a further 4 times.

CHEVRON SECTION 4

NEXT ROW (RS): [Work row 1 of Repeat
Pattern to marker, SM] 3 times, work row 1
of Edge Pattern resolving short rows together
with next st as you pass them.
NEXT ROW (WS): Work row 2 of Edge Pattern,
[SM, work row 2 of Repeat Pattern] 3 times.

Continue in patt as set to end of row 24 of
Edge Pattern and Row 4 of Repeat Pattern.
91 sts

At end of last row, turn, PM, using the
Cable Cast On method, cast on 24 sts. *115 sts*

Rep Chevron Section 1, working
Repeat Pattern 4 times per row. *133 sts*

Rep short rows 1-4, then rep short rows 3-4
a further 5 times.

Rep Chevron Section 2, working
Repeat Pattern 5 times per row. *151 sts*

Rep Chevron Section 3, working
Repeat Pattern 6 times per row. *169 sts*

Rep short rows 1-4, then rep short rows 3-4
a further 9 times.

Rep Chevron Section 4, working
Repeat Pattern 6 times per row. *187 sts*

Rep Chevron Section 1, working
Repeat Pattern 7 times per row. *205 sts*

Rep short rows 1-4, then rep short rows 3-4
a further 13 times.

Rep Chevron Section 2, working
Repeat Pattern 8 times per row. *223 sts*

Rep Chevron Section 3, working
Repeat Pattern 9 times per row. *241 sts*

Rep short rows 1-4, then rep short rows 3-4
a further 17 times.

BORDER
ROW 1 (RS): * K1, ssk, k8, [kfb] twice,
k to 2 sts before marker, k2tog, SM; rep
from * a further 8 times, k1.
ROW 2 (WS): Knit.

Rep rows 1-2 a further 3 times.

Cast off from RS as foll using using
Jeny's Surprisingly Stretchy Bind Off.

FINISHING

Weave in all ends and block to measurements.

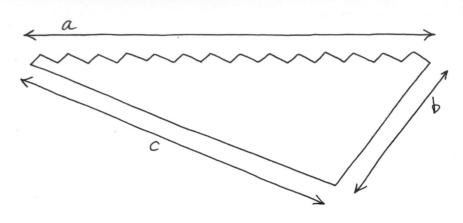

DRUYAN SCHEMATIC KEY

a. Wingspan: 218.5 cm / 86"
b. Cast off edge: 114.5 cm / 45"
c. Side edge: 186 cm / 73¼"

LILLEMOR
—
SHAWL

Lillemor Rachlew, *one of four Norwegians to be the first women to set foot on the Antarctic mainland*

The final project in this section is near and dear to my heart, because it's one that I've talked about making for many years now. Back in the winter of 2015, I took a photo of the snow outside my window. My apartment is in the basement, so my windows are often varying levels of snowed-in during wintertime. It was a typical late January day in Maine: windy, cold, and bright. The sun would melt the top layer of snow on the pile, turning it to ice, and just as quickly the wind would blow a fine new layer of snow on top of it. It created beautifully defined sculptures in the snow as it lay against my window, so I had to take a picture of it: the gentle curve of wind-blown snow against the stark, clean lines of the window frame. It didn't take me too long to realise (with some cajoling from friends who had seen the picture) that it would make a pretty cool shawl.

It took a few years to develop enough of an understanding of shaping in knitting to be able to tackle it. I figured out that I wanted to treat it like a Colouring Inside the Lines exercise, since the icy divisions in the snow lent themselves well to defined geometric shapes. My first step was to trace out the discernible shapes present in the photo. (I did this in Adobe Illustrator, but you could do something similar with tracing paper or just a permanent marker over the top of a printout of the image.) [fig 1 & 2]

Once this outline was complete, I took the background image away so I could focus on the aesthetics and practicality of the traced shape itself.

Now I had to ask myself a few questions. Did I want to keep this strictly representative of the original image, or were there places I should tweak it to make it easier to construct and knit? And if I did want to tweak it, did I want to let the technique dictate the shape by keeping it all to one shaping technique, such as all short rows or all increasing and decreasing? Or did I want to let the shape dictate the technique and work shaping techniques together at the same time?

I did a few more sketches to play with the former idea. Here's the one of the potential outcome of working the fabric with short rows only, and substituted cast-ons and cast-off at the beginnings and ends of shapes for the increasing and decreasing that would keep it going in a straight line. [fig 3]

It's an interesting shape, and one that might be interesting to play with parts of, but for me the overall impression was overwhelming and didn't feel particularly wearable. I did like the bottom edge, and that's something that would be fun to pull out and play with on its own, but it didn't work for this particular shawl. I decided that letting the shape dictate the technique and therefore using increases, decreases, and short rows in tandem was the best solution to get me where I wanted to go. [fig 4]

I also wanted to look at the image in terms of editing, to see where I might change lines to make it easier to knit. I experimented with moving the individual wedge points into a cluster, and shifting the final diagonal line on the bottom out to the corner. I liked the visual effect, but I also knew from previous knitting experience that there was no way to have several short rows end at the same place and not have it create a gap or puckering in the fabric. So I knew that probably wouldn't work out in this case, but I did like what changing the angle at the bottom corner did for both the aesthetic of the shawl and for the knittability: bringing that line out to the point meant that I wouldn't have to change technique in the middle of a section but could shift easily at the transition point between two.

I was going into these questions with a couple of assumptions in place. The triangle on the bottom left-hand corner was almost exactly a D triangle from the increase/decrease cheat sheet and all the other shapes built off of it, so I decided that would be the easiest place to start. From there, the short rows curve in a series of wedges around the corner and up the right edge, and then it ends with a curve that I decided would best be achieved by regularly placed decreases within the centre of the fabric and increases at the edges to maintain the straight outer lines. This seemed like it would work almost like the traditional lace stitch Feather and Fan, where stacking decreases in

fig 1

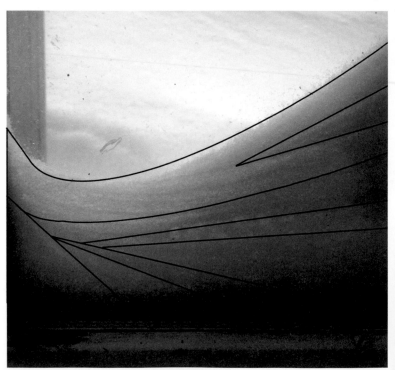

one location lowers it, and stacking increases in another location raises it. I had mapped out a few other options, but this was the one that made the most sense to me.

When it came to breaking the shawl down into the actual maths of stitch and row count, I decided the best way to tackle it would be to use ratios. I printed the sketch and used a good old fashioned ruler to help me sort out the proportions. Since everything was going to be based on of the originating D triangle, I knew that its stitch count and row count would dictate everything else that followed. I would like to say that I did a very long and complicated bit of calculation for that triangle based on my gauge swatch pre- and post-blocking, plus my intended finished dimensions for the shawl, minus the border I planned to add at the end, but the reality is that sometimes proportions are easier to understand when they're in your hands. For this triangle, I knew the regular and consistent increase rate

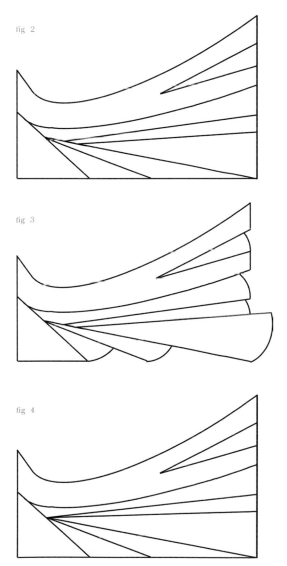

fig 2

fig 3

fig 4

would mean I could keep going until it was as big as I wanted it, and so I went for it.

Once I had knit that triangle and was comfortable with its size, I used its row and stitch count to help me figure out the maths for the rest of the shawl. So, for example, my original triangle serendipitously measured 1" along the bottom edge of my printout, so that made my base ratio of 1 very simple. The length of the line where my live stitches would be equated to 1.375. After knitting the triangle, I knew that 1 in terms of rows equalled 116, and 1.375 in terms of stitches equalled 121. My next wedge was 0.625 along the row edge. I did a little cross-multiplying and dividing to get 76 rows (116 x 0.625) / 1x) = 76). I also took a look at where the top point of the wedge intersected the original triangle, and the ratio of stitches used during the short rows for the new wedge was in between 0.5625 and 0.625, so I split the difference for 72 stitches. I knew that I was starting with 72 stitches and would continue the same increase rate as I had during the initial triangle to keep the line straight and smooth, and I had 76 rows to make 72 stitches worth of short rows happen. These ratios decided the structure of this short row wedge, and shaped the progression of the short rows for the rest of the shawl.

Luckily for me, most of the numbers in these equations worked out to be whole or close towhole numbers, but in other cases it wasn't so easy. In those cases, I tried to strike a balance between finding an easy, workable knitting repeat, something that meant I wouldn't have to have multiple sets of instructions per short row wedge, and staying true to the original shape.

I also got to choose how and when I would change the direction of my knitting: would I go large to small or small to large with my short rows? In the end, it worked out in terms of both aesthetics and knitting convenience. I liked how with small to large there was an automatic and instant change in direction, and I also liked that with small to large there was no point at which I had to work across a row resolving multiple short rows as I went. I wanted to work with Japanese Short Rows for this pattern (my favourite), which is a technique that uses locking stitch markers to hold your place in the turn. I knew that if I went large to small, that would involve a lot of locking stitch markers! So small to large felt like a good choice for multiple reasons.

Of all the patterns in the book, this one had probably the smoothest process. There was no ripping, there was no rethinking—just smooth sailing. It felt good that sometimes, just sometimes, you find the perfect marriage of yarn, inspiration, and implementation that makes the many hours of daydreaming and maths all worth it.

Lillemor

One size:

167.5 cm / 66" wide x 76 cm / 30" along right edge, 63 cm / 24¾" along left edge

Yarn A: Woolfolk

Sno (4 ply / fingering weight; 100% Ovis 21 ultimate merino; 204 m / 223 yds per 50 g skein)
Shade: 1+2; 4 skeins

Yarn B: Woolfolk

Tynd (4 ply / fingering weight; 100% Ovis 21 ultimate merino; 204 m / 223 yds per 50 g skein)
Shade: 2; 1 skein

Gauge:

21.5 sts and 40 rows = 10 cm / 4" over stocking stitch on 3.75 mm needles after blocking.

Needles:

3.75 mm / US 5 circular needle, minimum 80 cm / 32" length

Always use a needle size that will result in the correct gauge after blocking.

Notions:

Locking stitch markers, tapestry needle, t-pins and blocking wires

Notes:

Lillemor is constructed modularly and finished with a border picked-up after completion. Please refer to construction schematic for order and direction of knitting.

PATTERN BEGINS

Section 1

Using the long-tail method and yarn A, cast on 3 sts.
SET-UP ROW (WS): Purl.
ROW 1 (RS): K1, M1L, k to last st, M1R, k1. *2 sts inc*
ROW 2 (WS): Purl.

Rep rows 1-2 a further 55 times. *115 sts*

Break yarn A.

SECTION 1 EYELETS

Join yarn B.
ROW 1 (RS): K1, M1L, k to last st, M1R, k1. *117 sts*
ROW 2 (WS): Knit.
ROW 3: K1, yo, k1, [yo, k2tog] to last st, yo, k1. *119 sts*
ROW 4: Purl.
ROW 5: P1, M1P, p to last st, M1PR, p1, do not turn, break yarn B and slide sts to other end of needle ready to work a RS row. *121 sts*

SECTION 2

Join yarn A.
ROW 1 (RS): K1, M1L, k1, turn and PLM for JSR. *122 sts*
ROW 2 (WS): Purl.
ROW 3: K1, M1L, k to previous turn, resolve JSR with next st, turn and PLM for JSR. *1 st inc*
ROW 4: Purl.
ROWS 5-6: Rep rows 3-4 once more. *124 sts*
ROW 7: K1, M1L, k to previous turn, resolve JSR with next st, k1, turn and PLM for JSR. *1 st inc*
ROW 8: Purl.
ROWS 9-72: Rep rows 7-8 a further 32 times. *157 sts*

Break yarn A.

SECTION 2 EYELETS

Join yarn B.
ROW 1 (RS): K1, M1L, k to previous turn, resolve JSR with next st, turn and PLM for JSR. *158 sts*
ROW 2 (WS): Knit.
ROW 3: K1, yo, k1, [yo, k2tog] to 1 st before previous turn, yo, sl1, resolve JSR with next st, psso, turn and PLM for JSR. *159 sts*
ROW 4: Purl.
ROW 5: P1, M1P, p to previous turn, resolve JSR with next st, do not turn, break yarn B and slip sts from RH needle to LH needle ready to work a RS row. *160 sts*

SECTION 3

Join yarn A.
ROW 1 (RS): K1, M1L, k1, turn and PLM for JSR. *1 st inc*
ROW 2 (WS): Purl.
ROW 3: K1, M1L, k to previous turn, resolve JSR with next st, turn and PLM for JSR. *1 st inc*
ROW 4: Purl.
ROWS 5-44: Rep rows 3-4 a further 20 times. *182 sts*
ROW 45: K1, M1L, k to previous turn, resolve JSR with next st, k1, turn and PLM for JSR. *1 st inc*
ROW 46: Purl.
ROWS 47-114: Rep rows 45-46 a further 34 times. *217 sts*
ROWS 115-154: Rep rows 3-4 a further 20 times. *237 sts*

Break yarn A.

SECTION 3 EYELETS

Join yarn B.
Rep Section 2 Eyelets. *240 sts*

SECTION 4

Join yarn A.
SET-UP ROW (RS): K4, turn and PLM for JSR.
SET-UP ROW (WS): Purl.
ROW 1 (RS): K1, k2tog, k to previous turn, resolve JSR with next st, k3, turn and PLM for JSR. *1 st dec*
ROW 2 (WS): Purl.
ROW 3: K to previous turn, resolve JSR with next st, k3, turn and PLM for JSR.
ROW 4: Purl.
ROWS 5-70: Rep rows 1-4 a further 16 times, then rep rows 1-2 once more. *222 sts*

Break yarn A.

SECTION 4 EYELETS

Join yarn B.
ROW 1 (RS): K to previous turn, resolve JSR with next st, k3, turn and PLM for JSR.
ROW 2 (WS): Knit.
ROW 3: K2tog, [yo, k2tog] to 1 st before previous turn, yo, sl1, resolve JSR with next st, psso, k3, turn and PLM for JSR. *221 sts*

ROW 4: Purl.

ROW 5: P to previous turn, resolve JSR with next st, p3, do not turn, break yarn B and slip sts from RH needle to LH needle ready to work a RS row.

SECTION 5

Join yarn A.

SET-UP ROW (RS): K1, k2tog, k11, turn and PLM for JSR. *220 sts*

SET-UP ROW (WS): Purl.

ROW 1: K to previous turn, resolve JSR with next st, k13, turn and PLM for JSR.

ROW 2: Purl.

ROWS 3–6: Rep rows 1–2 twice more.

ROW 7: K1, k2tog, k to previous turn, resolve JSR with next st, k13, turn and PLM for JSR. *1 st dec*

ROW 8: Purl.

ROWS 9–18: Rep rows 1–8 once more, then rep Rows 1 and 2 once more. *218 sts*

ROWS 19: K to previous turn, resolve JSR with next st, k1, turn and PLM for JSR.

ROW 20: Purl.

ROWS 21–22: Rep rows 19–20.

ROW 23: K1, k2tog, k to previous turn, resolve JSR with next st, k1, turn and PLM for JSR. *1 st dec*

ROW 24: Purl.

ROWS 25–26: Rep rows 19–20.

ROWS 27–32: Rep rows 19–24. *216 sts*

Break yarn A.

SECTION 5 EYELETS

Join yarn B.

ROW 1 (RS): K to previous turn, resolve JSR with next st, k1, turn and PLM for JSR.

ROW 2 (WS): Knit.

ROW 3: K2tog, [yo, k2tog] to 1 st before previous turn, yo, sl1, resolve JSR with next st, psso, k3, turn and PLM for JSR. *215 sts*

ROW 4: Purl.

ROW 5: P to previous turn, resolve JSR with next st, k1, do not turn, break yarn B and slip sts from RH needle to LH needle ready to work a RS row.

SECTION 6

Join yarn A.

SET-UP ROW (RS): K4, turn and PLM for JSR.

SET-UP ROW (WS): Purl.

ROW 1 (RS): K to previous turn, resolve JSR with next st, k3, turn and PLM for JSR.

ROW 2 (WS): Purl.

ROWS 3–10: Rep rows 1–2 a further 4 times.

ROW 11: K1, k2tog, k to previous turn, resolve JSR with next st, k3, turn and PLM for JSR. *1 st dec*

ROWS 13–16: Rep rows 1–2 twice more.

ROWS 17–32: Rep rows 1–16. *213 sts*

ROW 33: K to previous turn, resolve JSR with next st, turn and PLM for JSR.

ROW 34: P54, turn and PLM for JSR.

ROW 35: Rep row 33.

ROW 36: P to 2 sts before previous turn, turn and PLM for JSR.

ROWS 37–84: Rep rows 35–36 a further 24 times.

ROW 85: K to previous turn, resolve JSR with next st, turn and PLM for JSR.

ROW 86: P to end, resolving JSRs with next st through the back loop as you pass it.

Break yarn A.

SECTION 6 EYELETS

Join yarn B.

ROW 1 (RS): K to previous turn, resolve JSR with next st, turn and PLM for JSR.

ROW 2 (WS): Knit.

ROW 3: K2tog, [yo, k2tog] to 1 st before previous turn, yo, sl1, resolve JSR with next st, psso, turn and PLM for JSR.

ROW 4: Purl.

ROW 5: P to previous turn, resolve JSR with next st, do not turn, break yarn B and slip sts from RH needle to LH needle ready to work a RS row.

SECTION 7

Join yarn A.

SET-UP ROW (RS): K to last st, resolving JSR with next st as you go, M1R, k1. *214 sts*

SET-UP ROW (WS): Purl.

ROW 1: K to last st, M1R, k1. *1 st inc*

ROW 2: Purl.

ROW 3: [K40, k2tog] twice, [k40, ssk] twice, k to last st, M1R, k1. *1 st inc, 4 sts dec*

ROW 4: Purl.

ROWS 5–8: Rep rows 1–2 twice more. *2 sts inc*

ROW 9: K20, [k2tog, k40] twice, [ssk, k40] twice, ssk, k to last st, M1R, k1. *1 st inc, 5 sts dec*

ROW 10: Purl.

ROWS 11–12: Rep rows 1–2. *1 st inc*

ROWS 13–24: Rep rows 1–12. *211 sts*

Break yarn A.

SECTION 8

SECTION 8 EYELETS 1

Join yarn B.

ROW 1 (RS): K96, turn and PLM for JSR.

ROW 2 (WS): Knit.

ROW 3: K1, [yo, k2tog] to 9 sts before previous turn, k1, turn and PLM for JSR.

ROW 4: Purl.

ROW 5: P to 8 sts before previous turn, do not turn, break yarn B and and slip sts from RH needle to LH needle ready to work a RS row.

SHORT ROWS

Join yarn A.

ROW 1 (RS): K8, turn and PLM for JSR.

ROW 2 (WS): Purl.

ROW 3: K to previous turn, resolve JSR with next st, k7, turn and PLM for JSR.

ROW 4: Purl.

ROWS 5–16: Rep rows 3–4 a further 6 times.

Break yarn A.

SECTION 8 EYELETS 2

Join yarn B.

ROW 1 (RS): K to previous turn, resolve JSR with next st, k7, resolve JSR with next st, turn and PLM for JSR.

ROW 2 (WS): Knit.

ROW 3: K1, [yo, k2tog] to previous turn, yo, k3tog next 2 sts with JSR, [yo, k2tog] 3 times, turn and PLM for JSR.

ROW 4: Purl.

ROW 5: P to previous turn, resolve JSR with next st, k7, do not turn, break yarn B and slip sts from RH needle to LH needle ready to work a RS row.

SECTION 9

Join yarn A.

SET-UP ROW (RS): K to last st, resolving JSR with next st as you go, M1R, k1. *212 sts*

SET-UP ROW (WS): Purl.

ROW 1: K to last st, M1R, k1. *1 st inc*

ROW 2 (WS): Purl.

ROW 3: [K39, k2tog] twice, [k39, ssk] twice, k to last st, M1R, k1. *1 st inc, 4 sts dec*

ROW 4: Purl.

ROWS 5-8: Rep rows 1-2 twice more. *2 sts inc*

ROW 9: K20, [k2tog, k39] twice, [ssk, k39] twice, ssk, k to last st, M1R, k1. *1 st inc, 5 sts dec*

ROWS 11-12: Rep rows 1-2. *1 st inc*

ROWS 13-24: Rep rows 1-12 once more. *206 sts*

Break yarn A.

SECTION 9 EYELETS

Join yarn B.

ROW 1 (RS): K to last st, M1R, k1. *207 sts*

ROW 2 (WS): Knit.

ROW 3: K1, [yo, k2tog] to last st, yo, k1. *208 sts*

ROW 4: Purl.

ROW 5: P to last st, M1PR, p1. *209 sts*

Cast off from WS as foll using Jeny's Surprisingly Stretchy Bind Off.

BORDER

Using yarn B, beg at top left edge, pick up and k117 sts down left edge to cast-on point of Section A, PM, pick up and k237 sts to end of Section C, PM, pick up and k163 sts along right edge to top right edge. *517 sts*

SET-UP ROW (WS): Knit.

ROW 1 (RS): [K1, yo, k1, (k2tog, yo) to 1 st before marker, yo, k1] 3 times. *523 sts*

ROW 2: Purl.

ROW 3: [P1, M1PR, p to 1 st before marker, M1P, p1] 3 times. *529 sts*

Cast off as for main shawl.

FINISHING

Weave in all ends and block to measurements.

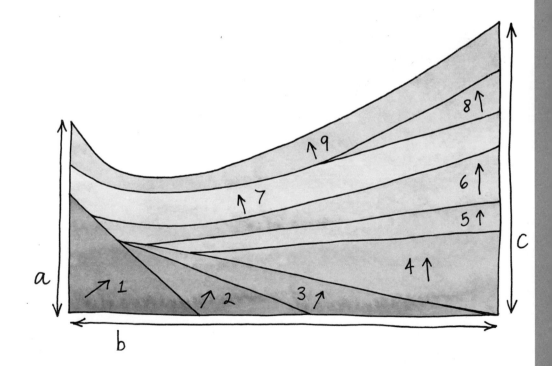

LILLEMOR SCHEMATIC KEY

a. Width: 63 cm / 24¾"

b. Length: 167.5 cm / 66"

c. Depth: 76 cm / 30"

Baa Ram Ewe
baaramewe.co.uk

Blacker Yarns
blackeryarns.co.uk

The Fibre Co.
thefibreco.com

Indigodragonfly
indigodragonfly.ca

Julie Asselin
julie-asselin.com

Madelinetosh
madelinetosh.com

Magpie Fibers
magpiefibers.com

Miss Babs
missbabs.com

Mrs. Crosby
mrscrosbyplays.com

Quince & Co.
quinceandco.com

Shibui Knits
shibuiknits.com

Spincycle Yarns
spincycleyarns.com

Sweet Fiber Yarns
sweetfiberyarns.com

The Uncommon Thread
theuncommonthread.co.uk

Woolfolk
woolfolkyarn.com

YOTH
yothyarns.com

1/1 LPC	sl1 to cn and hold to front, p1, k1 from cn
1/1 WSRC	sl1 to cn and hold to front, p1, p1 from cn
1/1 RPC	sl1 to cn and hold to back, k1, p1 from cn
1/2 LC	sl1 to cn and hold to front, k2, k1 from cn
1/2 LPC	sl1 to cn and hold to front, p2, k1 from cn
1/2 RC	sl2 to cn and hold to back, k1, k2 from cn
1/2 RPC	sl2 to cn and hold to back, k1, p2 from cn
1/3 LC	sl1 to cn and hold to front, k3, k1 from cn
1/3 RC	sl3 to cn and hold to back, k1, k3 from cn
2/1 LC	sl2 to cn and hold to front, k1, k2 from cn
2/1 RC	sl1 to cn and hold to back, k2, k1 from cn
2/2 LC	sl2 to cn and hold to front, k2, k2 from cn
2/2 RC	sl2 to cn and hold to back, k2, k2 from cn
3/2 LPC	sl3 to cn and hold to front, p2, k3 from cn
3/2 RPC	sl2 to cn and hold to back, k3, p2 from cn
3/3/2 LC	sl3 to first cn and hold to front, sl3 to second cn and hold behind first cn, p2, k3 from second cn, k3 from first cn
3/3/2 RC	sl2 to first cn and hold to back, sl3 to second cn and hold in front of first cn, k3, k3 from second cn, p2 from first cn
3/3 LC	sl3 to cn and hold to front, k3, k3 from cn
3/3 RC	sl2 to cn and hold to back, k3, k3 from cn
approx	Approximately
beg	Beginning
bor	Beginning of round
BRK	Knit slipped st and yo together
BRP	Purl slipped st and yo together
br-k3tog	Knit next 3 columns together: one brk column, one purl column, and one brk column (5 loops total) (2 columns dec; leans right).
br-sssk	Slip next 3 columns (5 loops total) knitwise individually to right needle, bringing slip stitch and yo together as a single st, then return sts to left needle in new orientation and knit together through the back loop (2 columns dec; leans left).
brkyobrk	Knit 1, keeping brk on left needle, yo around right needle, knit into brk once more and drop from left needle (2 sts inc). On next round, (sl1yo, p1, sl1yo) into three loops of increase.
cast off	Bind off
dec	Decrease
DPN(s)	Double-pointed needle(s)
e-k	knit, wrapping yarn twice around needle
e-p	purl, wrapping yarn twice around needle
est	Established
foll	Follow(s)/Following
g st	Garter stitch
inc	Increase

JSR	Work as specified to turn, turn and PLM on working yarn. Holding LM against WS of work, sl1, then work in pattern as specified. LM will now sit between the first and second stitches to the inside of the turn. To resolve on RS, pull LM, place resultant loop on left needle and work together with next st. To resolve on WS, pull LM, place resultant loop on right needle, sl1 knitwise, return slipped st in its new orientation and loop to left needle, work together with next st through the back loop
k	Knit
k1/L	(left lifted increase): With left needle, pick up the left leg of the stitch two rows below the stitch just worked on your right needle and knit. *1 st inc*
k1/R	(right lifted increase): With right needle, pick up the right leg of the stitch below the next stitch on left needle, place on left needle and knit. *1 st inc*
k1tbl	Knit 1 stitch through the back loop
k2tog	Knit 2 stitches together
k3tog	Knit 3 stitches together
kfb	Knit into the front and back of 1 stitch
k1-yo-k1	(k1, yo around right needle, k1) into next st
k1, p1, k1	(k1, p1, k1) into next st
LH	Left hand
LM	Locking marker
LT	Slip two sts knitwise individually as if to knit, replace in new orientation on left needle. Knit second st on needle through the back loop, leaving both sts on the needle, then k2tog both sts through the back loop
M1	Work as for M1L
M1L	Make 1 Left; pick up strand between the two needles from the front to back with the tip of left needle, knit into the back of this stitch M1P (make 1 purlwise): Insert LH needle from front to back under horizontal strand between st just worked and next st, purl lifted strand through the back loop.
M1R	Make 1 Right; pick up strand between the two needles from back to front with the tip of left needle, knit into the front of this stitch
M1P	(make one purlwise): Insert LH needle from front to back under horizontal strand between st just worked and next st, purl lifted strand through the back loop.
M3	(k1, yo, kfb) into next st
M6	(k1, yo, k1, yo, k1, yo, k1) into next st
p	Purl
patt	Pattern
pfb	purl into the front and back of the next st
PLM	Place locking marker
PM	Place marker
psso	Pass slipped stitch over
p1tbl	Purl 1 stitch through the back loop

p2tog	Purl 2 stitches together
p3tog	Purl 3 stitches together
p4tog	Purl 4 stitches together
prov co	Provisional cast on
RH	Right hand
rem	Remain(s)/Remaining
rep	Repeat
rev st st	Reverse Stocking stitch (stockinette): purl on RS rows, knit on WS rows
RS	Right side
RT	k2tog leaving both sts on the left needle, knit the first st on the left needle again taking st to right needle
sl	Slip
SM	Slip marker
ssk	Slip 2 stitches knitwise one at a time, knit them together through back loop
SSK	Cast Off Sl2 knitwise individually to right needle, *return 2 sts to left needle in new orientation and k2tog tbl, sl1 knitwise to right needle; rep from * to end
sssk	Slip 3 stitches knitwise one at a time, knit stitches together through back loop
ssp	Slip 2 stitches knitwise one at a time, slip stitches in new orientation back to left needle, purl stitches together through back loop(s)
st(s)	Stitch(es)
st st	Stocking stitch (stockinette): Knit on RS rows, purl on WS rows
s2kpo	Slip 1 stitch knitwise, knit next 2 stitches together, pass slipped stitch over. 2 stitches decreased
sk2po	Sl1 knitwise, k2tog, pass slipped st over. *2 sts dec*
sl1-yo	Bring yarn to front between needles, slip next st purlwise, bring yarn over needle and slipped stitch. If working a knit afterward, leave yarn in back ready to work knit stitch; if working a purl afterward, bring yarn to front between needles ready to work a purl
tbl	Through the back loop
tog	Together
WS	Wrong side
wyib	With yarn held in back of work
wyif	With yarn held in front of work
yo	Yarn over needle and into working position
yob	Take yarn from back to front over right-hand needle and into working position. Work the yarn over together with its stitch when you next pass it
w&t	wrap and turn short rows: To resolve on RS, insert RH needle into both the wrap an the stitch that it's wrapping and knit both together. To resolve on WS, slip to RH needle, lift wrap onto RH needle, return wrap and st to LH needle and p2tog tbl.

The following tutorials are available for techniques used in this book:

Backwards loop cast on Pom Pom Issue 13 and newstitchaday.com/backward-loop-cast-on

Cable cast on purlsoho.com/create/cable-cast-on

Jeny's Surprisingly Stretchy Bind Off knitty.com/ISSUEfall09/FEATjssbo.php

Long-tail cast on Pom Pom Issue 11 and purlsoho.com/create/long-tail-cast-on

Provisional cast on blog.ysolda.com/ysolda-blog/2014/10/23/technique-thursday-provisional-cast-on

Sewn cast off purlsoho.com/create/elizabeth-zimmermanns-better-bind-off

Three needle cast off on Pom Pom Issue 5 and vimeo.com/171071650

Kitchener stitch on Pom Pom Issue 3 and vimeo.com/158459385

This book would not have been possible without the kindness and generosity of many, many people.

To the dyers and yarn companies whose yarn was graciously donated for the patterns in this book, massive, unending thanks for sharing your beautiful and thoughtful work with me.

To Quince and Co., whose yarn appears in the stitch dictionary in section 2, profound thanks for your support, in this endeavor and over the many years I've gotten to work with you.

To my sample knitters, Addi, Averi, Minh, Jessica, Kathryn, Bonnie, and my mom Darlene, many, many thanks for your tireless work and patience, without which this book would be a rather pathetic pile of sketches, yarn, and long-passed deadlines.

To the brilliant and persevering tech editors, Jen, Kate, Rachel, Jemima, and Minh, thank you for never batting an eye at my crazy ideas.

To the incredible, mountain-moving, badass women of PomPom, thank you, thank you, THANK YOU for believing in me.

To the incredible, groundbreaking women whose names grace the titles of these patterns, thank you for pushing the boundaries of the world we know and standing up for your right to do and to be whatever we want. May we all continue to blaze trails for all the strong women to come.

And to my friends, to my family, and to Will, for always encouraging me to follow my own path, and for being proud of me when I do so (even if I get a little muddy or scratched up in the process). For listening to me when I talked through incomprehensible ideas, for feeding me when I was hangry and too busy to cook, and for still loving me when I was Deadlinezilla. I love you all so very, very much. The world is not wide enough to hold how much you mean to me.

Bristol Ivy is a knitting designer and teacher from Portland, Maine. Her work focuses on the intersection of classic tailoring and innovative technique, and has been published with Brooklyn Tweed's Wool People, Quince & Co., Pom Pom Quarterly, Interweave Knits, amirisu, and many more. You can find her at bristolivy.com and on Twitter and Instagram as @bristolivy.